Handbook of Behavioral Assessment *edited by Anthony R. Ciminero, Karen S. Calhoun, and Henry E. Adams*

Counseling and Psychotherapy: A Behavioral Approach *by E. Lakin Phillips*

Dimensions of Personality *edited by Harvey London and John E. Exner, Jr.*

The Mental Health Industry: A Cultural Phenomenon *by Peter A. Magaro, Robert Gripp, David McDowell, and Ivan W. Miller III*

Nonverbal Communication: The State of the Art *by Robert G. Harper, Arthur N. Weins, and Joseph D. Matarazzo*

Alcoholism and Treatment *by David J. Armor, J. Michael Polich, and Harriet B. Stambul*

A Biodevelopmental Approach to Clinical Child Psychology: Cognitive Controls and Cognitive Control Theory *by Sebastiano Santostefano*

Handbook of Infant Development *edited by Joy D. Osofsky*

Understanding the Rape Victim: A Synthesis of Research Findings *by Sedelle Katz and Mary Ann Mazur*

Childhood Pathology and Later Adjustment: The Question of Prediction *by Loretta K. Cass and Carolyn B. Thomas*

Intelligent Testing with the WISC-R *by Alan S. Kaufman*

Adaptation in Schizophrenia: The Theory of Segmental Set *by David Shakow*

Psychotherapy: An Eclectic Approach *by Sol L. Garfield*

Handbook of Minimal Brain Dysfunctions *edited by Herbert E. Rie and Ellen D. Rie*

Handbook of Behavioral Interventions: A Clinical Guide *edited by Alan Goldstein and Edna B. Foa*

Art Psychotherapy *by Harriet Wadeson*

Handbook of Adolescent Psychology *edited by Joseph Adelson*

Psychotherapy Supervision: Theory, Research and Practice *edited by Allen K. Hess*

Psychology and Psychiatry in Courts and Corrections: Controversy and Change *by Ellsworth A. Fersch, Jr.*

Restricted Environmental Stimulation: Research and Clinical Applications *by Peter Suedfeld*

Personal Construct Psychology: Psychotherapy and Personality *edited by Alvin W. Landfield and Larry M. Leitner*

Mothers, Grandmothers, and Daughters: Personality and Child Care in Three-Generation Families *by Bertram J. Cohler and Henry U. Grunebaum*

Further Explorations in Personality *edited by A.I. Rabin, Joel Aronoff, Andrew M. Barclay, and Robert A. Zucker*

Hypnosis and Relaxation: Modern Verification of an Old Equation *by William E. Edmonston, Jr.*

Handbook of Clinical Behavior Therapy *edited by Samuel M. Turner, Karen S. Calhoun, and Henry E. Adams*

Handbook of Clinical Neuropsychology *edited by Susan B. Filskov and Thomas J. Boll*

The Course of Alcoholism: Four Years After Treatment *by J. Michael Polich, David J. Armor, and Harriet B. Braiker*

Handbook of Innovative Psychotherapies *edited by Raymond J. Corsini*

The Role of the Father in Child Development (Second Edition) *edited by Michael E. Lamb*

Behavioral Medicine: Clinical Applications *by Susan S. Pinkerton, Howard Hughes, and W.W. Wenrich*

Handbook for the Practice of Pediatric Psychology *edited by June M. Tuma*

Change Through Interaction: Social Psychological Processes of Counseling and Psychotherapy *by Stanley R. Strong and Charles D. Claiborn*

Drugs and Behavior (Second Edition) *by Fred Leavitt*

(*continued on back*)

PROBLEM-SOLVING THERAPY
FOR DEPRESSION

Problem-Solving Therapy for Depression

Theory, Research, and Clinical Guidelines

ARTHUR M. NEZU
CHRISTINE M. NEZU
Beth Israel Medical Center and
Mount Sinai School of Medicine

MICHAEL G. PERRI
Fairleigh Dickinson University and
FDR Veterans Administration Hospital

WILEY

A WILEY-INTERSCIENCE PUBLICATION

JOHN WILEY & SONS

New York • Chichester • Brisbane • Toronto • Singapore

Library of Congress Cataloging in Publication Data:

Nezu, Arthur M.
    Problem-solving therapy for depression : theory, research, and
clinical guidelines / Arthur M. Nezu, Christine M. Nezu, Michael G.
Perri.
        p.   cm. -- (Wiley series on personality processes)
    Bibliography: p.
    Includes indexes.
    "A Wiley-Interscience publication."
    ISBN 0-471-62885-9
    1. Depression, Mental—Treatment.   2. Problem-solving therapy.
I. Nezu, Christine M.   II. Perri, Michael G.   III. Title.
IV. Series.
    [DNLM: 1. Depression—therapy.   2. Models, Psychological.
3. Problem Solving.   WM 171 N575p]
RC537.N495 1988
616.85'27—dc19
DNLM/DLC
for Library of Congress   88-17287
                                                               CIP

To Linda, Ali, and Frank
A.M.N. & C.M.N.

To Kathy and Katie
M.G.P.

Series Preface

This series of books is addressed to behavioral scientists interested in the nature of human personality. Its scope should prove pertinent to personality theorists and researchers as well as to clinicians concerned with applying an understanding of personality processes to the amelioration of emotional difficulties in living. To this end, the series provides a scholarly integration of theoretical formulations, empirical data, and practical recommendations.

Six major aspects of studying and learning about human personality can be designated: personality theory, personality structure and dynamics, personality development, personality assessment, personality change, and personality adjustment. In exploring these aspects of personality, the books in the series discuss a number of distinct but related subject areas: the nature and implications of various theories of personality; personality characteristics that account for consistencies and variations in human behavior; the emergence of personality processes in children and adolescents; the use of interviewing and testing procedures to evaluate individual differences in personality; efforts to modify personality styles through psychotherapy, counseling, behavior therapy, and other methods of influence; and patterns of abnormal personality functioning that impair individual competence.

IRVING B. WEINER

Fairleigh Dickinson University
Rutherford, New Jersey

Preface

Few areas of psychological inquiry can boast as massive a proliferation of empirical and theoretical attention as that which has accrued to the construct of problem solving (Mahoney, 1974). Much of this earlier research has emanated from several different fields, including experimental cognitive psychology, education, and industry. Although certain definable, albeit tentative, conclusions can be drawn from this research literature, psychologists and other mental health professionals have only recently started to consider its adaptive utility for real-life problems and its applicability to clinical and counseling settings (D'Zurilla & Goldfried, 1971; D'Zurilla & Nezu, 1982).

This situation is ironic in our complex present society, which continuously (and often rudely) confronts individuals with a wide variety of problematic situations that must be solved to maintain an adequate level of functioning. In order to help people cope with this continuous imposition and confrontation with difficult life problems, clinicians must formulate optimal therapeutic procedures. Additionally, such programs should incorporate various prophylactic components that enable individuals to prevent recurrence of the problems.

The urgency of such empirical endeavors was voiced by Mahoney (1974) over a decade ago: "... these cognitive skills may offer an invaluable personal paradigm for survival. Their potential contribution to therapeutic efficacy and independent self-improvement will hopefully become an issue of priority in future empirical scrutiny" (p. 212). In fact, the past decade has witnessed a substantial increase in research, theory, and clinical applications that address specifically this challenge (D'Zurilla, 1986). Many theorists (e.g., D'Zurilla & Nezu, 1982; Spivack, Platt, & Shure, 1976) have argued that distinctions must be made between the problem-solving processes inherent in impersonal or intellectual tasks and those processes necessary in real-life situations. Terms such as "social problem solving" and "interpersonal problem solving" have come into use to describe this area. Social problem solving, then, refers to the cognitive-behavioral process by which individuals identify, discover, or create effective strategies of coping with negative life events and problematic situations.

More recently, a growing body of literature has identified a strong relation between social problem solving and depression. For example, studies have indicated that depressed individuals show deficits in their ability to effectively resolve both interpersonal and social problems. Related research has also addressed the influence of successful problem-solving as a buffer against the depression-associated effects of negative life stress. Therapies aimed at building or increasing problem-solving skills have also been efficacious in reducing depressive symptoms, as well as in reducing a person's risk for depressive episodes.

This book presents a pluralistic model of depression that utilizes a problem-solving framework. Adoption of such a model provides a heuristic metaphor that describes how various current cognitive-behavioral theories of depression interact with each other. Research supportive of the problem-solving model will be described throughout. This book was written to facilitate empirical inquiries by researchers, teachers, and clinicians, as well as to provide specific guidelines for application of the model by mental health professionals working with depressed individuals. Thus, the hope is that this book provides not only important source material, but also stimulation for future research and novel clinical utilization. Although the literature concerning social problem solving and depression is growing, much work still needs to be accomplished.

Part One provides an overview of the construct of depression and descriptions of the various current cognitive-behavioral models of depression (e.g., Beck; Seligman & Abramson; Lewinsohn; Rehm). Overviews also delineate the relation between social problem solving and competence, and between social problem solving and depression. Each of the five stages of problem solving (problem orientation, problem definition and formulation, generation of alternatives, decision making, solution implementation and verification) are described, as well as the relation between these stages and depression. The focus is on the method of subsuming various cognitive-behavioral models of depression under a pluralistic problem-solving framework.

Part Two contains a "therapist's manual," detailing therapeutic applications of the model. This section highlights various clinical issues, such as the "therapist's decision making" and common problems that are experienced by depressed individuals (e.g., loneliness, relationship problems, suicidal ideation).

Because depression continues to be both a serious and prevalent mental health problem, we hope that this book will have some impact on its treatment. However, because research evaluating the effectiveness of this approach has thus far been limited to unipolar, major depressive disorder, we recommend caution concerning its use with other, more severe forms of mood disorders (e.g., bipolar depression, psychotic depression, melancholic depression; see Chapter 6).

We would like to acknowledge three individuals, originally our respective mentors, now colleagues and friends, who have served as excellent role models throughout our careers—Tom D'Zurilla, Mike Petronko, and Steve Richards. Tom, in particular, should be recognized as one of the hallmark influences in the field of social problem solving. Mike, in his unwavering efforts to find optimal solutions for both his own patients and the patients of his students, is an exemplary "problem solver." Steve's commitment to excellence has inspired us to go the "extra mile." We greatly appreciate their collective support and encouragement.

We also thank our friends at Wiley, Herb Reich and Judith Overton, without whose help this book would never have become a reality.

ARTHUR M. NEZU
CHRISTINE M. NEZU
MICHAEL G. PERRI

Teaneck, New Jersey
Teaneck, New Jersey
Oakland, New Jersey
November 1988

Contents

PART ONE

Problem-Solving Formulation of Depression

Theory and Research

CHAPTER 1

Depression

Symptomatology, Diagnosis, Assessment, and Current Cognitive-Behavioral Theories

I'm always tired. I wake up in the middle of the night and think about all my problems—both big and small. This usually leaves me completely depressed in the morning. I have no appetite—I don't want to eat. I can't concentrate, and I don't feel like doing anything. I'm indifferent to all the things I used to care about—I'm world-weary and cynical. No one understands me. I feel all alone. Nothing is going to change. I feel totally overwhelmed—like I'm constantly under stress. It seems like there's no way out. Maybe I'd be better off ending it all.

ANONYMOUS DEPRESSED PERSON

Feeling sad is virtually a universal experience. For most of us, feeling "down" or "blue" accompanies disappointments, setbacks, or losses in our lives. In most instances, the sad mood lasts for only a short time. It troubles our lives for a while and soon passes. For some people, the sad mood can become intense and long lasting, coloring every aspect of existence. They feel powerless to change, the future appears hopeless, and occasionally suicide seems to be the only answer. Depression of this type represents one of the most significant mental health problems facing our nation.

One out of every 5 women may experience clinical depression during her lifetime; among men the probabilities are 1 in 10 (cf. Secunda, Friedman, & Schuyler, 1973). The American Psychiatric Association (1980) has estimated that depression results in hospitalization for as many as 6% of all women and 3% of all men. The impact of this disorder is significant for both the individual experiencing depression and for society as well. For example, the costs to society in decreased work productivity and the expense of treatments have been estimated to be as high as $11 billion per year (Craighead, Kennedy, Raczynski, & Dow, 1984). On a personal level, the toll of psychological pain and anguish experienced by depressed persons and their families is underscored by the significant number of

3

suicides related to depression; some estimates suggest that as many as 15% of severely depressed people eventually commit suicide (Copas & Robin, 1982; Robins & Guze, 1972). Without a doubt, depression constitutes a common and serious problem of enormous personal and social significance.

In the past 20 years, research on depression has progressed at a dramatic pace. The advent of cognitive-behavioral theories of depression has generated exciting new perspectives for understanding depression as well as innovative and effective modalities for its treatment. One such approach is the recently articulated problem-solving formulation of depression (Nezu, 1987). This book describes in detail the problem-solving model for understanding and treating depression. The first chapter begins with an overview of the problem of depression and a review of definitions; a description of the major clinical instruments used to measure depression follows; and the chapter concludes with brief summaries of four contemporary cognitive-behavioral perspectives on the conceptualization of depression.

DEFINING DEPRESSION

Depression has proven to be remarkably difficult to define. Dozens of different definitions all puportedly describe the same phenomenon. In some, depression simply refers to the common feeling of sadness, but in others depression may refer to an abnormal mood state, a symptom, a clinical syndrome, or even a disease process (cf. Levitt, Lubin, & Brooks, 1983). Definitional problems have prompted the development of classification systems with specific criteria that can be applied in a consistent manner (Feighner et al., 1972).

The earliest psychiatric classification of mood disorders is attributed to Kraepelin, who in the 1890s based his classifications on both the similarities of symptoms and the eventual outcome of the disorder. Kraepelin separated manic-depressive psychosis from dementia praecox (i.e., schizophrenia). The distinction was based on observations that despite the severe disturbance that is apparent during clinical episodes, depression tends to remit, and periods of normal mood return. In the United States, Adolf Meyer criticized Kraepelin's system because it relied too heavily on prognosis and did not take into account environmental precipitants of psychological reactions. By 1935, the focus in classifying depression shifted to etiology. The category of reactive depression was distinguished from the psychotic mood disorders of manic-depression and depressive psychosis.

In 1952, the first *Diagnostic and Statistical Manual* (DSM-I) of the

American Psychiatric Association (APA, 1952) used the term affective reactions to include involutional melancholia and manic-depressive illness, but excluded psychotic depressive reactions. The influence of psychodynamic theory was evident in the relabeling of depressive reactions as "depressive neuroses," an approach which continued in a subsequent revision (DSM-II, APA, 1968).

Dissatisfaction with the lack of standardized, reliable criteria resulted in a dramatic shift in the approach to diagnosing mental disorders. Feighner and his colleagues (Feighner et al., 1972) developed a classification system that grouped diagnostic categories together if they shared important clinical descriptive features without making assumptions as to their etiology. The Feighner system, known as Research Diagnostic Criteria (RDC) served as the basis for DSM-III (APA, 1980).

DSM-III classified all depressions together, regardless of severity, chronicity, or apparent association with precipitating stress. A distinction was made between affect (i.e., an immediately observed emotion such as anger, fear, or sadness) and mood (i.e., a more pervasive and sustained emotion). Three further distinctions were made in mood disorders: first, whether they were episodic or chronic; second, whether the affective episodes were limited exclusively to depressive periods (i.e., unipolar) or included at least one manic phase (i.e., bipolar); and third, whether the affective disorder was manifest in a single episode or in recurring episodes.

In the most recent revision of the *Diagnostic and Statistical Manual* (DSM-III-R, APA, 1987) affective disorders are called *mood disorders* and are subdivided into bipolar disorders and depressive disorders. The essential feature of bipolar disorders is the presence of one or more manic episodes. The essential feature of depressive disorders is one or more periods of depression without a history of manic episodes.

DSM-III-R lists two depressive disorders: *major depression*, in which there is one or more major depressive episodes; and *dysthymia*, a less severe disturbance, in which there is a 2-year-history of a depressed mood, but the condition does not meet the criteria for a major depressive episode.

For a diagnosis of a major depression, at least five of the following symptoms must have been present during the same 2-week period, the symptoms must represent a change from previous functioning, and at least one of the symptoms must be either depressed mood, or loss of interest or pleasure:

1. Depressed mood (or can be irritable mood in children and adolescents) most of the day, nearly every day (as indicated either by subjective account or observation by others)

2. Markedly diminished interest or pleasure in all, or almost all, activities most of the day, nearly every day (as indicated by subjective account or observation of apathy by others)
3. Significant weight loss or weight gain when not dieting (e.g., more than 5% of body weight in a month), or decrease or increase in appetite nearly every day (in children, consider failure to make expected weight gains)
4. Insomnia or hypersomnia nearly every day
5. Psychomotor agitation or retardation nearly every day (observable by others, not merely subjective feelings of restlessness or of being slowed down)
6. Fatigue or loss of energy nearly every day
7. Feelings of worthlessness or excessive or inappropriate guilt (which may be delusional) nearly every day (not merely self-reproach or guilt about being sick)
8. Diminished ability to think or concentrate, or indecisiveness, nearly every day (either by subjective account or as observed by others)
9. Recurrent thoughts of death (not just fear of dying), recurrent suicidal ideation without a specific plan, a specific plan for committing suicide, or a suicide attempt

The diagnosis of major depression is appropriate only after establishing that an organic factor has not initiated and maintained the disturbance or that the condition is not the normal reaction to the loss of a loved one. In addition, the diagnosis is incompatible if the disturbance is superimposed on schizophrenia or on schizophreniform or delusional disorders, or if the criteria for schizoaffective disorder are met.

In DSM-III-R, the current state of mood disorders is subclassified as mild, moderate, severe without psychotic features, or severe with psychotic features. If the disorder fails to meet these severity criteria, it is then described either as being in partial or in full remission. In addition, a current major depressive episode can be specified as: *melancholic type*— a typically severe form of a major depressive episode that may be particularly responsive to somatic therapy; or *chronic type*—a current episode that has lasted 2 consecutive years without a period free of depressive symptoms for 2 months or longer.

Commonly associated features of depression include tearfulness, anxiety, irritability, brooding or obsessive rumination, excessive concern with physical health, panic attacks, and phobias.

Although a major depressive episode may begin at any age, the average age at onset is the late 20s. The onset of a major depressive episode is variable, the symptoms usually developing over days to weeks. In some cases, however, it may be sudden, especially when it is associated with severe psychosocial stressors. In some cases, other symptoms such as generalized anxiety, panic attack, phobias, or mild depressive symptoms, occur over a period of several months prior to the depressive episode itself.

The duration of a major depressive episode is also variable. Untreated, the episode typically lasts 6 months or longer. Usually there is a complete remission of symptoms, and the individual is able to revert back to a predepression level of general functioning. In chronic cases, however, some symptoms persist for as long as 2 years without a remission period of 2 months or longer.

Major depressive episodes almost always impede an individual's social and occupational functionings, but the degree of impairment varies widely. In severe cases, the person may be unable to function socially or occupationally, or even to eat, dress, or maintain minimal personal hygiene. The most serious complication of depression is suicide.

Summary

Depression, a prevalent and serious condition, is one of the most significant mental health problems facing our nation. It has often been referred to as "the common cold" of psychiatric disorders. Despite its prevalence and familiarity, depression has often been difficult to define. Recently developed classification systems, such as DSM-III and its revision, DSM-III-R, have provided specific criteria to improve the reliability and accuracy of the diagnosis of depression.

MEASURING DEPRESSION

The majority of instruments designed solely for the measurement of depression fall roughly into two classes. One consists of self-administered inventories of general statements similar to the ones in the Minnesota Multiphasic Personality Inventory (MMPI; Hathaway & McKinley, 1943). The second class includes rating scales primarily for diagnostic use or for applied research by professional raters in clinical settings.

Self-Report Instruments

MMPI DEPRESSION SCALE (MMPI-D).   The Depression scale, one of 10 clinical scales of the MMPI, has been used widely for the measurement of depression for clinical and research purposes. The MMPI-D is composed of 60 true/false items. Of the 60 items, 11 discriminate between depressed patients and other psychiatric patients. The remaining 49 items discriminate between a normal sample and a sample of patients diagnosed as manic-depressive—depressed type. The median split-half reliability of the Depression scale is .73, and the mean concurrent validity is .33 (Dahlstrom & Welsh, 1960). The MMPI-D scale has several limitations. First, factor analytic studies (e.g., Harris & Lingoes, 1955) have demonstrated that the scale is multidimensional. It includes such heterogeneous factors as "mental dullness" and "brooding" that are not reliably correlated with depression. Second, the MMPI instructions do not specify time frame. Consequently, responses to test items may more accurately represent a "trait" of depression than a description of the person's immediate mood "state." Third, since items for the MMPI were selected empirically, rather than on the basis of face validity, examination of a patient's specific test responses may offer little information about the specific symptoms experienced by the depressed person. Consequently, results from the MMPI-D provide little information for a treatment plan or a functional analysis of the depressive behaviors. As a means of addressing some of these limitations, Dempsey (1964) developed a 30-item version of the MMPI-D scale. Although this newer scale appears to be more of a homogenous inventory than the original 60-item scale, it still does not sample the complete range of depressive symptomatology (Hammen, 1981).

BECK DEPRESSION INVENTORY (BDI).   The BDI, perhaps the most widely used self-report measure of depression, was originally developed as a clinical rating scale (Beck, Ward, Mendelson, Mock, & Erbaugh, 1961). The BDI consists of 21 items representing the wide range of depressive symptoms. Each item consists of four statements listed in order of symptom severity and assigned an empirical scoring factor of 0 to 3. Item categories include mood, pessimism, crying spells, guilt, self-hate, irritability, social withdrawal, sleep problems, appetite disturbance, and loss of sexual interest. The time frame for the BDI, "the way you feel today, right now," clearly makes it a measure of state of depression. Factor analyses of the BDI have generally revealed three factors: "guilty depression," "retardation," and "somatic disturbance" (Mayer, 1977). Split-half reliability has been estimated to be .86 with test-retest reliability reported as .74 after 3 months (Miller & Seligman, 1973). Studies of its concurrent validity have yielded a mean coefficient of .54 (Rehm, 1976). The BDI, which has often been used as a pre- and posttreatment measure in research studies, can also be used in psychotherapy as a periodic measure of the severity of depression. In addition, it can provide useful information concerning the degree to which various depressive symptoms are troubling a patient. Of the various self-report measures of depressive *severity*, the BDI has had the most advocates (Hammen, 1981).

ZUNG SELF-RATING DEPRESSION SCALE (SDS).   The Self-Rating Depression Scale (Zung, 1965, 1973) consists of 20 statements. The test instructions do not indicate a specific time frame. Individuals completing this scale indicate the frequency with which each statement is applicable on a 4-point scale, from "none or a little of the time" to "most or all of the time." In scoring this scale, each response has a value of 1, 2, 3, or 4, depending on whether the statement was worded negatively or positively. Zung used previously reported factor-analytic studies to select symptoms and behaviors most characteristic of depression. The items tapped three areas that characterize depression: affective (2 items), biological (8 items), and psychological (10 items). Critics of the SDS have noted three shortcomings: (1) Answers can be easily faked, especially in the direction of symptom admission; (2) reliability data are not available for the instrument; and (3) normal adolescents and normal elderly adults tend to score in the clinical range (Glazer, Clarkin, & Hunt, 1981).

DEPRESSION ADJECTIVE CHECKLIST (DACL).   The DACL (Lubin, 1965, 1967, 1977) is a self-administered inventory that requires the respondent to indicate those adjectives that describe present mood. The DACL was derived from a list of 171 adjectives by using the responses of 95 severely depressed psychiatric patients and a matched normal group of 279 persons. The DACL consists of seven different forms (A through G). Forms A, B, C, and D each contain 32 adjectives and are equivalent, with 22 positive and 10 negative adjectives. Lists E, F, and G contain 34 adjectives, 22 positive and 12 negative, and also are equivalent. The DACL has a "general" form and a "today" form, in which only the instructions differ, so that the test may be used either as a state or a trait measure depending on the instructions to the respondent. For example, the state form asks individuals to "Check the words that describe how you feel now—today." The DACL has undergone considerable psychometric development, and normative data are available for various age groups, including adolescents as well as adults. Interlist correlations average about .87 and concurrent validity ratings have ranged from .30 to .71 (Lubin, 1967; Rehm, 1976). The availability of alternate forms and their brevity make the DACL especially useful for repeated measurement research. For example, it has been used to measure day-to-day fluctuations in mood level (e.g., Lewinsohn & Graf, 1973). The DACL differs from previously described self-report depression scales in sampling a much more limited range of depressed behavior—that is, depressed affect. This limitation is in contrast to the BDI and the SDS, which include items involving behavioral, physiological, and cognitive aspects of depression. The DACL is somewhat less valuable for pre- and posttreatment assessment because of the large day-to-day intrasubject variability of DACL scores.

Interviewer Rating Instruments

SCHEDULE FOR AFFECTIVE DISORDERS AND SCHIZOPHRENIA (SADS). The SADS (Endicott & Spitzer, 1978) is a semistructured interview guide that enables the interviewer to quantify symptoms and information related to both affective disturbances (depression and mania) and thought disorders (schizophrenia). The patient's functioning can be assessed in terms of three different time frames: the preceding week, the worst period of the most recent episode, and the patient's overall life history. The data obtained from this interview provide a quantified and detailed description of the patient's symptomatology. The information enables a clinician to determine a Research Diagnostic Criteria (RDC) categorization (Spitzer, Endicott, & Robins, 1978). The RDC system has gained prominence because of its reliability and usefulness for identifying homogenous groups for research, and it is almost synonymous with the DSM-III definitions.

HAMILTON RATING SCALE FOR DEPRESSION (HRSD). The original Hamilton Rating Scale (Hamilton, 1960) has 17 items, each of which is rated on either a 3-point or 4-point scale. The HRSD items represent cognitive, behavioral, and somatic symptoms of depression, with a somewhat greater emphasis given to behavioral and somatic areas. Newer versions have expanded the number of items up to 26 in order to increase the focus on cognitive aspects of depression. A trained clinician completes the HRSD after a structured interview. One study has indicated that advanced doctoral students in clinical psychology can obtain high levels of interrater agreement (O'Hara & Rehm, 1983). Further, Endicott, Cohen, Nee, Fleiss, and Santakos (1981) provide evidence that HRSD scores can be reliably derived from a SADS interview. As such, it is possible to conduct a single comprehensive interview to determine both diagnosis and severity of depressive sympotomatology. Because of its high reliability and sensitivity to fluctuations in depressive symptoms, the HRSD is the most widely used interviewer-rated assessment measure of depression in outcome studies (Hedlund & Vieweg, 1979).

Summary

Several self-report and interviewer-rated measures exist that help to assess the *severity* of depressive symptomatology. The following recommendations for clinical assessment procedures are based somewhat on convention, as well as on relevant research findings: (1) Use the SADS as an overall structured interview format to guide differential diagnosis; (2) use information gleaned from the SADS interview in order to complete the HRSD; and (3) have the patient complete the BDI. For research purposes, additional measures of depressive symptomatology may be added. Further, in conducting research with the HRSD, it is advisable to have two raters independently score this measure in order to determine whether a high degree of reliability exists between clinicians.

CONCEPTUALIZING DEPRESSION

Prior to the 1970s, research addressing the psychosocial aspects of depressive disorders was scant (Secunda et al., 1973). As mentioned previously, however, there has been an enormous increase in empirical attention to psychological theories of depression in the past 20 years. Cognitive-behavioral models of depression have stimulated much of this phenomenal growth. This section contains brief reviews of the following four major theories of depression—the behavioral, helplessness, cognitive, and self-control models. The chapter concludes by addressing the question—why another theory of depression?

Behavioral Model of Depression

Peter Lewinsohn (1974) and his colleagues have conceptualized depression within the framework of learning theory. Their approach extends earlier behavioral formulations (Ferster, 1966; Lazarus, 1968; Skinner, 1953) that emphasized the reduced frequency of overall activity as the primary defining characteristic of depression. The guiding theoretical assertions of Lewinsohn's work are (1) that depression is a function of the degree to which an individual's activity level is maintained by positive reinforcements, and (2) that deficits in social skills play an influencial role in determining the rate of positive reinforcement for one's behavior.

Lewinsohn defines reinforcement in terms of the quality of a person's interactions with the environment. A key assumption of this formulation is that the depressed person's behavior does not lead to a sufficiently high rate of positive reinforcement. As a result of this lowered rate, there is a decrease in the person's level of activity. The individual, thus, has few or no rewarding interactions, and consequently, experiences dysphoric feelings of depression. Learning theory terminology conceptualizes this process as an extinction phenomenon, with the depressed person's behavior and affect viewed as direct functions of decreases in response-contingent reinforcement.

The lower rate of behavior by the depressed person makes positive reinforcement less likely and consequently initiates a cycle of reduced activity and increasingly infrequent reinforcement. Significant others, such as friends and family members, often notice the individual's depressed behavior and provide the person with sympathy, increased attention, and a reduction in responsibilities. Unwittingly, they may actually reinforce the lowered rate of activity, and as a result, the frequency of the depressed behavior and affect increases.

According to Lewinsohn, a decrease in the quality of an individual's interactions with the environment may occur for several reasons. First, there may be either a decrease in the availability of positive reinforcers in the environment or an increase in the aversive aspects of the environment. Second, the individual may not possess adequate skills either to attain the available reinforcers or to cope with aversive elements (e.g., stressors) in the environment. Third, the positive impact of events that were previously reinforcing may be diminished, or the negative potency of aversive events may be strengthened.

Lewinsohn conceptualizes depression as occurring on a continuum ranging from mild states of occasional inactivity and unhappiness to the moderate and severe occurrences that are labeled as a psychiatric disorder. Both the severity and extensiveness of depressive symptoms are viewed as functions of low rates of positive reinforcement (and/or a high rate of aversive experience). Lewinsohn and his associates have conducted a series of studies (e.g., Lewinsohn & MacPhillamy, 1974; MacPhillamy & Lewinsohn, 1971, 1974) to examine the relation of decreased rates of activity and positive reinforcement to depression. For these investigations, MacPhillamy and Lewinsohn (1971) developed the Pleasant Events Schedule (PES). The PES contains a list of 320 pleasant events that individuals rate for both frequency and enjoyment. The PES responses of depressed individuals have been compared with the responses of nondepressed psychiatric patients and nondepressed normal individuals. Compared to the control groups, depressed subjects reported significantly fewer activities and found fewer events to be pleasurable (Lewinsohn & MacPhillamy, 1974; MacPhillamy & Lewinsohn, 1971, 1974). These findings lend support to the view that depression varies as a function of activity level and positive reinforcement. One limitation of these studies, however, is that they were based on subjects' recollections of pleasant events that occurred during the previous month. Consequently, the results may have been affected by group differences in recall. For example, the current mood of the depressed subjects may have influenced their recollection of both activity level and obtained pleasure, thereby producing discrepancies between the subjects' self-reports and their actual behavior (cf. Jacobsen, 1981).

Lewinsohn has also examined the relation between mood and activity level. In two studies (Lewinsohn & Graf, 1973; Lewinsohn & Libet, 1972) depressed, psychiatric control, and normal subjects self-monitored the daily frequency of pleasant events and mood over 30-day periods. The results indicated that daily ratings of depressed mood correlated significantly with a low frequency of pleasant events for all three groups. In addition, Lewinsohn and Talkington (1979) examined the relation between mood and the occurrence of unpleasant events and found that depressed mood significantly correlated with the frequency of unpleasant events. Collectively, these findings lend support to Lewinsohn's contention that activity and mood are functionally related.

Treatment studies that examine the effects of increased activity rates on changes in mood provide additional indirect support for Lewinsohn's model of depression. Several investigations have suggested that treatment strategies designed to increase pleasant activities can help to alleviate depression (e.g., Lewinsohn & Atwood, 1969; Lewinsohn & Shaw, 1969; Lewinsohn, Weinstein, & Alper, 1970; Turner, Ward, & Turner, 1979). It should be noted, however, that these studies used multifaceted interventions and included a variety of treatment procedures. Consequently, it is difficult to isolate the specific effect of increased pleasant activities on depression.

The ability to interact effectively in social situations also plays a prominent role in Lewinsohn's formulation of depression. Social skills are viewed as the means by which an individual obtains positive reinforcement from his or her environment. According to Lewinsohn, social competence mediates one's vulnerability to depression. The social interactional ability of depressed individuals is assumed to differ from that of nondepressed individuals. Direct empirical evidence for this major hypothesis is derived from comparisons of the social competence of depressed and nondepressed subjects.

In a series of studies, Lewinsohn and his associates (Lewinsohn, Mischel, Chaplin, & Barton, 1980; Libet & Lewinsohn, 1983; Youngren & Lewinsohn, 1980) have examined the nature of social competence in depressed persons. Collectively, depressed individuals, in comparison to nondepressed controls, were found to (1) initiate interpersonal behaviors at approximately half the rate of nondepressed individuals; (2) report more discomfort in interpersonal situations; (3) elicit less attention and less interest in social interactions; and (4) rate themselves and are rated by peers and observers as significantly lower in social competence during small group interactions.

Coyne (1976b) has also examined the interactional skills of depressed people. He concurs with Lewinsohn's hypotheses that a low rate of positive social reinforcement maintains depressed behavior and that deficits in social skills are partly responsible. In his research, Coyne has examined the impact that depressed persons have on others with whom they interact. For example, in one study, depressed persons talked by phone with non-depressed experimental subjects (Coyne, 1976a). In responding to the depressed persons, the normal subjects themselves reacted with increased feelings of depression, hostility, and anxiety. Coyne contends that stressful life experiences make depressed people especially prone to seek support and reassurance from others. However, although the depressed person is so needy of this type of support, he or she often doubts its sincerity when it is received and consequently, attempts to elicit additional reassurance. This demanding pattern of behavior is likely to be aversive to others, generating hostility, annoyance, and guilt. Although people may attempt to suppress direct expression of their annoyance, the depressed person may pick up subtle cues and, thus, becomes even more needy of reassurance and more prone to engage in the behaviors that others find aversive.

Helplessness Model of Depression

The learned helplessness phenomenon was first described systematically by Martin Seligman and his colleagues at the University of Pennsylvania (Overmier & Seligman, 1967; Seligman & Maier, 1967). These researchers found that dogs that experienced inescapable electric shock later failed to emit even the simplest of behaviors to terminate the shock. The dogs demonstrated significant motivational, learning, and emotional deficits. They rarely attempted to escape, did not follow an occasional successful escape response with another, and passively suffered the shock without any observable signs of emotionality. Seligman suggested that these deficits were a consequence of the dogs' learning that their behavior had no impact on the outcome of whether or not they received a shock. After experience with uncontrollable outcomes, they appeared to develop low expectancies for exerting control over later outcomes that, in fact, could be controlled. Moreover, these low expectancies appeared to produce a wide range of motivational, affective, and behavioral deficits strikingly similar to the state of depression observed in humans.

In a series of studies with humans, Seligman compared the responses of individuals experiencing feelings of helplessness through experimental manipulations in the laboratory setting with the behavior of individuals suffering from naturally occurring depression (cf. Seligman, 1975). The parallels between laboratory helplessness and depression appeared striking. Both groups demonstrated highly similar response patterns including passivity, slowed learning, lowered aggression, loss of appetite, negative expectations, and feelings of helplessness, hopelessness, and powerlessness.

Additional research with human subjects demonstrated that experience with uncontrollable outcomes did indeed produce depressionlike behavior in subsequent performance (Seligman, 1975). Nonetheless, a variety of complexities and problems with the learned helplessness formulation were noted in the studies with humans. For example, the original helplessness model viewed depression as occurring on a continuum ranging from the transient occurrence of sad mood to the severe states of psychiatric disorder. The original model did not specify explicitly which factors account for differences in the severity and chronicity of depression and offered no suggestions about classifying or distinguishing among types or categories of depression. Another shortcoming of the original helplessness model was its inability to explain salient symptoms of human depression such as guilt and self-blame. Indeed, as Abramson and Sackheim (1977) observed, it is logically inconsistent to predict that depressed persons will experience self-blame for events over which they believe they have no control. In addition, some puzzling findings were discovered in laboratory studies of learned helplessness in humans. For example, in some instances, uncontrollability of outcome not only failed to produce helplessness but actually facilitated subjects' subsequent performance (cf. Wortman & Brehm, 1975).

In response to the obvious need for a more complex model of human depression, Abramson, Seligman, and Teasdale (1978) reformulated the helplessness theory, placing a heavy emphasis on individual causal interpretation of uncontrollable events. Abramson et al. proposed that an individual's attribution for loss of control serves as a mediator between the absence of control and the emergence of helplessness-related deficits and depression. Specifically, they proposed that helplessness and depression are likely to occur after inability to produce a highly desired outcome or prevent a highly aversive outcome. When confronted by such circumstances, individuals attempt to explain why the circumstances have occurred. Their explanations determine how they will respond to the events. In the revised model, it is assumed that attributions are the primary determinants of an individual's actions and affect, and that behavior and emotion are logically consistent with the interpretation of events. In the reformulated model, three explanatory dimensions are relevant to understanding the individual's interpretation of events. First, the cause may be attributed to the person or to the situation (i.e., an internal vs. an external explanation). Second, the cause may be viewed as a factor that will either be transient or persistent across time (i.e., an unstable vs. a stable explanation). Third, the cause may be perceived to have an impact on a variety of outcomes or may be limited just to the event of concern (i.e., a global vs. a specific explanation).

Further, the revised helplessness model proposes that particular consequences are associated with the attributions made on each of these three dimensions. For example, an individual who attributes a negative event to an internal cause is likely to experience a loss of self-esteem; attribution to an external cause, on the other hand, is less likely to cause damage. The stability of causal beliefs affects the persistence of depression following negative events. If a transient factor is perceived to be the cause of the negative event, then depressive reactions to that event are unlikely to persist over time. If, however, the negative event is explained by a persistent cause, then depressive reactions are likely to be chronic. Finally, if an individual believes that a global factor has caused the negative event, then deficits associated with helplessness and depression are likely to occur in a variety of situations. On the other hand, if the person attributes the cause to a specific factor, then deficits will tend to be limited in scope.

The reformulated helplessness model postulates also that people demonstrate consistency in their explanatory styles. Individuals tend to invoke the same sorts of causal explanations for different negative events in their lives. Moreover, the reformulated theory predicts that an individual who regularly offers internal, stable, and global causes will be at a high risk for developing depression when faced with uncontrollable negative events. The theorists caution, however, that causal explanations and explanatory style are not sufficient in themselves to cause depression. Rather, attributions and style are risk factors that increase the likelihood that a person will experience deficits of depression and helplessness in response to negative events.

According to the reformulated model, the expectation of future uncontrollability is sufficient to produce most of the symptoms of depression, including a lowered rate of activity, cognitive deficits such as impaired learning, emotional responses of sadness and anxiety, and a lowering of appetitive drives. In addition, the expectation of uncontrollability may also bring about physiological consequences such as neurochemical changes and an increase in susceptibility to disease. The expectation of future uncontrollability is a sufficient condition for the production of all symptoms except self-esteem loss. As already noted, loss of self-esteem is a consequence of internal attributions for loss of controllability.

When the individual perceives negative events as beyond control through personal actions, the expectation of future uncontrollability is likely to occur. In such circumstances, the specific attributions that develop are influenced by two variables, namely, the reality of the particular circumstances and the individual's explanatory style. If the negative event that sets off the expectation of helplessness is the death of a close family member, reality dictates that the individual will experience a stable and global loss. The loved one will not return, and the scope of the loss will entail the many activities previously shared with the loved one. The second influence on attribution is explanatory style, the individual's tendency to choose certain kinds of explanations for bad versus good events. Explanatory style makes certain expectations more likely than others. Depression-prone persons exhibit a typical style, tending to give internal, stable, and global explanations for bad events. This style predisposes them to depression when they experience uncontrollable outcomes (e.g., "It's my fault; it's going to last for a long time; and it's going to have an effect on everything I do").

Thus, from the revised learned helplessness perspective, the inability to produce a highly desired outcome or to avoid a highly aversive outcome initiates cognitive processes aimed at developing an explanation for loss of control. The invoked attributions affect the individual's expectancy for control over future outcomes; and these expectancies, in turn, affect self-esteem, motivation, affect, and performance in later situations. The greater the internality of the attribution, the greater the loss of self-esteem; the greater the stability of the attribution, the greater the chronicity of the helplessness deficits; and the greater the globality of the attribution, the wider the range of behavioral domains affected by the sense of the helplessness.

Cognitive Distortion Model of Depression

According to Aaron Beck, a negatively biased cognitive set constitutes the core process in depression (Beck, 1976; Beck, Rush, Shaw, & Emery, 1979). When faced with stressful life events, depression-prone individuals experience negative thoughts. These thoughts, which typically consist of negative views of self, the world, and the future, predispose such persons to the experience of depression. To these individuals, the environment presents overwhelming obstacles that guarantee personal failure. Moreover, they view themselves as personally incapable of changing either their lives or their stressful circumstances. Consequently, they experience a sense of hopelessness about the future as well.

In conceptualizing depression, Beck utilizes three major concepts: (1)

the cognitive triad, (2) negative schemas, and (3) cognitive errors. The cognitive triad consists of three patterns of negative ideas and attitudes that characterize people who are depressed. The triad includes negative views of the self, the world, and the future.

The depressive view of the self includes negative evaluations of abilities and worth as a person. In comparing themselves to others, depressed individuals see themselves as defective and inadequate. This negative self-view pervades virtually all aspects of life and results in an overwhelming sense of worthlessness. In their early research (e.g., Beck, 1963; Beck & Hurvich, 1959; Beck & Ward, 1961), Beck and his associates observed that clinical interviews with depressed patients were dominated by themes of failure and personal inadequacy. Similar themes also seemed to characterize the dreams reported by depressed people. Other researchers (Hollon & Kendall, 1980) have documented the association of depression with self-reports of frequent automatic thoughts of personal inadequacy and maladjustment. In laboratory tasks, depressed individuals consistently expect their performance to be worse than average. Moreover, when asked to provide evaluative self-ratings, people who are depressed select trait descriptors with significantly negative connotations.

The second aspect of the cognitive triad is a negative view of the world. Here again, in both clinical interviews and in self-reports of their dreams (Beck, 1963, 1967), depressed persons indicated that they preceived their daily experience as permeated by themes of loss and stress (Beck, 1963, 1967). The view of the world, in this triad, is as an overwhelming burden, filled with excessive demands and daily defeats. Consequently, depressed individuals experience a pervasive sense of helplessness. They rate even the most common interpersonal problems as significantly more difficult to deal with than do people who are not depressed (Funabiki & Calhoun, 1979). Indeed, so far-reaching is this negative view of the world that individuals who have apparently recovered from depressive episodes continue to dream about problems and losses more often than do nondepressed people (Hauri, 1976).

The final facet of the cognitive triad is the depressive view that the future is hopeless. People who are depressed expect that their unpleasant condition will continue without any possibility of improvement. Researchers have consistently found a strong association between depression and measures of pessimism and hopelessness (e.g., Erickson, Post, & Paige, 1975; Gottschalk, 1974; Hollon & Beck, 1979). In addition, depressed persons show an idiosyncratic time orientation. They tend to dwell on past failures rather than to look toward future possibilities (Miller, 1975; Shaw, 1979). As a consequence of this orientation, depressed individuals typically report little motivation to act with energy or positive expectation.

Thus, they increase the likelihood that the future will indeed continue to be bleak and unchanged, and they find themselves trapped in a self-fulfilling prophecy of depression.

According to Beck, virtually all the symptoms of depression may be attributed to the negative cognitive triad. Sad affect, the hallmark of depression, is assumed to be a direct consequence of negative cognitions. For example, laboratory studies (e.g., Frost, Graff, & Becker, 1979; Teasdale & Fogarty, 1979; Velten, 1968) have shown that having subjects concentrate on depressive thoughts, such as "I am worthless," can induce a depressed mood. Likewise, other symptoms of depression are also viewed as consequences of the depressed person's cognitions. For example, it is possible to interpret decreased activity levels as the direct result of the pessimism and hopelessness that characterize a depressed person's thoughts. Similarly, if an individual views daily experience as oppressive and the future as hopeless, then suicidal wishes are logical consequences. Thus, in Beck's view, it is the exaggerated negative view of the self, the world, and the future that accounts for the various affective, motivational, and behavioral deficits of depression.

The second major component in Beck's theory involves the concept of cognitive structures or "schemas." Schemas are stable, long-standing thought patterns representing a person's generalizations about past experiences. According to Beck, schemas serve to organize from past circumstances information relevant to a current situation. They facilitate the processing of new information by directing attention selectively to certain aspects of a situation. Consequently, schemas determine the way selected information is perceived, remembered, and later recalled. Since any given situation may contain a myriad of stimuli, schemas are evoked to facilitate the processing of information. Depression-prone individuals develop schemas consisting of stable and pejorative views of themselves and their experience. The schemas that produce depression often involve the perception of a personal loss or damage to one's self-worth. Due to the negative nature of their schemas, depression-prone individuals tend to respond to their circumstances in a fixed, negative manner, independent of what is occurring in their environment.

Beck maintains that depressive schemas originate in childhood and adolescence. A person learns to construct reality through early experiences with significant others. Certain experiences (such as the death of a parent, repeated rejection by peers, or harsh criticism by teachers) may lead to the formation of attitudes and beliefs that will later prove maladaptive. For example, a child may develop the schema, "No matter what I do, I will never be accepted by others."

Once learned, a schema is usually out of awareness until the person encounters circumstances somehow reminiscent of the conditions in which the schema was learned. At that point, the person may employ the schema to organize and process information about the situation. The individual selects and categorizes information about the situation in a manner consistent with the schema. Depressive schemas predispose the individual to distort events so as to maintain a negative view of self, the environment, and the future.

Derry and Kuiper (1981) tested Beck's proposition that depressed individuals process information on the basis of negative schema. The researchers compared the memories of depressed and nondepressed subjects for adjectives that were either "meaningful" to them or "descriptive" of them. The depressed subjects recalled more adjectives with depressive content that they had judged descriptive of themselves than did nondepressed psychiatric patients or normal control subjects. These findings lend support to Beck's theoretical assertion that depressed individuals utilize a negative schema for processing and retaining personal information.

In a related study, Abramson, Alloy, and Rosoff (1981) examined the hypothesis that negative self-schema may prevent depressed persons from generating hypotheses about the contingencies between their behavior and outcome. The researchers found that when asked to develop generalizations for exerting control, depressed subjects underestimated the potential amount of control available to them. Thus, negative schemas appear to play an integral role in the depressive cycle. Schemas for lack of control result in an inability to develop hypotheses for exerting control, and this inability, in turn, leads to the behavioral deficits of depression.

According to Beck, stressful life events activate depressive schemas. These schemas, in turn, are responsible for distortions in the way the depression-prone individual perceives and interprets experiences. Interpretations based on depressive schema often result in conclusions that are logically inaccurate. Nonetheless, the individual maintains depressive schemas despite evidence disproving their validity. Beck et al. (1979) contend that the maintenance of depressive schemas is a consequence of a faulty system of information processing in which the individual draws illogical conclusions from six basic cognitive errors:

1. *Arbitrary inference*—drawing a specific conclusion in the absence of evidence to support the conclusion
2. *Selective abstraction*—drawing a conclusion based on a detail taken out of context
3. *Overgeneralization*—drawing a broad, global conclusion on the basis of one or more isolated pieces of information

4. *Magnification and minimization*—exaggerating the significance of negative events and minimizing the significance of positive events

5. *Personalization*—relating external events to oneself when there is no realistic basis for making such a connection

6. *Absolutistic, dichotomous thinking*—placing all experiences in one of two opposite categories

According to Beck, depressed individuals make these errors in logic when evaluating experiences. Consequently, their thoughts are characterized by extreme, negative, categorical, absolute, and judgmental cognitions. Their distorted perceptions serve to maintain negative views of themselves, the world, and the future.

According to Beck, the cognitive processes used by depressed people represent deviations from the logical thought processes of nondepressed people. Krantz and Hammen (1979) developed a laboratory paradigm to test this proposition. In the paradigm, subjects read a series of stories about people experiencing negative life events and were asked to indicate the reactions that they would have if they themselves actually experienced the events. The set of possible responses included four alternatives: (1) a "depressed-distorted" response (representing one of the cognitive errors suggested by Beck); (2) a depressive but relatively realistic response; (3) a nondepressed realistic response; and (4) a nondepressed but distorted response (e.g., gross underestimation of the negative aspects of an event). The results of studies using this paradigm (Blaney, Behar, & Head, 1980; Krantz & Hammen, 1979) have consistently shown that depressed individuals choose a greater number of depressed-distorted responses than nondepressed subjects. These findings support Beck's contention that cognitive errors characterize the thought processes of people who are depressed.

Finally, Beck suggests that the reciprocal nature of the interaction between a depressed person and the environment often reinforces depressive schemas and the negative view of the self, the world, and the future. The actions of the depressed person affect others, whose reactions in turn, have an impact on the depressed person (cf. Bandura, 1977). For example, crying spells and continuing complaints of unhappiness may alienate the depressed person from significant others (cf. Coyne, 1976b). Over time, family and friends may view the depressed individual as unpleasant company, and they may then reduce their contact with the person. Their actions, in turn, engender a response in the depressed individual, activating schemas of social alienation and self-rejection. The behavior of significant others in this instance may strengthen the depressive schema by creating a circular feedback system that deepens the downward spiral in depression.

Self-Control Model of Depression

Rehm (1977) asserts that depression is a consequence of deficiencies in self-control. Rehm's conceptualization of depression is derived from Kanfer's (1971) general self-control model that places major significance on an individual's ability to achieve goals through three sequential processes, namely, self-monitoring, self-evaluation, and self-reinforcement. Rehm contends that depressed individuals demonstrate deficits in each component of the self-control process. These deficits, in turn, produce the individual symptoms of depression, and collectively they account for all the manifestations of the depressive syndrome.

Within the perspective of social learning theory (e.g., Bandura, 1977), self-monitoring is a naturally occurring process in which a person observes his or her own behavior, its antecedents, and its consequences. Rehm contends that the self-monitoring of depressed individuals characteristically shows selective attention to negative rather than positive events and to immediate rather than long-term consequences of behavior. Selective attention to negative events in their experience accounts for the pessimism that is typical of depressed individuals. Selective attention to immediate consequences of behavior results in motivational deficits and precludes working toward long-term positive goals. Rehm (1981) notes that cognitive errors of selective abstraction and arbitrary inference (cf. Beck, 1974) are consequences of the selective attention that typifies the depression-prone individual. In addition, negatively biased self-monitoring increases the proportion of aversive material in the person's awareness and results in depressed mood.

The nature of monitoring processes in depressed persons has received considerable research attention. Laboratory studies (e.g., Nelson & Craighead, 1977; Wener & Rehm, 1975) have shown that depressed individuals tend to underestimate the amounts of positive feedback that they receive, particularly when feedback is given at high rates. In addition to memory distortions, other negative biases seem characteristic of self-monitoring processes in depressed persons. Roth and Rehm (1980) studied self-monitoring in depressed and nondepressed psychiatric patients. They found that when allowed to choose the type of performance feedback (e.g., correct versus incorrect responses), depressed patients more frequently selected negative feedback, whereas nondepressed patients more frequently chose positive feedback. Roth and Rehm also showed that when depressed subjects viewed videotapes of themselves in social interactions, they accurately identified the number of their own negative behaviors (as defined by the experimenters) but significantly underestimated the number of positive behaviors that they displayed on the tapes. Nondepressed pèrsons, on the other hand, accurately counted their own positive behaviors but underestimated the number of their negative behaviors. These findings support Rehm's contention that a strong negative bias typifies the self-monitoring process in depressed persons.

The second component of the self-control process is self-evaluation, which is conceptualized as a process of comparison. In this process individuals compare estimates of performance supplied by self-monitoring with internal criteria for success or failure. According to Rehm, depressed persons set overly stringent, perfectionistic standards. The standards are so high, that mismatches between performance and standards are inevitable. Depressed persons discount the importance of intermediate or short-term progress. According to the stringent criteria that they have set for themselves, anything less than complete accomplishment of their final goal is viewed as a failure. In contrast, nondepressed people appear to discriminate among several levels of relative or partial success or failure.

Rehm contends that, as a consequence of excessively stringent, dichotomous evaluation standards, depressed individuals experience a much higher ratio of negative to positive self-evaluations than do nondepressed individuals. Moreover, Rehm posits that the combination of negatively biased self-monitoring and unrealistically high self-evaluative criteria produces the low self-esteem that typifies depression.

Empirical support for Rehm's assertions regarding self-evaluation and depression has been derived from a variety of studies. Golin and Terrell (1977) examined the aspiration levels of mildly depressed and nondepressed college students. They found that depressed students gave higher levels of aspiration for performance that involved skill, but not for tasks determined by chance. The investigators concluded that the high levels of aspiration set by the depressed students may cause them to perceive average performances as failure experiences.

Depressed college students also seem to set more unrealistic academic goals for themselves than do nondepressed college students (Schwartz, 1974). Studies using clinical samples have also shown that high evaluation criteria are characteristic of depressed patients. For example, Loeb, Beck, Diggory, and Tuthill (1967) found that depressed and nondepressed psychiatric patients obtained identical performances on a laboratory task, yet self-ratings indicated that members of the depressed group gave their performances significantly poorer evaluations than the ones given by the nondepressed patients. Other studies have also shown that depressed subjects give themselves lower self-evaluations than nondepressed subjects give themselves even when the objective performances of both groups have been identical (Ciminero & Steingarten, 1978; Lobitz & Post, 1979; Smolen, 1978).

A key aspect of the self-evaluation process involves attributing responsibility for success or failure to internal or to external causes. In revising Kanfer's self-control model, Rehm includes self-attributions as modifiers of self-evaluation. According to Rehm, only internal attribution of success or failure has significance in the self-evaluation process. People are unlikely to see a success that is attributable to external cause as an appropriate opportunity for self-reinforcement. Likewise, they are unlikely to feel that a poor performance due to external factors should be an occasion for self-punishment (cf. Bandura, 1978). Rehm hypothesizes that depressed persons make attributions that are consistent with negative expectancies. Consistent with the revised helplessness model (Abramson et al., 1978), Rehm also suggests that depressed persons are likely to attribute success to external, unstable, specific factors, and failure to internal, stable, and global causes (cf. Rehm & O'Hara, 1980).

Self-reinforcement, the final step in the self-control process, represents the mechanism by which a person influences his or her own behavior. The individual compares the self-monitored performance with the standard for self-evaluation. How well the performance and the standard correspond determines the likely consequence. If the performance meets or exceeds the standard, there is likely to be a positive self-evaluation resulting in contingent self-reward. If the performance fails to match the standard, there is likely to be a negative self-evaluation resulting in contingent self-punishment. It is assumed that although self-reinforcement and self-punishment may occasionally include tangible reinforcers, cognitive consequences, such as self-satisfaction and self-criticism, more typically regulate behavior (cf. Bandura, 1978).

Rehm posits that low rates of self-reinforcement and high rates of self-punishment characterize depression. Since self-reinforcement is crucial to the achievement of delayed reinforcement and long-term goals, low rates of self-reinforcement may account for the overt symptoms of depression involving reduced activity level (e.g., reduced participation in previously enjoyable activities, lack of initiation, and psychomotor retardation). Frequent self-punishment may also contribute to these deficits, may be responsible for self-deprecating thoughts and low self-esteem, and may discourage future goal-directed behavior. Furthermore, when the overall pattern of reinforcement is no longer sufficient to maintain rates of behavior necessary for functioning in a given environment, the individual experiences an aversive state. Overt signs of depressed affect, such as crying spells, may communicate this state to others.

A number of studies have examined the self-reinforcement styles of depressed and nondepressed persons. A comparison of depressed and nondepressed psychiatric patients showed that although the two groups had equivalent performances on a memory task, depressed individuals punished themselves more and rewarded themselves less than did the nondepressed patients (Rozensky, Rehm, Pry, & Roth, 1977). Partial replications of these findings were reported in two additional studies. Nelson and Craighead (1977) found that depressed college students rewarded themselves less, although no differences in self-punishment were identified. On the other hand, Roth, Rehm, and Rozensky (1980) found that depressed persons were not significantly different in their use of self-rewards, but engaged in self-punishments more frequently. Rehm (1980) suggested that these differences may be attributed to task differences in the two studies.

SUMMARY

Over the last 20 years, several promising psychological models have been developed to account for the etiology of depression and to suggest strategies for the treatment of depression. Lewinsohn's behavioral model equates depression with a pervasive reduction in the individual's instrumental activity, caused by a reduced rate of positive reinforcement. In Seligman's revised helplessness model, attributions for lack of control over negative outcomes are viewed as the determinants of an individual's affective reactions. Beck's cognitive model considers depression to be a consequence of distorted cognitions, which predispose the individual to negative views of the self, the environment, and the future. Finally, Rehm's self-control model suggests that depression results from deficits in self-monitoring, self-evaluation, and self-reinforcement.

Given the vast amount of research engendered by these four theories, a reasonable question from the reader is—"Why another theory of depression?" Although a complete delineation of the research concerning these theories is beyond the scope of this book, it should be noted that each one of these popular theories has engendered both supportive *and* conflicting empirical evidence concerning the model's validity (cf. Coyne, 1982; Coyne & Gotlib, 1983; Craighead et al., 1984; Hammen, 1985). As such, it is difficult to ascertain which theory most adequately accounts for the pathogenesis of depression. Further, whereas recent descriptions of treatment programs for depression emanating from these models have tended to incorporate a wider variety of both cognitive and behavioral techniques (Craighead et al., 1984), each theory still purports to explain the pathogenesis of depression based on a *unitary* etiological pattern. Very little theoretical integration of these models has occurred (Nezu, 1987). Moreover, based on a critical review of various psychological models of depression, Hammen (1985) suggests the following reasons for newer comprehensive theories of depression: (1) to delineate ways of integrating various critical vulnerability factors identified by each theory, as well as their manner of operation at different levels of analysis; and (2) to specify a multivariate model that also describes the interactional process that exists among these variables over the course of time.

A major thesis of this book is that adoption of a problem-solving framework of depression provides a useful metaphor to integrate these existing theories in a meaningful manner. As will be described in Chapter 5, the overall problem-solving process, in fact, incorporates several variables that cognitive-behavioral models identify as major etiologic factors (i.e., negative causal attributions, decrease in positive reinforcement, self-control difficulties). Moreover, the problem-solving model attempts to join the bodies of literature on stress-related depression and cognitive-behavioral theories of depression in a more explicit fashion. Therefore, a "meta-model" of depression is being proposed that incorporates and integrates several existing models. Consonant with Hammen's (1985) call for an integrative, "transactional" approach to depression, this volume describes the pathogenesis in terms of reciprocal relations among stressful events, problem solving, and depressive symptomatology as they occur and change over time. Specifying the etiological importance of this overall process, as compared to a single vulnerability factor, is consistent also with a pluralistic approach, which views unipolar depression as a multi-dimensional phenomenon with many causes (Craighead, 1980). As such, this framework can provide a heuristic model of both assessment and therapy that considers idiographic differences *among* individuals, as well as differences *within* a particular person across time and differing situations (Nezu, Nezu, & Perri, in press). Preliminary to discussion of the problem-solving model of depression, the next chapter considers social problem solving in general.

CHAPTER 2

Problem Solving, Social Competence, and Mental Health

The major thesis of the problem-solving conception of mental health is that specific sets of cognitive and behavioral skills play a mediating role in both emotional reactions and the quality of overall psychological adjustment (D'Zurilla, 1986; D'Zurilla & Nezu, 1982; Nezu & D'Zurilla, in press). This chapter begins with an examination of social problem solving and its relevance to psychological well-being, including definitions of the terms "social problem solving," "problems," and "solutions." Next is an overview of the social problem-solving process, followed by a review of several procedures used to assess problem solving in adults. The chapter concludes with an examination of problem solving as related to social competence and mental health.

DEFINITIONS

Social Problem Solving

In the literature of clinical and counseling psychology, problem solving of real-life difficulties has been referred to as "social problem solving" (cf. D'Zurilla & Nezu, 1982). Other terms that have also been used include "interpersonal problem solving" (Shure, 1981), "interpersonal cognitive problem solving" (Spivack, Platt, & Shure, 1976), "personal problem solving" (Heppner & Peterson, 1982), and "applied problem solving" (Heppner, Neal, & Larson, 1984). We prefer to use the term social problem solving to highlight the social context in which real-life problem solving takes place.

In simplest terms, *social problem solving* may be viewed as the process by which people both understand, and react to, problems in living. More formal definitions have been offered by D'Zurilla, Nezu, and their associates. For example, D'Zurilla and Goldfried (1971) defined problem solving as "a behavioral process . . . which (a) makes available a variety of

27

potentially effective response alternatives for dealing with a problematic situation, and (b) increases the probability of selecting the most effective response from among those alternatives" (p. 108). D'Zurilla and Nezu (1982) refer to social problem solving as the " . . . process whereby an individual identifies or discovers effective means of coping with problem situations encountered in day-to-day living" (p. 202). More recently, Nezu (1987) defined problem solving as " . . . the metacognitive process by which individuals understand the nature of problems in living and direct their attempts at altering either the problematic nature of the situation itself or their reactions to them" (p. 122).

One implication of these definitions of social problem solving is that the process may be viewed simultaneously from varying perspectives. On a basic behavioral level, it is possible to conceptualize problem solving as a form of learning in which the individual's response to a problem situation constitutes a change in behavior (cf. Gagne, 1966). From a social learning perspective, problem solving is a self-management process, wherein the individual becomes the principal agent in guiding those features of personal behavior that might eventually lead to a desired positive outcome (Goldfried & Merbaum, 1973). Finally, from a mental health perspective, problem solving serves as a general coping strategy whose goal is the discovery of a wide range of effective behaviors, thereby contributing to the facilitation and maintenance of general social competence (D'Zurilla & Nezu, 1982; Lazarus & Folkman, 1984).

Problems

Within this model, *problems* are defined as specific life situations (either present or anticipated) that demand responses for adaptive functioning, but which do not receive effective coping responses from the persons confronting the situations because of the presence of various obstacles (D' Zurilla & Goldfried, 1971; Nezu & D'Zurilla, in press). These obstacles can include ambiguity, uncertainty, conflicting demands, lack of resources, and/or novelty.

Essentially, problems often represent a discrepancy between the reality of a situation and desired goals (D'Zurilla, 1986; Nezu, 1987). Problems are likely to be stressful if they are at all difficult and relevant to well-being (D'Zurilla, 1986; Nezu, 1986b; Lazarus & Folkman, 1984). A problem can be a single event (e.g., loss of one's wallet or purse), a series of related events (e.g., a boss repeatedly making unreasonable demands), or a chronic situation (e.g., continued unemployment). The demands in the problematic situation may originate in the environment (e.g., objective task requirement) or within the person (e.g., a personal goal, need, commitment). As a function of individual differences that exist among differing people experiencing similar situations, the specific nature of these demands is influenced strongly by one's perceptions. As such, these demands are best characterized as *perceived* demands.

According to the definition, a problem is *not* a characteristic of either the environment or person alone. Rather, a problem is a particular type of person-environment relation that reflects a perceived imbalance or discrepancy between demands and adaptive response availability. This imbalance is likely to change over time, depending on changes in the environment, the person, or both.

Solution

A *solution,* in this model, is defined as any coping response designed to alter the nature of the problematic situation, one's negative emotional reactions to it, or both (D'Zurilla, 1986; Nezu, 1987). *Effective* solutions are those coping responses that not only achieve these goals, but simultaneously maximize other positive consequences (i.e., benefits) and minimize other negative consequences (i.e., costs) (D'Zurilla & Nezu, 1987). These associated costs and benefits involve the short- and long-term implications of the solution, as well as both the personal consequences for the individual and the impact that the solution has on significant others. The adequacy or effectiveness of any potential solution varies from person to person and from setting to setting because the perceived effectiveness of a particular problem-solving response depends also on values and goals of the problem solver or significant others in the environment.

This model's perspective of social problem solving also distinguishes among the concepts of problem solving, solution implementation, and social competence (D'Zurilla, 1986; D'Zurilla & Nezu, 1987; Nezu, 1987). As noted earlier, problem solving is a process of *discovery,* specifically, the finding of an effective solution to a problem situation. Solution implementation, on the other hand, entails the actual coping *performance* of the chosen solution response. Thus, coping performance is the *outcome* of the problem-solving process. The term ''problem-solving coping'' refers to the combination of problem solving and coping performance with regard to a particular problem. The implementation of a solution is dependent not just on problem-solving ability, but on other factors, including deficiencies in performance skills, emotional inhibitions, and deficits in motivation (or reinforcement). This distinction between problem solving and coping performance becomes particularly important for research on the relation between the problem-solving process and problem-solving outcomes (D'Zurilla & Nezu, 1987; Nezu & D'Zurilla, in press). In other words, process measures should focus on the skills and abilities that enable individuals to solve problems effectively, whereas outcome measures should focus on either their reported solutions (specific coping responses or techniques) or their actual coping performance. In clinical practice it is also important to have different treatment strategies available for the individual who may be good at discovering an effective solution but poor at carrying it out.

Social competence has been defined as "the effectiveness or adequacy with which an individual is capable of responding to various problematic situations which confront him" (Goldfried & D'Zurilla, 1969, p. 161). Social competence, generally considered an evaluative term, entails the wide range of social skills that enable an individual to deal effectively with the demands of everyday living. Social problem solving is only one component of social competence, albeit a very significant one (D'Zurilla & Nezu, 1982, 1987; McFall, 1982; Sarason, 1981; Wrubel, Benner, & Lazarus, 1981).

THE SOCIAL PROBLEM-SOLVING PROCESS

There are two overriding assumptions in a problem-solving model of mental health. First, by virtue of complex cognitive abilities and the demands of society, human beings are active problem solvers. Second, psychological adjustment is related to adeptness at solving problems of both an intrapersonal and interpersonal nature (cf. D'Zurilla & Nezu, 1982). Certain cognitive and behavioral skills mediate both emotional reactions and overall psychological adjustment, depression in particular. Among these skills are the individual's general approach and sensitivity to problems, whether he or she considers potential solutions and anticipates the consequences of different actions, and how the individual decides to react when faced with a problematic situation. Furthermore, this model postulates that problem-solving skills are significant determinants of social competence (defined as the capacity to deal effectively with the wide range of problems in daily living) and that social competence is a key component of overall psychological adjustment (D'Zurilla & Goldfried, 1971; D'Zurilla & Nezu, 1982).

Overall problem-solving capacity comprises a series of specific skills rather than a single unitary ability. According to D'Zurilla and Nezu (1982; see also D'Zurilla & Goldfried, 1971), "effective" problem solving requires five interacting component processes, each of which makes a distinct contribution toward effective problem resolution. They include (1) problem orientation, (2) problem definition and formulation, (3) generation of alternatives, (4) decision making, and (5) solution implementation and verification.

The problem-orientation component is different from the other four components in that it is a *motivational* process, whereas the other components consist of specific *skills* and *abilities* that enable a person to solve a particular problem effectively. *Problem orientation* may be described as a set of orienting responses representing the immediate cognitive-affective-behavioral reactions of a person when first confronted with a problematic situation. These orienting responses include a particular type of attentional set (i.e., sensitivity to problems) and a set of general beliefs, assumptions, appraisals, and expectations concerning life's problems and one's own general problem-solving ability. This cognitive set is based primarily on the person's past developmental and reinforcement history related to real-life problem solving. Depending on the specific nature of these cognitive variables, they may produce positive affect and approach motivation, which can likely facilitate problem-solving performance, or they may produce negative affect and avoidance motivation, which can inhibit or disrupt problem-solving performance.

The remaining four components of the problem-solving process constitute a set of specific skills or goal-directed tasks that enable a person to solve a particular problem successfully. Each task makes a distinct contribution toward the discovery of an adaptive solution or coping response in a particular problem-solving situation. The goal of *problem definition and formulation* is to clarify and understand the specific nature of the problem. This includes a reappraisal of the situation in terms of its significance for well-being and changeability. (The initial problem appraisal involves the person's immediate response to an undefined problem based primarily on experiences with similar problems.) After defining and formulating the nature of the problem more clearly and concretely, the person can then appraise the problem more accurately.

The goal of the third component, *generation of alternatives,* is to make available as many solutions as possible in order to maximize the likelihood that the "best" (most preferred) solution will be among them. The purpose of *decision making* is to evaluate (judge and compare) the available solution alternatives and to select the best one(s) for implementation in the actual problem situation. Finally, the purpose of *solution implementation and verification* is to monitor the solution outcome and evaluate the effectiveness of the solution in managing the problematic situation.

Solution implementation, or coping performance, is included with verification in the problem-solving performance because it is the necessary prerequisite for verification. As noted earlier, however, solution implementation is separated from the problem-solving process when assessing problem-solving skills or abilities. Verification skills encompass self-monitoring and evaluation of the actual solution outcome.

These five processes are not based on a natural classification of cognitive-behavioral strategies used by individuals in the real world. Rather, they represent a prescriptive model of effective or successful problem solving, based on both clinical judgment and available research. Further, the sequence in which these components are presented reflects a logical and useful format for training individuals in effective problem resolution and coping. It does not, however, represent an assessment of how successful problem solvers in real life generally or typically go about solving problems. Nor does it imply that real-life problem solving should proceed in such an orderly, unidirectional fashion. Instead, effective problem solving is likely to involve continous movement between and among the five components before actual resolution of a problem. For example, one important aspect of the third component, generation of alternatives, involves brainstorming an exhaustive list of potential solution possibilities. Such an approach, however, can also be used during previously ordered problem-solving processes, as in generating a list of possible reasons why the situation is actually a problem (a problem-definition-and-formulation task).

In addition to specific problem-solving component skills, D'Zurilla (1986) suggests that certain specific abilities underlie the overall process of learning and implementing various problem-solving operations. These abilities include certain cognitive skills identified by Spivack et al. (1976): (1) *problem sensitivity*, an awareness that problems are a common feature of human interactions, coupled with a willingness to examine difficulties when they arise; (2) *causal thinking*, an appreciation of one's own motivations as well as the motivations of others; (3) *alternative-solution thinking*, an ability to produce a variety of potential problem solutions by suspending judgment and withholding censorship of ideas; (4) *consequential thinking*, the capacity to consider the personal and social consequences of one's behavior prior to deciding which action to take; and (5) *means-end thinking*, the ability to spell out the step-by-step requirements needed to accomplish an objective, including the recognition of potential obstacles, available alternatives, and likely consequences.

Rather than conceptualizing social problem-solving skills as personality traits or as facets of general intelligence, this model considers them to be a set of social skills learned through direct and vicarious experience with other people, particularly significant adults (e.g., parents or child-rearers) in one's life (Spivack et al., 1976; Spivack & Shure, 1974). The degree to which the developing child learns these skills will mirror the degree to which the adults at home model various problem-solving skills. The manner in which significant adult models cope with actual problems probably plays a key role in a child's acquisition of problem-solving abilities (Nezu & Kalmar, in press).

There are two main reasons why people may be ineffective problem solvers. First, the person simply may not have learned the necessary skills. Second, the individual may have acquired the skills but fail to demonstrate effective problem solving in a particular situation due to negative emotions (e.g., anxiety or depression) that inhibit the performance of any or all of the various problem-solving operations.

ASSESSMENT OF SOCIAL PROBLEM SOLVING

Measurements of social problem-solving skills and abilities, or assessment procedures, are useful in determining both generalized and specific problem-solving deficits, so as to plan appropriate treatment interventions. Whereas a wide variety of specific measures currently exist, they can be categorized into two general assessment approaches (D'Zurilla, 1986; D'Zurilla & Nezu, 1982): (a) self-report or verbal methods, and (b) observational procedures. Of the first type, two popular and widely used measures include the Means-Ends Problem-Solving Procedure (MEPS; Platt & Spivack, 1975) and the Problem Solving Inventory (PSI; Heppner & Peterson, 1982).

Means-Ends Problem-Solving (MEPS) Procedure

As noted earlier, Spivack and his associates (cf. Spivack et al., 1976) conceptualize means-ends thinking as the ability to articulate the step-by-step means needed to successfully resolve a problem situation. The delineation of the means to achieve a goal incorporates recognition of obstacles that must be overcome and implies an awareness of how others may react to the problem-solving process. Spivack and his associates describe means-ends thinking as an "interpersonal road map" that lays out, in some detail, the direction to take in solving a problem and possible alternative routes if a detour occurs along the way.

In order to assess means-ends ability, Platt and Spivack (1975) developed a method called the Means-Ends Problem-Solving (MEPS) Procedure. The MEPS test utilizes an "open-middle format" whereby the test taker receives a written or verbal description of a problematic interpersonal situation, as well as a successful solution to the problem. The task for the test taker is to use imagination to fill in the middle of the story and to supply the means by which the successful objective was achieved.

The MEPS consists of 10 problematic situations such as getting to know a beautiful girl, successfully stealing a diamond, getting along with one's boss, or finding a lost watch.

The subject's responses to each story can be scored for number of (1) *relevant means* (discrete steps that facilitate achievement of the successful outcome); (2) *irrelevant means* (steps judged to be ineffective for goal achievement in the particular situation); (3) *no-means* (a restatement of the story, or a "miraculous" resolution of the problem); (4) *enumerations* (elaborations or specific examples of a more basic means); (5) *obstacles* (the acknowledgement of potential impediments to goal achievement); and (6) *time references* (recognition that time may be a factor in the resolution of the problem). It is also possible to score the thematic content of means. The scores most commonly reported are the number of relevant means and the ratio of relevant to total means.

Two types of data have been offered in support of the validity of the MEPS test. The first set rates MEPS performance of normal subjects versus various samples of psychiatric patients. In a series of studies (Platt & Spivack, 1972a, 1973, 1974; Siegel, Platt, & Peizer, 1976), researchers examined performance scores on the MEPS of adult psychiatric patients and nonpatient controls. Compared to the normal sample, the psychiatric patients were found to be deficient in means-ends cognition. More specifically, the patient group produced significantly fewer relevant means and significantly greater irrelevant-to-relevant means. Furthermore, means-ends thinking ability was inversely related to two indices of degree of psychopathology: premorbid social competence (Platt & Spivack, 1972b) and MMPI scale elevations and configurations indicative of psychosis (Platt & Siegel, 1976).

Treatment outcome studies showing improvements in MEPS test performance after problem-solving training have provided additional (indirect) validational support for the MEPS procedure. For example, Coche and his colleagues demonstrated that problem-solving training for hospitalized psychiatric patients produced positive changes in MEPS test performance (Coche & Flick, 1975) and in self-report indices of impulse control, self-esteem, and feeling of competence (Coche & Douglas, 1977) relative to no-treatment and placebo control groups.

However, close examination of the assumptions and procedures of the MEPS raises several important issues in the assessment of problem-solving skills (cf. Butler & Meichenbaum, 1981; D'Zurilla & Nezu, 1982). For example, the MEPS test format is somewhat unusual for a test of abilities, in that the MEPS is essentially a projective test. The test is presented as a storytelling exercise and no effort is made to induce a problem-solving set within the subject. It is unclear whether the test assesses the subject's problem-solving skill (i.e., abilities in the individual's repertoire) or problem-solving performance (i.e., the implementation of problem-solving skills). Consequently, although psychiatric patients differ from normal subjects in the quantity and quality of the means they produce on the MEPS test, the difference may represent a lack of motivation to utilize problem-solving skills rather than an actual deficit in problem-solving abilities. Presumably, the MEPS assessment provides information about the way an individual *typically* responds in problem situations. Butler and Meichenbaum (1981) have suggested that a preferable assessment modality would be that of a capabilities test (e.g., a subtest of a general intelligence measure), which is designed to assess *maximal* performance with respect to specific areas of ability.

Further, the open-middle format of the MEPS test contributes a degree of artificiality to the testing situation. Each problem situation of the MEPS test item has a happy ending, a format that is not representative of the complexities of real-life situations. Furthermore, the open-middle format does not permit an assessment of the individual's problem-solving orientation. An individual's expectancies and general approach to problem situations can play an important motivational role in the generation of problem-solving cognition and behavior (D'Zurilla, 1986; Nezu & D'Zurilla, in press).

An additional concern is the content validity of the MEPS items. Some of the problem situations have little relevance to real-life circumstances. For example, it is a rare individual who might experience "stealing a diamond" or "gaining revenge on an SS trooper." The objectives in such problem situations are unlikely to have personal significance for the test taker, and may even inhibit problem-solving as a reaction to questionable goals (Nezu & Ronan, 1988). Consequently, the individual's storytelling efforts on the MEPS may not be indicative of cognitive and behavioral reactions in real-life problematic situations (cf. D'Zurilla & Nezu, 1982; Meijers, 1978).

Finally, the scoring of the MEPS raises concern as well. Means, obstacles, and time references scores presumably reflect the hypothetical components of means-ends thinking, namely, steps in planning, awareness of obstacles, and a recognition that the solving of problems may be a time-consuming endeavor. Platt and Spivack (1972a) have shown, however, that the score on the means component is more crucial than either the obstacles or time references score in discriminating psychiatric patients from normal subjects on the basis of MEPS test performance. Similarly, Butler and Meichenbaum (1981) have suggested that a qualitative assessment of MEPS test performance (e.g., the *effectiveness* of alternatives and decisions) might capture the key difference between effective and ineffective problem solvers more readily than a mere quantitative scoring (e.g., number of relevant means).

Problem Solving Inventory (PSI)

A somewhat different perspective on problem solving is provided by Heppner and Petersen's (1982) Problem Solving Inventory. This self-report instrument provides information about individuals' attitudes toward social problem solving and their perceptions of their problem-solving styles. The PSI has been described both as a measure of *self-appraised* problem-solving ability (Heppner, Neal, & Larson, 1984) and as a measure of problem-solving style (Sherry, Keitel, & Tracey, 1984). The PSI consists of 35 randomly ordered, Likert-type items chosen by the authors as representative of D'Zurilla and Goldfried's (1971) five problem-solving stages (general orientation, problem definition, generation of alternatives, decision making, and evaluation). Sample PSI items include: "I am usually able to think up creative and effective alternatives to solve a problem"; "I generally go with the first good idea that comes to my mind"; "When I am confused by a problem, one of the first things I do is survey the situation and consider all the relevant pieces of information."

Validational support for the PSI has come from two general sets of studies, which primarily have used college students as subjects. In one set of studies, significant differences between self-appraised effective problem solvers and self-appraised ineffective problem solvers have been found on measures of social competence, positive adjustment, and psychopathology (Heppner & Anderson, 1985; Heppner, Baumgardner, & Jackson, 1985; Heppner, Kampa, & Brunning, 1987; Heppner, Reeder, & Larson, 1983; Nezu, 1985, 1986d; Nezu, Kalmar, Ronan, & Clavijo, 1986; Nezu, Nezu, Saraydarian, Kalmar, & Ronan, 1986; Nezu & Ronan, 1985, 1988). In addition, Heppner and Petersen also conducted a series of problem-solving training programs based on the D'Zurilla and Goldfried (1971) model and found that subjects trained in problem-solving techniques differed significantly from controls in self-reports of problem-solving behaviors on the PSI, particularly in the decreased use of implusive strategies (Dixon, Heppner, Petersen, & Ronning, 1979; Heppner, Baumgardner, Larson, & Petty, 1983). Further, as described in Chapter 5, studies focusing on the efficacy of problem-solving therapy for clinically depressed individuals have found the PSI to be sensitive to changes in problem-solving ability and depressive sypmtomatology (Nezu, 1987; Nezu & Perri, 1987). Moreover, researchers have found the PSI to be correlated with behavioral measures of problem-solving competence (Heppner, Hibel, Neal, Weinstein, & Rabinowitz, 1982) and unrelated to social desirability factors (Heppner & Petersen, 1982).

Additional Measures

Additional self-report measures exist that require subjects to demonstrate problem-solving skills by performing specific tasks designed to test such skills. For example, to address some of the concerns regarding the MEPS, Nezu and D'Zurilla developed measures that test two specific problem-solving skills: (1) generating effective solutions to real-life problems, and (2) making effective decisions (D'Zurilla & Nezu, 1980; Nezu & D'Zurilla, 1981a, 1981b; Nezu & Ronan, 1987). These measures were developed in accordance with the behavioral-analytic method espoused by Goldfried and D'Zurilla (1969) involving test construction. This approach involves five steps: (1) *situational analysis* (identification of significant problematic situations relevant to a particular population under study); (2) *response enumeration* (determination of a range of possible responses or solutions for each of these problems); (3) *response evaluation* (evaluation of these solutions by appropriate judges); (4) *development of a measuring instrument format;* (5) *evaluation of the measures* (assessment of the instrument's psychometric properties).

By using the behavioral-analytical method, these measures by Nezu and D'Zurilla become more relevant to real-life problems and permit an assessment of the *quality* or effectiveness of the task response (either generating alternatives or making decisions). Additional measures of problem solving based on this format of test construction include the Adolescent Problem Inventory (Freedman, Rosenthal, Donahoe, Schlundt, & McFall, 1978), the Family Problem Questionnaire (Claerhout, Elder, & Janes, 1982), the Interpersonal Problem Solving Assessment Technique (Getter & Nowinski, 1981), the Situational Competence Test (Chaney, O'Leary, & Marlatt, 1978), the Problem Solving Performance Evaluation Test (Bedell, Archer, & Marlowe, 1980), and the Problem Inventory for College Students (Fisher-Beckfield & McFall, 1982). Unfortunately, the majority of these instruments were designed for a particular research study and due to the low frequency of their use in other investigations, little is known about their psychometric properties.

An additional concern regarding these verbal or self-report measures of problem solving involves their limited scope. Most tests currently used to assess problem solving focus on only a limited number of component abilities. D'Zurilla (1986) suggests that this limitation may be responsible for the occasional failure to demonstrate a strong relation between test performance and real-life problem-solving performance, as well as for conflicting results concerning the relation between these measures and psychopathology (cf. Butler & Meichenbaum, 1981; D'Zurilla & Nezu, 1982).

To address this concern, D'Zurilla and Nezu (1988) are currently testing the psychometric properties of the recently developed Social Problem Solving Inventory (SPSI). This self-report measure was designed to provide for a comprehensive assessment of problem-solving abilities across the five major component processes. Further, subscales encompass cognitive, behavioral, and affective aspects of problem orientation. With such a measure, it may be possible to develop valuable information about specific problem-solving deficits. This type of data becomes extremely useful in guiding treatment planning.

Observational Approaches

The second general approach toward problem-solving assessment uses procedures (D'Zurilla & Nezu, 1982) involving observation and evaluation of overt problem-solving performance either in the natural environment or in laboratory settings. For example, a person might participate in a role-play situation depicting an interpersonal problem, such as difficulties in the relationship with a supervisor at work. Although this approach may reflect a higher degree of ecological validity, it is also limited in its ability to directly assess the *process* of problem solving. Failure to effectively resolve the problem may not be a function of deficits in problem-solving abilities, but rather the result of ineffective communication, assertiveness, or role-play skills. Therefore, this overall approach may be more useful in the assessment of problem-solving performance or the *products* of the problem-solving process (see D'Zurilla, 1986; D'Zurilla & Nezu, 1982, for discussions concerning the relative merits of each general assessment approach).

Perhaps the most advantageous overall approach toward assessment of problem-solving skills and abilities lies in combining the advantages of both verbal and observational methods (D'Zurilla & Nezu, 1982). One excellent example is the problem-solving discussion method (cf. Kendall & Fischler, 1984). According to this format, subjects talk about and solve either hypothetical or real-life problem situations. These discussions are either directly observed or tape-recorded and then later coded and analyzed. Measures can include both the problem-solving process (i.e., method by which problems were defined) and the products (i.e., reported chosen solutions).

A second promising approach recently articulated by D'Zurilla (1986) incorporates subjects' engaging in self-observation and monitoring. Based on previous suggestions by D'Zurilla and Nezu (1982), the Problem-Solving Self-Monitoring (PSSM) method asks subjects to provide information in the following five areas with regard to a particular problematic situation: (1) the problem itself, (2) one's emotional reaction to the problem, (3) alternative coping responses or solutions that were considered, (4) the actual solution that was chosen, and (5) the nature of solution implementation and the actual outcome. Research concerning the validity and utility of the PSSM method is currently in progress.

PROBLEM SOLVING, SOCIAL COMPETENCE, AND MENTAL HEALTH

Now that we have defined problem solving and have reviewed some of the ways in which it is measured, we can ask the key question of how it relates to mental health. As noted earlier, the basic assumption underlying the problem-solving approach to clinical intervention and prevention is that problem solving is positively related to social competence and inversely related to psychopathology or maladaptive behavior. About 30 years ago, Jahoda (1953, 1958) argued that problem-solving ability is a critical component of positive mental health. Jahoda also suggested that deficits in problem-solving skills were associated with inadequate psychological adjustment and psychopathology. A number of other investigators (D'Zurilla & Goldfried, 1971; D'Zurilla & Nezu, 1982; Mechanic, 1968, 1970; Phillips, 1978; Spivack et al., 1976) have elaborated and extended this perspective. These theorists have contended that psychological adjustment should not be defined simply as the absence of psychopathology, but rather as the presence of specific forms of *effective functioning*. This position argues that social competence is an indicator of positive mental health (e.g., Jahoda, 1953, 1958; White, 1959). Moreover, these authors hypothesize that social competence is inversely correlated with psychopathology.

In the 1960s and 1970s, Zigler, Phillips, and their associates conducted a series of studies which provided support for this hypothesis. These researchers reported two major findings: (1) Level of social competence among psychiatric patients was inversely related to the degree of psychopathology exhibited by these patients; and (2) premorbid levels of social competence were found to be significant predictors of positive adjustment following hospitalization (Phillips & Zigler, 1961, 1964; Zigler & Phillips, 1961, 1962; Levine & Zigler, 1973). In these studies, level of social competence was derived from a scoring system based on six variables, including age, IQ, education, occupation, employment history, and marital status.

During the 1970s, Spivack and his associates conducted a series of studies using the MEPS procedure to examine directly the relation between problem solving and psychopathology (cf. Spivack et al., 1976). These investigators studied the problem-solving performance of a variety of clinical samples and compared them to matched control groups. Adult psychiatric patients (Platt & Spivack, 1972a, 1973), substance abusers (Platt, Scura, & Hannon, 1973), and adolescent psychiatric patients (Platt, Spivack, Altman, Altman & Peizer, 1974), all demonstrated significant deficits in MEPS test performance compared to appropriately matched, nonclinical control subjects. Moreover, a higher level of premorbid social competence was significantly correlated with a higher number of means and higher relevancy scores (Platt & Spivack, 1972b). Further, among male psychiatric patients, low scores on the MEPS were associated with MMPI profiles suggestive of psychotic symptomatology (Platt & Siegel, 1976).

Other researchers have conducted studies of problem solving and psychopathology and have reported findings similar to those of Spivack and his colleagues. For example, Gotlib and Asarnow (1979) used the MEPS in studying the problem-solving performance of depressed and nondepressed subjects. They reported significant between-group differences on several MEPS measures and also found significant correlations between MEPS measures and scores on the Beck Depression Inventory. The latter finding provides additional support for the hypothesized negative relationship between problem-solving ability and degree of psychopathology.

The relationship between problem solving and psychological adjustment has also been examined using the PSI. In a number of studies researchers have investigated the differences between individuals who appraise themselves as "effective" or as "ineffective" problem solvers. Self-ratings by effective problem solvers indicate that they are more motivated to solve problems, have higher expectations of success, are less impulsive and avoidant, are more systematic and persistent, and have a clearer understanding of problems (Heppner et al., 1982) than their ineffective counterparts. Effective problem solvers are also more assertive and less anxious (Neal & Heppner, 1982), have a more positive self-concept, fewer dysfunctional thoughts, fewer irrational beliefs (Heppner, Reeder, & Larson, 1983), and tend to employ more rational decision-making strategies (Phillips, Pazienza, & Ferrin, 1984) than ineffective problem solvers.

Furthermore, when compared to effective problem solvers, ineffective problem solvers report a greater number of life problems (Heppner et al., 1982; Nezu, 1985), more health and physical symptoms (Sherry et al., 1984), more anxiety (Neal & Heppner, 1982; Nezu, 1985, 1986d; Sherry et al.), more depression (Heppner, Baumgardner, & Jackson, 1985; Heppner et al., 1987; Nezu, 1985, 1986a; Nezu, Kalmar, Ronan, & Clavijo, 1986; Nezu, Nezu, Saraydarian, Kalmar, & Ronan, 1986; Nezu & Ronan, 1985), more psychological stress symptoms as measured by the SCL-90 (Heppner et al., 1987), and more psychological maladjustment as measured by the MMPI (Heppner & Anderson, 1985).

The findings from the studies using the PSI suggest a strong relationship between self-appraised problem solving and psychological adjustment. D'Zurilla (1986) has noted that self-appraisal of problem-solving ability can affect adjustment directly by influencing a person's self-esteem and feelings of well-being. Heppner et al. (1982) have suggested that it can also have an impact on adjustment by influencing actual problem-solving performance which, in turn, affects adaptive functioning (cf. Butler & Meichenbaum, 1981). From the perspective of transactional theory, the positive consequences of effective performance on the environment would then reinforce and maintain positive self-appraisal (cf. Lazarus & Folkman, 1984). Positive self-appraisal alone, however, cannot produce effective problem-solving performance unless the person also has the particular problem-solving abilities needed to resolve the problematic situation. Consequently, it is reasonable to expect that specific problem-solving skills should also be related to psychological adjustment or psychopathology (cf. D'Zurilla, 1986; Nezu, 1987).

Another avenue of empirical inquiry provides additional support for the relation between problem solving and mental health. This line of research involves controlled outcome studies that evaluated the efficacy of problem-solving therapy with a wide variety of clinical groups. These investigations indicate that this therapy approach has been successful with psychiatric inpatients (Siegel & Spivack, 1976; Coche & Flick, 1975), alcoholics (Intagliatia, 1978; Chaney et al., 1978), academic underachievers (Richards & Perri, 1978), obese persons (Black & Scherba, 1983; Black & Threlfall, 1986; Perri et al., 1987; Perri et al., in press), agoraphobics (Jannoun, Munby, Catalan, & Gelder, 1980), and persons experiencing anxiety (D'Zurilla, 1986). Although certain methodological problems exist with a handful of these studies (see D'Zurilla, 1986; D'Zurilla & Nezu, 1982, for critical evaluations of the problem-solving therapy outcome literature for adults), collectively these studies strongly suggest that increasing the effectiveness of problem-solving skills serves to decrease the severity of various clinical problems.

SUMMARY

This chapter began with operational definitions of the terms *social problem solving, problems,* and *solutions.* A brief overview of the social problem-solving process was then presented, including descriptions of the five major problem-solving components (problem orientation, problem definition and formulation, generation of alternatives, decision making, solution implementation and verification). Problem orientation was conceptualized as a set of orienting responses that include an attentional set (i.e., sensitivity to problems) and a group of general beliefs, assumptions, appraisals, and expectations concerning life's problems and one's problem-solving ability. The remaining four problem-solving operations were described as a set of specific skills or goal-directed tasks enabling a person to solve a particular problem successfully. These components were characterized as making distinct contributions toward the discovery of an adaptive solution or coping response in a particular problem-solving situation. The *prescriptive* nature of this model was underscored by stating that the delineated sequence reflects a logical and useful format for training purposes.

A description of various assessment measures such as the MEPS and PSI followed, highlighting strengths and weaknesses. In general, measures of social problem solving fall into two categories: (1) verbal or self-report measures and (2) observational formats. The overall best approach is to use procedures that combine the advantages of both types of measures, such as D'Zurilla's (1986) PSSM (problem-solving self-monitoring) method.

This chapter concluded with a discussion of the relation between social problem solving and mental health. Theoretically, a *positive mental health* perspective suggests that psychological adjustment should not be defined simply as the absence of psychopathology, but rather as the presence of specific forms of effective functioning. Further, social competence should be viewed as an indicator of positive mental health. This perspective also postulates that there is an association between deficits in problem-solving skills and inadequate social adjustment and psychopathology.

Studies that provide support for this conceptualization were briefly highlighted. Although this literature is not without both empirical and theoretical difficulties (cf. Durlak, 1983; Tisdelle & St. Lawrence, 1986), the research findings on the relation between social competence and psychopathology lend themselves to two general interpretations. First, pathological behavior may result directly from deficiencies in the problem-solving abilities that contribute to social competence (D'Zurilla & Goldfried, 1971; D'Zurilla & Nezu, 1982; Phillips, 1978; Spivack et al., 1976). As D'Zurilla and Goldfried noted in 1971, much of what has been viewed clinically as abnormal behavior or emotional disturbance might also be classified as ineffective problem solving and its consequences.

Second, problem solving may be an integral component of social competence and thereby may serve as a preventive factor or as a buffer against the development or progression of psychopathology and maladaptive psychological adjustment. The next chapter examines the relation between problem solving and depression and begins the presentation of the theoretical model positing that depression can be activated by the interaction of stressful events and ineffective problem-solving coping.

CHAPTER 3

Toward a Problem-Solving
Formulation of Depression

The problem-solving model of unipolar depression focuses on the reciprocal relations among negative life events, current daily problems, immediate and long-term emotional reactions, and problem-solving coping
activities. This "transactional" perspective represents a primary level of
analysis concerning the pathogenesis of depression. However, the overall
approach includes two additional focal areas: (1) the influence of biological
vulnerability factors and previous learning history; and (2) the specific
relations between the various problem-solving processes and depression.
It is within this latter microanalysis, as contained in Chapter 4, that various
cognitive-behavioral theories of depression will be integrated under a
general problem-solving rubric. The present chapter will address transactional analysis and biological factors.

Models of Stress

Before describing the problem-solving formulation of depression, a brief
overview of the concept of stress will be useful. Scientific investigators
have been interested in this construct for more than 50 years. During this
period, both the definition and understanding of the stress concept have
undergone substantial changes (Nezu & D'Zurilla, in press).

The early dominant stress paradigm incorporated a stimulus-response
(S-R) conceptualization based on a view of humans as organisms that
simply react passively to environmental stimuli. Within this general approach, the stress construct was defined as both an external stimulus and
as a response. Stimulus definitions of stress involved major life events
that placed strong demands for readjustment on individuals (cf. Dohrenwend & Dohrenwend, 1974). The research based on this approach has
tended to focus on broad-scale stressful life events, such as extreme
physical dangers (e.g., war, natural disasters, severe illnesses) and major
life changes (e.g., divorce, death of a loved one, change in careers).

Response definitions of stress within this overall approach have focused on the physiological and emotional sequelae of exposure to a laboratory or naturalistic stressor (cf. Brady, 1980; Ciaranello, 1983; Selye, 1983).

Although the S-R model of stress has contributed substantially to our general knowledge about stress and its relation to adaptational outcomes, the model has also received severe criticism in recent years because of its limited explanatory and predictive power and its simplistic, mechanistic view of human nature (D'Zurilla, 1986; Lazarus & Folkman, 1984). Both stimulus and response definitions of the stress construct have ignored or deemphasized important person variables (e.g., internal demands for readjustment, perceptions, appraisals, coping) that can moderate various physiological and emotional stress responses.

This early dissatisfaction with S-R definitions prompted development of more sophisticated stimulus-organism-response (S-O-R) interactional approaches to stress. S-O-R models attempted to incorporate important mediating organismic variables (Cofer & Apply, 1964; Levine, Weinberg, & Ursin, 1978; Spielberger, 1972), such as perceptions, appraisals, coping skills, and various personality characteristics. Researchers working with this model have tried to determine the separate and interactional influences of different environment and person variables on various types of emotional and physiological stress reactions (cf. Hamberger & Lohr, 1984).

Although the S-O-R interactional model of stress represented a significant improvement over previous formulations, such an approach continued to characterize humans as relatively passive organisms. Further, a one-directional mode of determinism was usually postulated as the primary pathway among variables. For example, causal influence was described as beginning with an environmental event, which activated certain organismic variables (e.g., Type A behavior pattern). These in turn affected certain response variables (e.g., increased blood pressure). As such, this framework presented a static picture of stress-related phenomena that failed to recognize the important *reciprocal relations* among person and environmental variables in stressful life experiences, including the important role of *active coping* in mediating stress responses (D'Zurilla, 1986; Lazarus & Folkman, 1984; Nezu & D'Zurilla, in press). It is interesting to note that many current cognitive-behavioral models of depression are primarily based on such unidirectional, diathesis-stress formulations (cf. Hammen, 1985).

A *transactional* model of stress, proposed by Richard Lazarus and his associates, attempts to correct the limitations of the more traditional stress models. This approach represents a relational, process-oriented view of stress that incorporates and emphasizes both appraisal and coping processes (Lazarus, 1981; Lazarus & Lanier, 1978; Lazarus & Folkman,

1984). Within this framework, stress is defined as a particular person-environment relation in which demands (external and/or internal) are appraised by the person as taxing or exceeding coping resources and as influencing well-being (Lazarus & Folkman, 1984). This relational view of stress assumes that people are active, thinking, problem-solving organisms that *interact* with their environment, instead of passive organisms that simply *react* to environmental stimuli. Within this model, the concept of a person-environmental *interaction* involves the process of *reciprocal determinism* (Bandura, 1977), where person and environmental variables constantly influence and change each other over time. The term "transactional" has been used to describe this dynamic, interactional process. Our problem-solving formulation of depression does incorporate a transactional perspective of stress (D'Zurilla, 1986; Nezu, 1987; Nezu & D'Zurilla, in press) in which *social problem solving* plays a prominent role as an adaptive and flexible, general coping strategy.

A PROBLEM-SOLVING MODEL OF DEPRESSION

The primary level of analysis within the overall model focuses on transactional relations among four variables: (1) major negative life events; (2) current problems; (3) problem-solving coping; and (4) depressive symptomatology (Nezu, 1987; Nezu, Nezu, & Perri, in press). As described later in this chapter, a second level of analysis involves genetic and biological vulnerability factors, as well as an individual's previous developmental and learning history. A third level of analysis, delineated in the next chapter, focuses on the relation between each of the major problem-solving components and depression.

Major Negative Life Events

Over the past several decades, a substantial body of research has documented the extent to which major negative life events affect psychological distress patterns, particularly depression (Billings & Moos, 1982; Nezu, 1986b; Nezu & Ronan, 1985). Although various discrepancies can be found among studies, literature reviews in general support the existence of a strong association between increased frequencies of negative life events and the onset of depressive disorders. For example, depressed patients have been found to report more previous negative life events than do schizophrenic patients, patients with anxiety disorders, and normal controls (Rabkin, 1982). Additional studies have suggested that the *type* of life event is often important in determining the probability of consequent depression. For example, depression has been suggested to most likely occur as a function of events involving a significant loss (e.g., divorce, death of a family member, becoming unemployed) (cf. C. Costello, 1980; Lloyd, 1980).

Whereas negative life events have been linked consistently to the onset of depressive illness, the actual relation appears rather modest, with correlations centering around .30 (Christensen, 1981). Thus, over 90% of the variance in the occurrence of psychological distress, as a consequence of major life changes, remains unexplained. Moreover, both research and clinical experience clearly indicate that many individuals, even under severely stressful circumstances, do not necessarily experience depressed mood (Sarason, Levine, & Sarason, 1982). For example, Clayton (1979) found that 1 year after bereavement, only 16% of a studied sample showed clinical depression.

These limitations have led to various attempts to refine the stress-dysfunction paradigm in order to better understand varying individual reactions to equivalent levels of negative life change (Nezu, 1987; Nezu & Roman, 1985). One promising approach is to study the *cumulative* effects of daily problematic situations (Nezu, 1986b). For example, frustrations or strains from ongoing problematic situations with a co-worker (e.g., competition for a promotion), even though not as dramatic as getting fired, can represent a significant source of stress. Difficulties in resolving differences with one's spouse over financial plans, although not as major as a divorce or separation, also may serve as a significant stressor. Thus, within our model, both types of stressors (i.e., major life events and daily problems) should be included to obtain a more comprehensive understanding of individual differences in depressive reactions to stressful life experiences.

Current Problems

As defined in Chapter 2, problems within the model are specific life situations (either present or anticipated) that demand a response for effective or adaptive functioning, but due to the presence of various obstacles, effective or adaptive coping responses are not immediately apparent or available to the person confronted with these situations (D'Zurilla & Goldfried, 1971; Nezu & D'Zurilla, in press). Recent research has suggested that these less dramatic daily stressful events *cumulatively* have an important influence on long-range health and emotional well-being (DeLongis, Coyne, Dakof, Folkman, & Lazarus, 1982; Kanner, Coyne, Schaefer, & Lazarus, 1981; Nezu & Ronan, 1985). With specific regard to depressive symptoms, Nezu (1986b) evaluated the stressful effects of self-defined problematic situations on consequent depressive symptom-atology. A prospective design was utilized to evaluate the hypothesis that the frequency of experienced problems would be a significant predictor of distress *apart* from the distress associated with major life events. Ad-ditionally, prior levels of depressed mood served as a relevant covariate to methodologically control for the influence of premorbid status. Results of data obtained from 129 university students were supportive of the major hypothesis. Results from related investigations provide further converging evidence in support of a positive correlation between the frequency of current problems and depressive symptomatology (Nezu & Ronan, 1985; Nezu, Perri, & Nezu, 1987).

Problem-Solving Coping

The third and most important component within this level of the overall problem-solving model of depression is *problem-solving coping*. Accord-ing to various stress researchers, the term *coping* refers to the cognitive and behavioral activities by which a person attempts to manage a stressful problematic situation. Coping serves two purposes: problem solving and emotional regulation. With specific regard to depressive reactions, coping responses function to help people avoid depression by moderating the potential effects that stressors have on functioning, as well as by avoiding future stressors (Billings & Moos, 1982). Whereas various definitions of the single term coping continue to exist, investigators have found it useful to distinguish between two general categories of coping reactions: prob-lem-focused and emotion-focused.

Problem-focused coping seeks to improve the objective problematic situation (i.e., the imbalance between demands and adaptive response availability). The function of *emotion-focused coping,* on the other hand, is to manage the emotional distress associated with the problematic sit-uation. Lazarus and Folkman's (1984) transactional stress theory treats problem solving as a form of problem-focused coping whose adaptive utility is limited to problematic situations appraised as *changeable*. When a stressful situation is appraised as *unchangeable*, the individual must rely on emotion-focused forms of coping in order to manage stress effectively.

In contrast with Lazarus and Folkman's view of problem solving as a form of problem-focused coping, we conceive problem solving as a more versatile, flexible, and adaptive set of coping strategies. More specifically, within the present model, problem solving is defined as the *general coping process* by which a person attempts to identify, discover, or invent a "solution," or adaptive coping response, for a particular problematic life

situation (D'Zurilla, 1986; Nezu, 1987; Nezu & D'Zurilla, in press). Solutions might involve either active attempts to change the problematic
nature of the situation, one's emotional reaction to it, or both (Nezu,
1987). Therefore, problem-focused coping may be only one alternative
set of strategies that might result from an individual's engaging in the
problem-solving process. Given the highly variable nature of the reciprocal relations between people and their environments across individuals,
situations, and person-situation interactions, attempts to alter the source
of stress may not always be the most appropriate and effective coping
strategy. For example, dealing with the loss of a spouse does not always
require active behavioral attempts; engaging in acceptance, prayer, or
mourning may be more helpful. Problem solving, then, should not be
simply equated with active efforts to change the problematic situation.
Rather, the "solutions" emanating from the problem-solving process might
include strategies for changing one's reactions to a problem, as well as
attempts to alter the problematic nature of the situation. Depending on
the nature of the stressful situation, *both* sets of strategies in tandem may
be the most effective approach for overall coping.

For example, in cases where the problematic situation is appraised
initially as changeable, but later (due to unsuccessful problem-solving
attempts) reappraised as unchangeable, it is helpful to reformulate the
problem to include emotion-focused goals, such as minimizing emotional
distress, enhancing personal growth in some fashion, or maintaining a
sense of self-worth. Thus, problem-solving coping is a *general* coping
approach that can help people manage or adapt to most stressful situations, thereby enhancing perceived controllability and minimizing emotional distress, even in situations that cannot be changed for the better
(D'Zurilla, 1986; Nezu, 1987; Nezu & D'Zurilla, in press).

Depressive Symptomatology

In the present problem-solving model, because of the reciprocal causal
influence that depressive symptoms may have on the other three components, they are included as a major variable within the transactional
perspective. Depressive reactions within this model include both the immediate *and* long-term symptoms that may result as a function of experiencing stressful events. Depressive responses include various somatic,
behavioral, cognitive, and affective aspects (see Chapter 1). The specific
symptom picture of depression may vary in the pattern, intensity, and
subjective quality of the experience within the same person while in the
same problematic situation, as well as across persons and situations depending on other aspects of the model, such as the person's cognitive

appraisal of the stressor, biological vulnerability, and the quality of one's coping attempts (Nezu, 1987; Nezu & D'Zurilla, in press).

Pathways to Depression: Interactions Among Negative Life Events, Problems, and Problem-Solving Coping Activities

In the problem-solving model of depression, reciprocal relations among major negative life events, daily problems, problem-solving coping activities, and depressive symptomatology are of major importance (Nezu, 1987). These four variables are postulated as constantly interacting. Thus, in this approach, the concept of stress and the experience of depression are dynamic processes that change in intensity and quality over time, depending on the changes that occur in major life events, current problems, and problem-solving coping activities.

Figure 3.1 represents the descriptive pathways that indicate reciprocal relations among negative life events, problems, problem-solving coping,

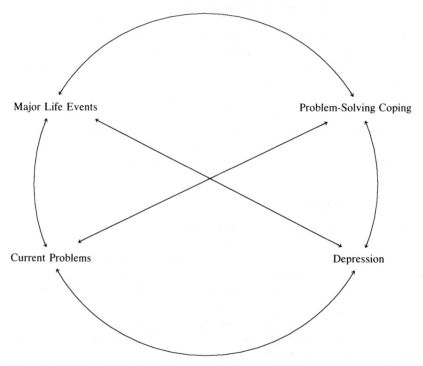

Figure 3.1. Reciprocal Relations Among Major Life Events, Current Problems, Problem-Solving Coping, and Depression.

and depression. According to this model, a major negative life event can lead to the occurrence of a wide range of daily problematic situations (e.g., getting fired leads to problems of job hunting, limited funds, difficulties with family and friends, lowered self-esteem, etc.). Similarly, on-going problems may lead to a major life change (e.g., difficulties with communicating with a spouse may lead to a divorce). Major life events and daily problems are both stressors that potentially engender a variety of negative consequences. As such, they require some attempts at coping. These negative consequences, whether perceived or real, serve three possible functions: (1) They lead to a decrease in perceived and/or actual positive reinforcement and an increase in aversive stimulation; (2) they exacerbate the stressful nature of problems and increase the likelihood that future problems (or major life events) may occur; and (3) they have an impact on the motivation of individuals to engage in subsequent problem-solving attempts. In this manner, negative consequences can make people vulnerable to a depressive episode.

Whether such consequences are perceived as negative in valence depends upon the importance of such effects to a particular individual. These idiosyncratic appraisals of importance are strongly influenced by one's learning history, personal goals, and current life circumstances. For example, certain people who lose their jobs may appraise the potential consequences of such a stressful event as highly negative because of their particular life circumstances (i.e., no immediate job prospects, limited financial resources, lack of substantial job experience), whereas others may perceive the subsequent effects of getting fired as neutral due to different life circumstances (i.e., plentiful jobs in related field, substantial financial resources). On the other hand, still others who get fired, even with new jobs available, may appraise the consequences as negative due to the impact on their self-esteem. Because achievement of personal career goals is highly important for these individuals, such consequences become particularly salient, and thus receive more attention.

If these negative consequences lead to a decrease in positive reinforcement (either external, internal, or both) and an increase in aversive stimulation, a dysphoric, or sad, mood is likely to occur, especially if self-esteem or feelings of self-worth are affected (e.g., "My girlfriend just broke up with me because she said I was not 'right for her'—now what am I going to do? I am really going to miss being with her!"). If the negative consequences serve to exacerbate the stressful nature of the experience either by prolonging the difficulties associated with the original problem or by increasing the imminence of additional problems, it is likely that feelings of being overwhelmed will occur. These feelings in turn may lead to perceptions of future hopelessness (e.g., "Too many things are going on—I don't feel that I can ever cope with all of it!''). When either emotional sequela to a stressful event occurs, the likelihood increases that the other will also occur thus leading to several potential negative effects on one's overall coping attempts.

First, strong initial dysphoric reactions to a stressful situation can have a negative effect on various problem-orientation variables. For example, a strong initial depressive response might influence a person to (1) label the problem as "emotional" or "psychological," (2) attribute the problem to some personal defect or inadequacy (e.g., lack of courage, emotional hypersensitivity), (3) appraise the problem as a significant threat to well-being (e.g., threat to self-esteem), (4) have self-doubts about ability to solve the problem or cope with the situation effectively, and/or (5) give up hope and do nothing about the problem instead of committing time and effort toward its resolution (D'Zurilla, 1986; Nezu, 1987; Nezu & D'Zurilla, in press).

Second, an initial depressive response can also influence the efficiency of problem-solving task performance, such as defining the problem, generating alternatives, and/or making effective decisions (D'Zurilla, 1986; Nezu, 1987). For example, in a study evaluating the effects of inducing differential moods (elative, neutral, and depressive) on problem-solving effectiveness, Mitchell and Madigan (1984) found that subjects in the depressive mood condition performed less effectively on a measure of problem-solving ability (i.e., MEPS), compared to the other two groups. Further, their findings suggest that even if no interpersonal problem-solving skill deficit existed prior to the depressive induction procedure, the negative mood that resulted might have significantly impaired subsequent problem-solving performance.

Third, strong initial depressive reactions can also serve to narrow attention to cues noted at the first perception of the problem (cf. Mandler, 1982). If most of these salient cues are task *relevant*, then performance efficiency may improve, due to the activating effects of emotional arousal. However, if many cues are task *irrelevant* and distressing, such as worries, negative self-appraisals, or aversive autonomic responses, then they are likely to disrupt task performance. This disruptive effect is more likely to occur with difficult or complex problems than with simple problems because the former require more concentration and attention to a wider range of cues (Nezu & D'Zurilla, in press).

Immediate depressive reactions to a problem situation can also affect the problem-solving process by influencing (a) the choice of problem-solving goals (emotion-focused goals), (b) the preferences for different solution alternatives (anticipation of positive or negative emotional consequences), (c) evaluations of actual solution outcome (positive or negative emotional outcomes), and (d) the strength of future problem-solving efforts (D'Zurilla, 1986; Nezu, 1987; Nezu & D'Zurilla, in press).

Finally, depressive reactions to stressful events can also disrupt or inhibit *specific coping performance* (i.e., implementation of coping responses). For example, a person may engage in effective problem-solving thinking and choose an assertive coping response for a particular problematic situation, but because of intense emotional distress, may be unable to perform the assertive response effectively.

If this sequence of events continues unchanged, long-term negative affect (major depressive episode) becomes highly probable, owing to the unresolved problem(s). More specifically, unresolved problems represent the continued influence of negative consequences. Overall, initial dysphoric reactions can ultimately lead to more problems (e.g., not looking for a job because of decreased motivation leads to greater financial problems), which in turn may lead to the occurrence of a major life event (e.g., bankruptcy; separation from spouse). Thus, a vicious cycle that maintains the depressive symptoms can occur in the absence of any intervention or change. The more prolonged the duration of the problems, the likelier that clinical depression will result. On the other hand, successful problem-solving coping attempts by reducing the situation's stressful nature or by resolving the problem itself will likely eliminate or decrease immediate negative emotional distress and prevent long-term affective reactions.

For example, the nature of one's overall problem orientation can influence both the stressful nature of a problematic situation and the associated negative emotions. One orientation variable, termed *problem perception* (recognition and labeling of the problem), influences the nature of the problem directly, because it is impossible to completely separate the objective problematic situation from the person's perception of the situation (Lazarus & Folkman, 1984; Levine et al., 1978). Problem-orientation variables can also affect the nature of stressful situations indirectly by influencing the person's emotions and both the problem-solving process and coping performance. For example, depressive symptoms and a disruption in problem-solving coping performance are likely to result when the individual (1) attributes the cause of the problem to some permanent internal defect or abnormality (e.g., lack of intelligence), (2) appraises the problem as a serious threat to well-being (e.g., job security), (3) suffers serious self doubt about ability to solve the problem or cope with the situation effectively, and/or (4) is not willing to commit the necessary time and effort to independent problem solving (D'Zurilla, 1986; Nezu & D'Zurilla, in press).

Depending on the problem-solving goals (problem-focused, emotion-focused, or both), problem-solving task performance (problem definition and formulation, generation of alternative solutions, etc.) and the quality of the resultant coping attempts can also affect the probability of depressive symptoms. For example, studies have demonstrated that the inability (or perception of inability) to solve problems involving the control of aversive events and/or positive outcomes results in a sense of helplessness and hopelessness, which in turn, leads to depressive symptoms (cf. Abramson et al., 1978; Halberstadt, Andrews, Metalsky, & Abramson, 1984). On the other hand, several process and outcome-oriented studies have demonstrated the positive effects of problem-solving coping in prevention or attenuation of depression caused by stressful events (Nezu, 1987; Nezu & D'Zurilla, in press; see Chapter 5 in this volume for an overview of such research).

The reciprocal nature that exists among these major variables (negative life changes, problems, problem-solving coping, depressive symtomatology) suggests the creation of additional major pathways. First, problem-solving ability can moderate the actual occurrence, nature, and number of problems that result as a consequence of a major life event. Conversely, ineffective problem solving in general can lead to the actual occurrence of both negative life events and problem situations. For example, poor problem-solving coping on a new job can increase the likelihood that problems will occur.

Additionally, since many negative consequences of a problem may be long-term in nature, it is possible to activate or maintain depression in the absence of an *immediately* preceeding stressful event. Conversely, negative consequences associated with a problem may be alleviated by one of two processes: effective problem-solving coping or factors related to, but outside, the individual. The latter case may involve changes in the problem made by significant others; such changes are not a direct function of the individual's own attempts at coping. For example, an individual may become depressed as the result of losing a job. Family members or friends who provide this person with new employment serve to change the problem, even though the individual has made no attempts at problem resolution. In this manner, depressive symptoms may spontaneously remit as a function of the decreased impact of the negative consequences.

In essence, the preceding formulation proposes that each variable within the model can influence the others to produce and/or to maintain depression. More specifically, whether one becomes clinically depressed depends upon the nature of the outcome of the reciprocal relations among stressful events, problem-solving coping, and one's immediate emotional response. This particular analysis, however, focuses on the pathogenesis of depression as it occurs at a particular point in time. In order to answer questions concerning how a given individual might develop the vulnerabilities specified within this formulation (i.e., problem-solving deficits, vulnerabilities to stressful events), a second level of analysis regarding genetic and biological factors and prior learning and development histories becomes a necessary supplement.

BIOCHEMICAL ASPECTS OF DEPRESSION: RELATION TO THE PROBLEM-SOLVING FORMULATION

Because attempts to integrate genetic, biological, and psychosocial bodies of research on depression have been quite rare (Thase, Frank, & Kupfer, 1985), the specific relation between the problem-solving model depicted thus far and various biochemical aspects of depression can only be speculative. Yet, certain recent advances concerning the neurochemistry of stress and the biology of affective disorders provide intriguing points of intersection that may be relevant to the present formulation.

Recent research has indicated that several common features exist between the neurochemical changes produced by stress and the biochemical factors found to be associated with depression (Anisman & LaPierre, 1982). For example, a relationship has been found between clinical depression and depletion of the brain amines norepinephrine and serotonin, with some evidence suggesting the involvement of acetylcholine (Schildkraut, 1974).

Several studies have also indicated that uncontrollable stress can result in the depletion of brain norepinephrine (Weiss, Glazer, & Pohorecky, 1976) and serotonin (Thierry, Blanc, & Glowinski, 1971) and can produce an increase in acetylcholine (Anisman, Pizzino, & Sklar, 1980). It is likely that moderate to severe stress can induce neurochemical and biological changes related to depressive symptomatology (Anisman & LaPierre, 1982; Sackheim & Weber, 1982). For example, Cartwright (1983) found that among a sample of community volunteers, more than 50% of a subgroup of women going through divorce proceedings showed both clinical evidence of consequent depression and changes in biological patterns.

It is important to note that collectively, this research does not point simply to the presence of a particular abnormality of any of these neurotransmitters as involved exclusively in the pathology of depression. Instead, it is more likely that they act in combination (Anisman & LaPierre, 1982). In other words, the *balance* among neurotransmitter systems provides the most appropriate framework from which to understand the relation between biochemical factors and depression.

Further, research also has indicated that most processes of neuronal impulse transmission are under genetic regulation (Ciaranello, 1983). Although the exact mechanisms involved in the genetic transmission of clinical depression are unknown at this time (cf. Mendlewicz, 1985), it is possible that genetic vulnerability to depression lies in the inheritance of specific depression-related patterns in neurotransmission (cf. Ciaranello).

With specific regard to the present discussion, additional research has indicated that *control,* or the ability to engage in coping activities during stressful situations, is a critically important factor in reducing maladaptive physiological and neurochemical reactivity in response to stressful stimuli (Levine, 1983). For example, control over stressful stimuli has been found to be crucial in determining whether or not an amine depletion occurs (Anisman et al., 1980). Further, Henry (1980) has postulated that the routing of neuronal impulses associated with feelings of helplessness, or loss of control over stressful events, occurs via the hippocampus and septum, which then activate stimulation of the hypothalmic-pituitary-adrenal system, leading to increased production of acetycholine and secretion of corticosterone. The behavioral manifestation of this biochemical pattern is depression. If effective problem-solving skills help individuals maintain control over aversive events, and thereby serve to moderate the stressful effects of such events (Nezu, 1986c, 1987; Nezu & D'Zurilla, in press), it is likely that problem-solving coping can also function as a moderator of the stress-induced neurochemical changes associated with depression. In other words, effective coping with stressful situations may raise the threshold at which the deleterious effects of stress produce depression-related neurochemical changes.

Consistent with this formulation is a model of depression postulated by Akiskal and McKinney (1975). In reviewing the relevant psychochemical literature, these authors propose that a variety of stressors can induce changes in biochemical amines and that any assumed deficit in biogenic amine metabolism can be *secondary* to interpersonal events. Moreover, they suggest that these secondary biochemical alterations can induce and maintain depressive behavior as a function of their effects on the neurophysiological mechanisms of reinforcement. As such, certain biogenic amine deficiencies may be a predisposing, rather than a causal, factor in depressive disorders (cf. van Pragg, 1979).

The interactions among stress, biological propensity, and problem-solving coping may also have an impact on the probability of individuals experiencing various subtypes of depression (unipolar vs. bipolar; dysthymic disorder vs. psychotic and melancholic major depressive disorder). Biological factors may account for more of the variance in predicting certain subtypes of depression (i.e., psychotic depression, bipolar depression, melancholia) than psychosocial factors. For other subtypes (i.e., unipolar nonpsychotic depression, dysthymic disorder), psychosocial variables may be more influential than biological propensity in moderating the onset of depression. Problem solving may be involved in all types of depressive disorders, but only in an interactive capacity with stress, biochemical phenomena, and other psychosocial variables. In other words, the presence of severe neurochemical abnormalities may require only minimal amounts of stress to induce a depressive reaction (as a function of a genetically transmitted lowered threshold), regardless of a person's ultimate problem-solving effectiveness. Conversely, effective problem solving may inhibit depression if one's biological propensity is moderate, regardless of the severity of psychosocial stressors. This speculation is consistent with the observation that patients with milder, nonpsychotic, nondelusional, major depression are less likely to show evidence of biological dysfunction (Thase et al., 1985). Thus, in predicting the different depressive subtypes, the actual amount of the variance accounted for by problem-solving coping might depend upon the interaction with various neurochemical factors.

THE ROLE OF PREVIOUS LEARNING EXPERIENCES

This section briefly explores the role of previous learning experiences with regard to the problem-solving model. It is suggested that prior learning and developmental history can exert a strong influence in determining the behavioral expression of individual differences concerning the problem-solving formulation of depression. Such influences can occur at all sites within the model, including stressful events, problem-solving coping, and depression.

With regard to stressful events, there are several ways that previous learning experiences may make one especially vulnerable to depression when facing particular types of problems. First, reinforcing or punishing experiences with similar problems in the past can modify the importance, salience, and impact potency of a current problem for a particular individual. For example, a male rejected for dates several times in the past may be especially sensitive to feeling sad and worthless in response to a current rejection. More importantly, individuals who have experienced a significant interpersonal loss at a young age (e.g., death of a parent) may develop a depression-related vulnerability to future losses, such as death of a spouse or divorce (Wallerstein, 1983).

Second, complex learning that occurs throughout development into adulthood produces differences in the meaning and importance of various events. Through a variety of social learning processes (i.e., respondent, operant, and vicarious learning procedures), differences in the personal meaning attached to particular events can produce idiosyncratic vulner-abilities to such events. As an example, for one individual, situations characterized by achievement may be particularly important, whereas for another, events involving interpersonal relationships and affiliations are more critical. These differences in personal importance can lead to dif-ferences in vulnerability to depression when losses, disappointments, or problems in such areas occur (cf. Hammen, Miklowitz, & Dyck, 1986). In other words, not all depressed individuals respond in the same way to similar problems (cf. Horowitz, Weckler, & Doren, 1983).

Third, lack of similar prior experiences with a problematic situation can increase the ambiguity, uncertainty, and novelty of a current stressful event. Such novel problems, if perceived as personally important, can have an impact on self-efficacy perceptions. According to Bandura (1977), the single most important influence on self-efficacy beliefs is prior suc-cessful behavioral attempts. Conversely, lack of prior experience with similar situations may produce lowered perceptions of ability to cope with a stressful situation.

Previous learning history can also influence problem-solving coping attempts in response to current stressful situations. Developmentally, differences in learning histories, to a large extent, contribute substantially to the variability in people's overall problem-solving abilities (Spivack & Shure, 1974; Spivack et al., 1976). The quality of an adult's social problem-solving skills is likely to reflect prior direct and vicarious learning expe-riences from problems that have occurred throughout cognitive and emo-tional development.

Socialization and cultural factors are also likely to influence variability in the quality of people's overall coping abilities. One important example is the influence of sex-role orientation. One study found that sex roles serve as an important moderator of depressive symptoms related to the experience of stressful events (Nezu, Nezu, & Peterson, 1986). Under high levels of stress, subjects with high scores on a masculinity dimension reported lower depression scores than subjects with low masculinity scores, regardless of actual gender. The sex-role dimension of femininity appeared to contribute little to the prediction of depressive symptomatology. In a subsequent study (Nezu & Nezu, 1987b), the correlation between differences in sex-role orientation and distress was strongly related to differences in problem-solving coping ability. This finding is suggestive that differences in depression prevalence rates between men and women may be related to variables associated with sex-role differences, such as coping.

Even if a person's basic problem-solving ability is high, previous un-successful attempts at coping with a particular type of event are likely to influence current attempts to deal with a stressful situation. For example, prior difficulties with problems related to interpersonal relationships can affect the quality of current attempts to cope with a similar event by (1) influencing orientation to the problem (e.g., decreased motivation, negative appraisal of the situation), and/or (2) impacting on one's actual attempts (e.g., inhibiting effective coping attempts, ineffectively implementing a potentially effective solution).

Previous experience with a similar problem may also influence one to be more impulsive and less thoughtful in relation to current problem-solving attempts. An individual who has successfully resolved an interpersonal problem in the past by being assertive, is more likely to believe that a similar coping response would be effective for a current interpersonal problem, without assessment of the specific context of the current situation.

Prior learning history can also affect the specific pattern, intensity, and duration of a depressive reaction to a current stressful life event. In general, observations from a variety of research studies inadvertently indicate that the best predictor of depression is a past history of depressive episodes (cf. Hammen, 1985; Nezu & Ronan, 1988). This suggests a variety of possible pathogenic processes involving the etiologic role of previous depressive reactions. First, both respondent and operant conditioning processes may operate to influence the likelihood that a person will experience depressive symptoms in reaction to a current stressor if such an emotional reaction has been associated with similar situations in the past. Second, research has indicated that depressed individuals, in comparison to nondepressed persons, tend to remember more negative events in general, as well as negative aspects of a particular event (Breslow, Kocsis, & Belkin, 1981; Derry & Kuiper, 1981). If several prior problems are associated with depressive mood states, and the current problem is similar to the previous situations, a current depressive reaction is likely to be stronger. Memories of prior events, also having depressive content, are likely to influence one's perception of self and the future (cf. Kuiper, Olinger, & MacDonald, 1985). Third, previous depressive episodes can affect current depressive reactions by reinforcing the belief that the future is especially hopeless. In other words, if a person remembers being depressed in the past concerning similar situations, a current dysphoric reaction may provide "proof" that such responses are inevitable, which in turn can lead to perceptions of uncontrollability and helplessness.

Lastly, it is probable that biological vulnerability to depression, if present, interacts strongly with the wide range of experiences encountered throughout an individual's developmental history. This interaction effect could influence the potency and saliency of particular types of stressful situations, impact on one's overall problem-solving coping effectiveness, and provide for more frequent depressive episodes prior to adulthood.

INTEGRATIVE SUMMARY

The "big picture" of the problem-solving model of depression includes three major levels of analysis. This chapter has presented two of these focal areas. The first one is a transactional perspective, which specifies the reciprocal relations among major negative life events, daily problems, problem-solving coping, and depressive symptoms. Long-term negative affective states (i.e., clinical depression) can result from the interactions among two different sources of environmental stress (major life events and daily problems), immediate emotional reactions, and the nature of the problem-solving coping process. More specifically, if the outcome of interactions within this model, primarily as a function of problem-solving coping, is negative (i.e., unsuccessful problem resolution), then depression is likely to occur. If attempts at problem solving, on the other hand, lead to effective problem resolution, then the probability of long-term negative affective states occurring is minimal.

The second level of analysis addresses the influence of genetic and biological vulnerabilities, as well as the role of previous learning and developmental history. It appears that biological vulnerabilities to depression, which may be genetically transmitted, lie in a person's neurochemical reactivity threshold to stressful events. More specifically, biological correlates of depression may be the neurochemical sequelae to stressful events. Biological propensity to depression, thus, may represent a heightened sensitivity (or lower threshold) to stressful situations. However, whether this threshold in fact is reached depends also on various psychosocial variables, control in particular. Effective problem-solving coping with stressful situations may serve to inhibit activation of such depression-related neurochemical patterns. Further, individual differences in the complex interplay among environmental stress, coping, and biological propensity may explain the variability in differential types of depressive disorders, as well as in the severity of the actual experience of depression.

Prior learning experience may have a strong influence on each of the major variables within the transactional model (i.e., stressors, problem-solving coping, and depressive reactions). Prior history can affect the perceived importance, potency, and impact of a particular stressor, as well as the overall quality of an individual's problem-solving ability. Previous depressive episodes can also influence the nature, pattern, and severity of current depressive reactions, especially if the prior experiences are associated with similar circumstances.

At this juncture, it is important to point out the speculative nature of certain aspects of the preceding formulations, especially concerning the relation between biochemical correlates of depression and the problem-solving model. However, as with any attempt to integrate diverse bodies of research, certain leaps of inference become inevitable. This book began by highlighting the need to develop more comprehensive models of depression as a means of accounting for diverse research findings and providing for better explanatory approaches concerning the variability found among depressed persons, as well as within an individual across time and situations (cf. Hammen, 1985). To accomplish such a task often involves treading on "thin ice." Delineating this model may engender research addressing the complexities involved in a comprehensive understanding of depression, rather than research that attempts to isolate a single vulnerability marker based on the guise that parsimony should be a priority.

CHAPTER 4

Problem-Solving Component Processes

Relation to Depression and Cognitive-Behavioral Theories of Depression

This chapter describes the purposes, underlying processes, and training goals of the five major problem-solving components (problem orientation, problem definition and formulation, generation of alternatives, decision making, solution implementation and verification). By highlighting the relation of each problem-solving process to depression the chapter completes the description of a problem-solving formulation of depression. As a function of the nature and purposes of these components, problem solving actually encompasses several composite processes that several cognitive-behavioral theories identify as their major etiologic factors (i.e., causal attributions, cognitive distortions, self-control difficulties). As such, this third level of analysis within the problem-solving framework provides for a useful metaphor to integrate these existing theories in a meaningful manner. Such a comprehensive understanding of depression becomes particularly important in light of the existing explanatory limitations characteristic of current models when considered separately (Hammen, 1985; Nezu, 1987). The chapter describes applicable research addressing the effectiveness of training in the individual problem-solving components, relevant to a social problem-solving context. Various clinical examples taken from our collective experience in applying this model illustrate various important points. Lastly, the general implications of a problem-solving formulation of depression will be articulated.

PROBLEM ORIENTATION

The first problem-solving component reflects a general response set that individuals use in relation to understanding and reacting to perceived or actual stressful situations. This orientation serves as a motivational process which can have either a generalized facilitative or inhibitory effect on the remaining four problem-solving tasks. The major purposes of this orientation are to (1) increase one's sensitivity to problems in living; (2) minimize the influence of immediate emotional states and thoughts (self-statements) that are likely to disrupt further problem-solving activities; (3) increase one's approach motivation to engage in subsequent problem-solving coping attempts; and (4) focus on the stimulus determinants of the problem and on self-statements that are likely to facilitate effective problem-solving behavior (D'Zurilla, 1986; D'Zurilla & Nezu, 1982).

To achieve this purpose, training in this component is geared toward helping individuals to (1) correctly identify and recognize problems when they occur; (2) adopt the philosophical perspective that problems in living are normal and inevitable and that problem solving is a viable means of coping with them; (3) increase their expectation of engaging in successful problem-solving activities (i.e., perceived self-efficacy); and (4) inhibit the set to engage in automatic response habits based on previous experiences in similar situations (D'Zurilla & Nezu, 1982). The orientation process includes five specific variables: problem perception, problem attribution, problem appraisal, personal control beliefs, and approach/avoidance style.

Problem Perception

This process first focuses on the accurate recognition of stressful problems when they occur. It is only when individuals recognize a problem and attend to the relevant information that they can prepare to deal with it effectively. This sensitivity to problems is an important prerequisite for later problem-solving activities because it helps to activate the self-statement, "I need to do something about this situation."

In addition to identifying a problem situation, individuals also have to appropriately label it as such. Since stressful situations are often difficult and engender immediate negative emotional reactions, it is important that the problem solver also accurately label the *situation* as the problem, and not the affective response. This allows the individual to later correctly identify the specific problem-causing parameters of the situation. It is not necessary at this point for individuals to define the problem accurately, but they need to focus on the problem situation, rather than on their concurrent emotional state. Emotions, within this context, should be used as cues or signals that a problem exists, because labeling the emotional reaction as the problem can lead to later ineffective coping attempts. For example, instead of focusing on difficulties in finding a job right after college and labeling this situation as a problem, Jane S., a recent college graduate, reported her problem as "being down in the dumps all the time." Her previous way of coping with this problem had been to engage in short-term attempts at "feeling better," such as increasing social activities, going on shopping sprees, and eating more. By relabeling her problem more accurately (i.e., job-finding difficulties which impacted on her self-esteem), she was able to generate more appropriate, and therefore, more effective, alternative solutions to her problem (i.e., explore graduate education possibilities, reprioritize her career goals, seek employment in other less competitive geographical locations, etc.).

D'Zurilla (1986) also points out that previous learning experiences may cause individuals to vary in the idiosyncratic significance or meaning they attach to certain labels. For example, financial problems to John F. signified threats to his self-esteem and activated feelings of inadequacy. As a consequence, any time financial difficulties occurred (e.g., overdraft at the bank, rejection of credit application, occasional limited resources to meet monthly expeditures), he would tend to avoid thinking about them, which led to the creation of additional problems, rather than to the resolution of the original situation. By using the distressing feelings as cues that "something is going wrong—I need to solve these problems," John was able to engage in attempts to actively engage in further problem-solving activities.

Problem Attribution

This problem-orientation variable reflects the attributions of causality that individuals make in relation to problems in living. The circumstances under which a stressful event occurs can be initially construed along the dimension of internality-externality. More specifically, the causal explanations of problems can include either environmental factors or stable personality characteristics. A facilitative problem attribution involves an overall accurate focus on the reasons why a problem occurred. A general style that attributes the cause to internal factors can lead to unnecessary increases in responsibility, stress, and feelings of being overwhelmed. When this internal attributional focus involves negative assessments, depressive reactions can increase, especially if lowered self-esteem leads to decreases in motivation to engage in further problem-solving activities. For example, when Sally T., a newly appointed office manager, had difficulties with her boss, she often attributed this problem to internal personality defects—"I'm just stupid, I'll probably lose this promotion." Instead of attributing the real cause, a lack of specific training in relation to her new responsibilities, her self-statements of blame inhibited attempts to solve her problem.

Such attributional biases can lead to ineffective attempts at problem-solving coping. Heppner, Reeder, and Larson (1983), for example, found that ineffective problem solvers, as compared to effective problem solvers, tended to blame themselves more frequently. Further, this negative attributional style has shown a strong correlation with depressive affect and is a central etiological concept in explaining depression within the attributional reformulation of learned helplessness theory (Abramson et al., 1978).

On the opposite extreme, individuals may attribute the cause of problems solely to external, as compared to intrapersonal, factors—"It's all my wife's fault, if only she would see things my way, everything would be okay." This type of generalized attributional style again inhibits effective problem-solving activities. If a person continues to ascribe the causes of problems to external sources, there is little motivation to try and solve them. Further, this approach increases the probability that future problems will occur.

Therefore, a facilitative attributional style within this context involves the philosophical belief that problems in living are normal and inevitable and a willingness to engage in a reality-based search for the appropriate causes of any particular problem. Given the variable nature of person-situation interactions, the causes of various problematic situations can at times be attributable to the individual, at times to other external factors, and at times to a combination of both. Either extreme causal ascription is likely to inhibit effective problem-solving performance.

Problem Appraisal

This problem-orientation process involves the idiosyncratic evaluations of problems concerning (1) their importance or significance to a particular individual, and (2) if important, their valence with regard to one's personal well-being. Research addressing the impact of stressful events has pointed to the need to include assessment of the event with regard to its idiosyncratic importance for a particular individual (cf. Nezu & Carnevale, 1987). For example, the death of a distant relative or the loss of a job to one individual may be highly significant events, whereas to another, due to differential life contexts, they are not.

This initial judgment concerning an event's importance parallels one of the cognitive errors or distortions that Beck (Beck et al., 1979) identifies as characteristic of information processing in depression—*magnification and minimization*. Magnification involves the error in judgment that causes an overemphasis of a trivial event's significance, whereas minimization concerns underestimating the importance of an event when in fact it is significant. Either error in judgment can lead to later ineffective problem solving, because these distortions could influence the manner in which the problem is later defined and formulated.

The second judgment is an evaluation of the *valence* of the event concerning one's personal well-being. This concept is similar to Lazarus' (Lazarus & Folkman, 1984) notion of *primary appraisal*. Upon evaluating an event to be personally significant, the individual then appraises the problem as either positive or negative. A positive appraisal involves perceiving the event as a challenge or opportunity to benefit, whereas a negative appraisal entails viewing the problem as harmful or threatening. For example, Tom J. and Bob A., two employees of a company that had announced possible layoffs, had different appraisals of the problem. Both initially perceived this situation as significant and important. However, Tom viewed it as an opportunity to change careers and get a better job. Bob, on the other hand, viewed the potential layoff as extremely threatening. As a function of Tom's appraisal, he engaged in effective attempts at problem-solving coping and did not become depressed when the layoffs occurred. Bob's appraisal of the problem, however, served to inhibit his problem-solving performance, which then led to feelings of anxiety and depression.

Personal Control Beliefs

People's beliefs regarding both the likelihood that a problem is solvable and that they are capable of coping with the problematic situation effectively form one of the most important variables underlying the problem-orientation process (Nezu, Kalmar, Ronan, & Clavijo, 1986; Rotter, 1978). In other words, the expectancy of being able to affect or control, at least in part, events that happen in their lives can help determine people's responses to problems. For example, Bloom and Broder (1950) found that successful problem solvers had greater confidence in their ability to solve the problems presented to them than did unsuccessful problem solvers. Individuals who appraise themselves as effective problem solvers, compared to self-appraised ineffective problem solvers, tend to view common life problems as being caused by controllable factors (Baumgardner, Heppner, & Arkin, 1986). Further, research addressing the construct of one's locus of control consistently indicates that the general expectation of being able to control his or her environment greatly increases the likelihood that an individual will attempt to cope with actual situational problems (Lefcourt, 1966; Rotter, 1966). As will be described in Chapter 5, one study evaluating the effectiveness of social problem-solving therapy for unipolar depression found that training in problem-solving skills led to a decrease in depressive symtomatology, as well as an increase in personal control expectancies (Nezu, 1986c).

Personal control beliefs constitute the central construct within Bandura's (1977) self-efficacy theory. According to Bandura, personal judgments concerning ability to execute specific behaviors moderate the initiation, perserverance, and accomplishment of such behaviors, as well as actual behavior change. These evaluations are further distinguished from outcome expectations, concerning the actual impact of the specific behaviors. This second set of judgments has particular importance in later decision-making activities that assess the probability of a particular solution actually resolving the problem.

It is also important to note at this point that *extreme* beliefs in one's ability to control the environment may also be detrimental to later problem-solving activities and consequent emotional reactions. Problem solving has been defined previously as a broad-based coping process, where possible effective solutions may be geared toward active attempts to change the problematic nature of the situation, one's emotional reaction to it, or both (Nezu, 1987). A person who defines successful solutions only as those that change the nature of the situation may encounter bitter disappointments, which could also lead to depressive reactions. Believing that at times, certain problems cannot be solved (i.e., the stressful situation is unchangeable) allows an individual to also include emotion-focused goals as viable alternatives. For example, Matt D., a successful business executive, often became depressed when confronted with stressful situations over whose occurrence he had little control (e.g., various interpersonal difficulties involving women). Continuous attempts to change the nature of the situation, when the problem in fact was unchangeable (e.g., ex-fiancée falling "out of love" with him) led to feelings of disappointment and inadequacy. Problem-solving therapy, in part, for Matt focused on changing his belief that he could totally control every problematic situation he encountered and helping him to focus, at times, on changing his emotional reactions to unchangeable problems.

Approach/Avoidance Style

This problem-orientation variable concerns the manner in which individuals tend to either (1) commit themselves to solving problems, or (2) deny or avoid their existence. In general, it is better to approach or confront a problem than to avoid it. Denying that a problem exists only increases the likelihood that the problem will not be resolved and that future problems will also occur (D'Zurilla & Nezu, 1982). Avoidance of problems can further inhibit or disrupt later problem-solving activities. For example, Heppner et al. (1983) found that ineffective problem solvers engaged in more irrational beliefs concerning problem avoidance as compared to effective problem solvers. Further, effective problem solvers more often consider *effort* to be an important determinant of their performance as compared to ineffective problem solvers (Baumgardner et al., 1986).

Janis (1982) describes three forms of defensive avoidance behavior with regard to decision making: procrastination, shifting of responsibility, and selective exposure. Defensive avoidance in general involves the suppression of disturbing thoughts, selective inattention to cues that arouse negative emotions, and biased processing of information that directly deals with the problem situation. Procrastination, characterized by a general ignoring of disturbing information, is a pattern that can emerge when there are no deadline pressures to solve the problem.

A person can also avoid a problem by shifting responsibility onto others. For example, Gary C., parent of two adolescent daughters, tended to avoid making decisions concerning their upbringing and shifted responsibility for problem solving onto his wife, Ellen. This pattern eventually led to serious marital difficulties between them, increasing the possibility of a divorce or separation. Gary even attempted to avoid the martial problems. Problem-solving therapy for Gary, then, first involved encouraging him to take more responsibility in mutual decision making and entailed intensive problem-solving sessions between the couple.

In the third form of avoidance, selective exposure, the individual actively searches for and prefers information that supports the idea that there really is no problem to solve and avoids information to the contrary.

Depending on the specific nature of the stressful situation, however, either style may be adaptive or maladaptive. Denial in the form of minimizing the magnitude of a threat when the dangers are nonambiguous may be adaptive at times (Janis, 1982). For example, in the case of patients suffering from inoperable cancer, with little realistic hope for survival, denying the imminence of death may prove to be an effective coping strategy.

On the other hand, an extreme form of approach behavior may also be maladaptive. This situation might exist when an individual wants to solve the problem immediately, without taking the time or effort often necessary to engage in thoughtful and systematic problem solving. Due to previous experiences with similar problems, a person may "jump the gun" and attempt to implement a solution that worked in the past. Unless the situations are identical, it is likely that different problem parameters require different solutions. Therefore, it is important for individuals, when confronted with stressful problems, to inhibit the tendency to respond impulsively and automatically. Instead, they should stop and think. For example, Platt and Spivack (1974), in a study that compared psychiatric patients with normal controls on a variety of problem-solving parameters, found the controls included in their responses to hypothetical problems the notion that one should *think* before acting. On the other hand, the patient group showed more concern for taking immediate action. Further, research by Bloom and Broder (1950) indicates that less successful problem solvers tend to be impulsive and impatient. Studies by Heppner and his colleagues (Heppner et al., 1982; 1983) additionally characterize effective problem solvers as showing less impulsiveness, being more insightful, and rating themselves as more likely to engage in and enjoy thinking.

Research on Training in Problem Orientation

A study conducted by Cormier, Otani, and Cormier (1986) was designed to specifically address the effects of training in various problem-solving components. With regard to the problem-orientation process, graduate student subjects who received instructions in the content of this component performed significantly better than control subjects on two problem-solving tasks. One task required selecting the best alternative from a list of possible solutions to several interpersonal and social problems. In the second problem-solving measure, subjects described in detail the actual behaviors used to solve a series of six additional problems.

As will be described in more detail in Chapter 5, one purpose of an outcome study by Nezu and Perri (1987) involved testing the relative contribution of the problem-orientation component in treating clinically depressed individuals. A dismantling strategy was used to address this goal by randomly assigning 39 diagnosed depressed subjects to one of three conditions: Problem-Solving Therapy (PST—training in the entire model); Abbreviated Problem-Solving Therapy (APST—entire model minus training in the orientation process); and a Waiting-List Control (WLC). Results indicated that whereas APST subjects reported significantly lower posttreatment depression scores than WLC members, PST subjects evidenced significantly lower levels of depressive symptomatology than both the APST and WLC participants. It was concluded that although APST members were taught various problem-solving coping skills (i.e., defining problems, generating alternative solutions, decision making), not specifically addressing their problem-solving set may have led to less effective treatment. In a sense, having certain coping skills does not automatically guarantee their implementation. Because the goal of training in the problem-orientation process is to facilitate adoption of a positive set towards problems in living, thereby increasing motivation to engage in the remaining problem-solving tasks, negative orientation may have caused APST subjects to be inconsistent in implementing their learned skills.

These two studies provide strong support for the inclusion of training in problem orientation within the overall problem-solving therapy model. Equivocal results from problem-solving training that address other adult and child psychological disorders have in part been due to omission of the orientation process.

Relation to Depression

It has been argued in Chapter 3 that depression can result as a function of deficiencies in, or ineffective application of, any or all of the five major problem-solving components. The specific importance of the problem-orientation process to this depression-associated vulnerability lies in its impact on the likelihood that an individual will engage in further problem-solving activities. When a negative problem-solving set reduces the probability of an individual actively attempting to cope with stressful situations, the likelihood of negative consequences is greatly increased. This state of affairs then reinforces the negative set (i.e., ''I knew I shouldn't try and do anything about this problem, things turned out badly anyway''), thus beginning the process of the ''vicious cycle'' phenomenon (i.e., negative orientation leads to a lack of problem-solving attempts, which leads to negative consequences, which leads to an exacerbation of the negative set, which impacts on further problem-solving activities, etc.).

As stated previously, the problem-orientation component appears to describe a response set that incorporates several cognitive variables causally related in the literature to emotional distress and depression. These include cognitive appraisal (Lazarus & Folkman, 1984), irrational beliefs (Ellis, 1962), self-efficacy (Bandura, 1977), causal attributions (Abramson et al., 1978), and cognitive distortions (Beck et al., 1979). In these terms a negative or maladaptive problem orientation might include the following: appraising the situation as a threat instead of a challenge; maintaining a set of irrational beliefs about problems in general (e.g., ''Problems shouldn't happen to me''); evaluating one's sense of competence as ineffective; attributing the problem's cause to internal, stable, or global factors underlying a sense of hopelessness and helplessness; and/or magnifying or exaggerating the intensity, value, or significance of the problem. Taking into perspective the entire literature on these variables, such cognitions are not discrete phenomenon; rather the presence of one serves to facilitate the onset of another (Nezu, 1987). Further, it is not the presence of a negative problem-solving set *per se* that activates depression, but the influence that such an orientation has on the likelihood that people will engage in further problem-solving activities. In other words, cognitive-based theories of depression provide a partial explanation of the pathogenesis of depression, but not the entire picture (cf. Coyne, 1982; Coyne & Gotlib, 1983; Craighead, 1980; Nezu, 1987). For example, even if a person maintains a depressive attributional style, the interaction with the effectiveness (or ineffectiveness) of other problem-solving components is a better predictor of the likelihood of depression than the attributional style itself (Nezu, Kalmar, Ronan, & Clavijo, 1986).

PROBLEM DEFINITION AND FORMULATION

Although this operation can be considered the most important component within the social problem-solving process, it is probably also the most difficult and complex (D'Zurilla & Nezu, 1982). The purpose of this process is to assess the nature of the problem situation and to identify a realistic goal or objective for problem solving. Its importance for guiding effective latter problem-solving activities cannot be overemphasized. To paraphase a quote from John Dewey (1910)—"A problem well defined is half solved". In other words, a well-defined problem is likely to generate relevant solutions, improve decision-making effectiveness, and contribute to the accuracy of solution verification. In real-life situations, stressful problems are far from clear and well defined. Instead, they are often vague, ambiguous, and contain partial information that can lead to vague goals. Therefore, training in this initial problem-solving task has five components: (1) seeking all available facts and information about the problem; (2) describing these facts in clear and unambiguous terms; (3) differentiating relevant from irrelevant information and objective facts from unverified inferences, assumptions, and interpretations; (4) identifying the factors and circumstances that actually make the situation a problem; and (5) setting a series of realistic problem-solving goals.

Gathering Information

Rarely are problems in living well defined and delineated. Often individuals must seek additional information about vague and complex problem situations. This concept is a fundamental maxim of clinical assessment, diagnosis, and research. Attempting to understand the specific nature of a stressful problem without gathering information is analogous to diagnosing a patient as depressed without the benefit of interview data. This point is particularly important when the problem involves other people.

Difficulties in accurately identifying the emotions of others within relationships can lead to misunderstandings concerning the actual contributions an individual might be making toward causing a problem. For example, Janice G., a young woman, often felt disturbed and depressed because of her difficulties in maintaining close friendships. When newly developed friends appeared to become distant, she attributed this problem to personal defects (e.g., "I'm a boring person"), which further reinforced her feelings of sadness. This also led her to talk a lot about her own interests during conversations as a means of proving that she was not a boring person. Since this solution did not appear to be successful, it was recommended to Janice to better define her problem and to seek more information. She then asked a fellow worker, who confided in her that she often "came on too strong and opinionated." Rather than perceiving her as boring, then, her friends felt that they were unable to talk to her. By redefining her problem more accurately, Janice was able eventually to focus on the real problem.

Using Clear and Unambiguous Language

The use of concrete, clear, and unambiguous terms to describe a problem can help to minimize inaccurate definitions. This emphasis on objectivity and specificity is analogous to the use of operational definitions in behavioral assessment. Concrete and unambiguous language helps in all aspects of latter problem-solving activities (D'Zurilla & Nezu, 1982). Stating the problem specifically and concretely forces an individual to make relevant what may have appeared initially to be irrelevant (D'Zurilla & Goldfried, 1971; Skinner, 1953). For example, Bloom and Broder (1950) found that successful problem solvers tended to translate difficult and unfamiliar terms into simpler, more concrete language. On the other hand, unsuccessful problem solvers tended to accept vague concepts without attempting to reformulate them into more understandable terms.

Using more descriptive and specific language also minimizes the probability that vague and ambiguous terms will elicit emotional reactions associated with former learning processes. More specifically, if a vague term, such as "I feel all screwed up" leads to associations of previous situations that were similarly labeled, the probability of mood congruent memories occurring is increased. This only serves to maintain or exacerbate current feelings of depression. For example, Mike T. came to therapy for help with his "relationship problem." By using this ambiguous label for his difficulties, he associated them with previous problems with people in general and was overwhelmed by feelings of hopelessness. Accurately defining and concentrating on the current problem that led him into therapy at the time (i.e., recent breakup with a girlfriend) proved to be more manageable.

Minimizing Distortions in Information Processing

In defining and formulating problematic situations individuals often use processed information based on idiosyncratic judgments, inferences, valuations, assumptions, and interpretations. Whereas it is rare to have totally accurate information about a situation at hand, given the complex nature of real-life problems, this information may be subject to distortions in processing. When the definition of a problem is based upon inaccurate or distorted information, it is likely that individuals will attempt to solve "pseudoproblems," instead of real problems (D'Zurilla & Nezu, 1982). These pseudoproblems, however, are insoluble since solutions identified to deal with them are likely to be inappropriate or irrelevant for the actual problem. For example, Dana Z., a woman in her late 50s, continued to feel depressed and lonely. Initially, she defined her problem as being "old and out of touch with today's culture." This led her to refuse social invitations from younger co-workers. Dana would always think, "They're just trying to be nice—why would they want to hang out with an old person like me?" Upon realizing in therapy that this *arbitrary inference* was incorrect, she began to discover that her younger co-workers in fact perceived her as wise and experienced and valued her companionship. Accepting their invitations led to increased social activities and the resolution of Dana's pseudoproblem.

Other types of cognitive distortions identified by Beck (see Chapter 1, this volume), such as selective abstraction, overgeneralization, magnification, and minimization, can also influence the process of problem definition. Related to these mistakes in information processing is the selective attention to negative versus positive events and to immediate versus long-term consequences that is characteristic of depressed individuals (Rehm, 1981). Selective attention to the negative aspects of a stressful situation during self-monitoring may result in inaccurate definitions of problems. A negative attributional style (Abramson et al., 1978), whereby an individual consistently ascribes a problem's cause to himself or herself will also likely define the problem inaccurately. Intervention in this area should focus on the identification and amelioration of such distortions in information processing.

Another type of mistake that individuals may make in defining problems involves means-end thinking (i.e., identifying cause-effect relations, anticipating the consequences of behavior). In particular, this error concerns the overestimation or underestimation of the probability that a particular effect will follow a certain previous event or that certain consequences will result as a function of certain behaviors (D'Zurilla & Nezu, 1982). As Rehm (1981) notes, depressed individuals characteristically show selective attention to immediate consequences instead of long-range effects. Further, according to self-efficacy theory (Bandura, 1977), an individual's estimate of the likelihood that a certain response will result in certain effects (i.e., outcome expectations) is an important predictor of behavior and emotion. Errors in over- or underestimating the impact of certain consequences may also result in the creation of pseudoproblems (D'Zurilla & Nezu, 1982). For example, Dan P., who recently married into a stepfamily, felt extremely concerned and worried that his new stepchildren were not accepting him as a father. Upon discussing his problem, it became apparent that he underestimated the long-term impact that his attempts to bring the family close together had on his stepchildren. Instead of focusing on the positive aspects of their relationship, he attended to the negative events (e.g., his 7-year-old stepdaughter had a temper tantrum) and the short-term consequences, thus creating a pseudoproblem. In reality, Dan's pseudoproblem appeared to cause an actual problem for the family when he responded to each minor negative event as a crisis. Moderating his expectations and more accurately perceiving the effects of his behavior on the family led to the resolution of his original problem.

Understanding the Nature of the Problem

This aspect of the overall problem-definition-and-formulation process is perhaps the most difficult to conduct. It is during this procedure that individuals actually use the information previously gathered in order to best conceptualize *why* a given situation is a problem. Remember that a problem has been previously defined in Chapter 2 as a discrepancy between the demands of a situation and the availability of effective responses. Essentially, at this point the problem solver needs to identify specifically what it is about the situation that causes this discrepancy. This requires answers to questions such as: "What are the present conditions that are getting me upset?" "What would I like to have happen?" "What are the changes necessary to reach these goals?" "What are the obstacles that I have to overcome in order to reach these goals?" "Who is creating these obstacles?" "Are there any conflicts involved?" and "Who do these conflicts involve?" Although the following categories may overlap and are not exhaustive, it is helpful to classify critical problem situations in the following manner (D'Zurilla & Nezu, 1982):

1. *Presence of Aversive Stimuli.* Aversive problem situations entail the presence (or threat) of various negative consequences or punishing

stimuli. These include continued arguments with one's spouse, getting fired from a job, failing an exam, receiving a severe traffic violation, receiving rejections from potential dating partners, and prolonged medical complications.

2. *Loss of Reinforcement.* This type of stressful situation entails the decrease or loss of actual or expected positive reinforcement from one's immediate environment or life circumstances. These might include the death of a family member, unwanted divorce or separation, loss of a close friend who moves away, unexpected limitation in various abilities (e.g., athletic injuries, poor eyesight emanating from physical disability), decreased finances, job demotion, and aging. These types of problems are particularly relevant for engendering depressive reactions (see Chapter 3).

3. *Presence of Obstacles.* Often the emotions that individuals experience in reaction to problems are due to frustration over the existence of various obstacles that prevent them from obtaining desired goals. For example, a highly motivated teenager may have the ability to succeed at a prestigious university but cannot attend because of inadequate funds. Obstacles may also involve a person's idiosyncratic emotional reaction to potentially stressful situations (see Chapter 3). For example, Steve K. often experienced anxiety during job interviews. Although his educational background and previous work experiences were sufficiently impressive to provide him with several interview opportunities, he was unsuccessful in obtaining jobs due to his overt anxiety when asked various questions. For Steve, the obstacle to overcome was his own anxiety reaction.

4. *Presence of Conflict.* Conflictual aspects of problematic situations can be either *interpersonal* or *intrapersonal* in nature. Interpersonal problems involve differences in the interests or expectations between two or more people within various types of relationships. Friends may disagree about how to spend an evening together. A husband and wife might differ concerning the way to raise their children. Co-workers may have conflicting ideas about various business strategies to increase productivity. Intrapersonal conflicts involve differences in stimulus demands or goals that originate from either the environment or within the person. A young woman who wants to actively pursue a career might experience postpartum depression after the birth of her baby when the demands of raising a child conflict with her interest in doing well on a job.

Additionally, problems can vary in their degree of novelty, magnitude of seriousness, complexity, and depth. Unfamiliar or novel situations are likely to be particularly problematic because they involve aspects of uncertainty. As the degree of unfamiliarity of a situation increases, so does the number of decisions that need to be made. This often requires more active and concerted attempts at problem solving and an increased vigilance toward adopting the problem-solving set of "Problems in living are normal and inevitable."

It is especially important to highlight this point when the novel situation is originally perceived as positive in nature. For example, Jim D., a consumer project engineer, received a substantial promotion and raise with his company that necessitated a move to a new city in a different part of the country. Jim's initial reaction to the promotion was elation. However, after a few weeks on the new job, he started to feel depressed and overwhelmed with all the changes that occurred in his life-style. Jim needed to locate a new house, make new friends, become familiar with a wide range of new stores, and relate to new co-workers. Because he had not planned for all these changes, the stress associated with these new problems led to feelings of inadequacy and second thoughts about his ability to perform well within his new position. What had originally been evaluated as a positive decision now became a negative one.

Problems also vary in their degree of seriousness concerning the magnitude of the actual and potential negative consequences. Assessment of this component of a problem requires an appreciation of both immediate and long-term consequences and helps the problem solver to develop a time plan for achieving various subgoals and objectives. The immediate consequences of a problem may be minimal but may have serious long-range effects. For example, continuing to purchase material goods on credit may have a positive effect on an individual's immediate cash flow but can potentially affect greatly the amount of money owed on credit.

Another important parameter of a problem involves varying degrees of complexity. Complex problems are those situations that either overlap other significant problems or encompass several smaller subproblems. With regard to the first type, it is extremely important for an individual to understand how one problem may be intertwined with another. In such a case, the consequences of one situation will have a great bearing on the effects of the second. For example, Joan S., a middle-aged wife, felt that she had difficulties relating to her husband, in addition to problems raising her children. Her husband frequently complained that they did not have a "fulfilling social life." Further, Joan believed that her two teenaged children had suddenly lost all respect for her, and she continuously entered into loud arguments with them. The manner in which she dealt with either situation tended to affect the other problem. Joan would often cancel social plans with her husband due to feelings of being overwhelmed and tired after arguing with their children. Conversely, she often blamed her children for causing her difficulties with her husband. Upon realizing the interrelatedness of these situations, Joan was able to guide subsequent problem-solving activities toward the resolution of both situations.

The second type of complex problem concerns large, general, and sometimes overwhelming situations. For example, Jack B., a lawyer, came to therapy depressed as a result of what he perceived as a mid-life crisis. Initially, he stated that he hated the entire law profession and that he continued to have major problems working in that field. In essence, he defined his problem simply as "hating what I do!" In attempting to break this problem into smaller components, it appeared that several subproblems existed: (1) discontent with present salary; (2) difficulties in starting his own private practice; (3) persistent stress symptoms (headaches, gastrointestinal problems); and (4) overload of clients. By breaking the complex problem into smaller ones, it was possible for Jack to cope with each one more effectively.

The last problem parameter involves depth. Essentially, it is important for the individual to get at the real problem. Because there are several ways that any particular problem can be defined and formulated, different individuals may focus on varying levels of the problem. The real problem (or problems) is the one that is primary, basic, or fundamental. This might be the first problem in a chain of events. For example, general difficulties in relating to people may influence one to have problems in communicating with co-workers, which in turn may engender work problems that can lead to decreased effectiveness on the job (i.e., Problem A causes Problem B, which causes Problem C, etc.). Instead of only focusing on the problem of decreased work productivity, it is imperative to address also the original problem of difficulties relating to people. The success of any solution implemented to resolve Problem C or D may thus only be short-lived. Further, resolving Problem A may also resolve the remaining problems.

The real problem may also involve a larger, broader situation. By focusing only on one aspect of this problem, an individual may develop solutions that will ultimately fail. Other conflicts or obstacles that remain unattended to can render such solutions ineffective. Especially when a problem is complex, the individual needs to formulate the "big picture." Such a conceptualization of a problem situation requires awareness of both the "forest" *and* the "trees." For example, for Joan's problem described previously, she needs to be aware of the difficulties involved in relating to her husband and her children, and how each situation affects the other. The "forest" might be difficulties in relating to or communicating with significant others in general. Some "trees" may include specific ways in which she reacts to positive and negative feedback from people, expectations about how people should relate to her, expectations about marriage and child rearing, and difficulties managing various commitments.

Setting Goals

After engaging in the previous problem-definition-and-formulation operations, the problem solver is ready to delineate a set of goals or objectives. In essence, goals are an overall description of the desired outcome of a problem situation (D'Zurilla & Nezu, 1982). However, as defined earlier in Chapter 2, an effective solution not only changes the nature of the situation so that it is no longer a problem but in addition maximizes associated positive consequences and minimizes any negative consequences. Therefore, goals should also encompass a statement concerning the *overall* desired outcome.

In specifying goals, the problem-solver should (1) state the objectives in concrete and unambiguous terms, and (2) avoid stating unrealistic or irrational goals. The value of using specific and concrete language and terms has been espoused earlier. Unrealistic goals actually change the problem from a potentially solvable one to an insoluble situation. Such goals are impossible to attain and thus render the problem hopeless of resolution. Further, the impact on one's orientation (self-efficacy beliefs in particular) is great. In other words, attempts to reach an unattainable goal are doomed to failure. Such unsuccessful attempts may then reinforce any perceptions of inability to cope with a problem and can even lead to generalized beliefs about uncontrollability in general (cf. Seligman, 1975; Rotter, 1978).

For example, Mary and Joe C., a couple who had been married for only seven months, came to therapy seeking marriage counseling. A major concern involved frequent violent arguments about a wide variety of issues (e.g., finances, use of leisure time, future plans). After such an argument, Joe would become extremely withdrawn and depressed, and would not talk to Mary for days. In attempts to define and formulate the specific nature of some of their problems, it became apparent that one of Joe's unspoken goals in marriage was never to fight with his wife. Based on witnessing his own parents' frequent arguments, he had vowed that his marriage would be different. By trying to avoid arguments with Mary, he denied feelings of anger at her, which often led to explosive behavior when she did something that "broke the camel's back." Among various strategies to increase their mutual marital satisfaction, one focal issue during problem-solving therapy addressed changing his unrealistic goal. By reformulating his goal, Joe was eventually able to accept the realistic possibility that most couples have disagreements and arguments. The very (unrealistic) goal that he had been attempting to achieve within his marriage had turned out to be influential in *creating* the conflicts between them.

Goals should be stated in the form of "how can I . . .?" or "what can be done to . . .?" For example, "How can I meet more people in order to become less lonely?" or "What can be done so that I argue less with my husband?" With complex problems, subgoals should be specified in order to address the various trees within the larger forest. For example, in writing this book, completion of each chapter represented a subgoal. It is often possible to delineate a sequence whereby various subgoals need to be attained in order to proceed toward additional goals.

In setting goals, the problem solver now has the opportunity to reappraise or evaluate the overall nature of the problem situation with regard to its importance and significance for well-being. With vague and undefined problems, an individual may have previously perceived the problem to be quite threatening and potentially harmful. After clarifying the nature of the situation, it may be possible that a more complete picture emerges, and the problem then becomes less significant or less negative in valence. It is only with a well-defined problem that such appraisals can in fact be accurate (D'Zurilla, 1986).

Research on Problem-Definition-and-Formulation Training

Effectively engaging in this component of problem solving is hypothesized to have a major impact on latter problem-solving operations. In other words, accurately defining and formulating a problem situation should influence the quality of the other problem-solving tasks, such as generating alternatives and making decisions. Several investigations have been conducted to test this particular hypothesis.

In one study, Nezu and D'Zurilla (1981b) studied the effects of training in problem-definition-and-formulation (PDF) skills on the generation-of-alternatives process. College student subjects were divided into three conditions representing various levels of training in PDF (specific training, general training, and no training). Further, half of the members from each group received training in generating alternatives according to the "quantity principle" (i.e., the more ideas produced, the higher the likelihood of generating more effective alternatives; see next section in this chapter, Generation of Alternatives). The other half were given no instruction in applying this principle. After training, all subjects were asked to generate solutions for one of two socially oriented test problems. Problem-solving goals were experimentally determined to ensure common objectives for guiding the generation of alternatives for all subjects. Results of this study provide confirming evidence for the major hypothesis. More specifically, subjects trained in PDF skills produced significantly more effective solutions than the ones generated by both the subjects who received either general training or no training. Results of this investigation also indicated that subjects who received instruction in the use of the quantity principle produced significantly better solutions than the subjects who did not receive such training.

In a second study conducted by Nezu & D'Zurilla (1981a), the effects of training in PDF skills were evaluated with regard to improving decision-making effectiveness. College student subjects were randomly assigned to one of the three groups described previously, reflecting different levels of training in PDF skills. However, in this study, half of the subjects in each condition also received special training in the utility model of decision making (D'Zurilla & Nezu, 1982; see later section in this chapter, Decision Making), whereas the second half were given no specific decision-making aids. After training, all subjects were presented with eight intrapersonal and interpersonal test problems (e.g., how to avoid fights with a friend), along with a list of possible solutions for each. These potential alternatives varied in their degree of effectiveness. Subjects were asked to choose the best solution for each problem. Results of this investigation indicated support for the major hypothesis. More specifically, subjects who received specific training in PDF skills did significantly better on the decision-making task than subjects who did not receive such training. Further, specific training in PDF also resulted in significantly better decision making than simply teaching general PDF guidelines. Additionally, general guidelines in PDF resulted in better decisions than not providing any guidelines in PDF at all. Finally, this study also found that subjects who were given training in decision making chose more effective solutions than subjects who received no training in decision making.

The Cormier et al. (1986) study noted previously also provides evidence in support of the importance of PDF training. In this study, subjects who received instructions in certain PDF skills selected significantly better solution alternatives for six test problems than participants who did not receive such training. Research by Hansen, St. Lawrence, and Christoff (1985), which utilized a multiple-baseline design with seven chronic psychiatric patients to evaluate the effectiveness of training in several problem-solving skills, also provides similar supportive evidence.

Relation to Depression

The problem-definition-and-formulation component contributes importantly to a problem-solving-associated risk factor for depression because of the impact on the effectiveness of latter problem-solving operations (i.e., generating alternatives, decision making, solution implementation and verification). In other words, depression can be activated by deficiencies (or decreased effectiveness) in this process when an ill-defined and poorly formulated problem leads to an ineffective coping response.

Many operations within problem definition and formulation involve objectivity and specificity (i.e., separating facts from assumptions and inferences, using concrete and unambiguous terms to describe the problem, identifying the cause of the problem). Depression-related cognitive distortions, irrational thoughts, and causal attributions can influence the nature of defining a problem in objective and specific terms (Nezu, 1987). For example, distortions of information relating to a problem, such as those identified by Beck (1967), are likely to lead to an inaccurate definition of a stressful situation, which can then lead to ineffective problem resolution. Always attributing the cause of a problem to oneself can also lead to ineffective problem formulation. In other words, failure to properly identify the source of the problem (either internal, external, or both), decreases dramatically the probability of generating effective solutions at a latter point. If this state of affairs engenders a preponderance of negative consequences as a result of unresolved problems, then the individual's difficulties in accurately defining problems may also be a source of risk for a depressive reaction.

Related to problem definition is the setting of realistic goals or objectives. As noted earlier, the effective setting of such goals is extremely important because it serves to guide subsequent attempts at solution generation and decision making. It also provides for the use of criteria and performance standards. Rehm (1977), in delineating a self-control model of depression, discusses the liability of unrealistic goal setting. If the objectives are too high, attempts at problem resolution are likely to fail, again resulting in potential negative consequences for an individual, as well as influencing problem-solving orientation (i.e., self-efficacy beliefs). Essentially, unattainable goals change the situation from a solvable problem to an insoluble one, because it would be impossible to find a satisfactory solution.

GENERATION OF ALTERNATIVES

The purpose of this component is to make available as many solution alternatives or coping strategies as possible and to maximize the likelihood that the best or most effective solution will be among them. The theoretical underpinnings associated with this problem-solving component are related to the brainstorming method (Osborn, 1963; Parnes, 1967), which was originally developed to facilitate idea finding in group sessions and which has been widely used in industrial and management settings (Mahoney, 1974). Brainstorming is based primarily on two general principles: (1) the quantity principle, and (2) the deferment-of-judgment principle (D'Zurilla & Nezu, 1982). The use of a *strategies-tactics* procedure has also been advocated by social problem-solving theorists (cf. D'Zurilla & Goldfried, 1971; D'Zurilla & Nezu, 1982).

Quantity Principle

According to this principle, the more alternative solutions that individuals produce, the more likely they are to arrive at the potentially best ideas for a solution. Parnes (1962) has demonstrated that persons following such brainstorming instructions tend to contribute significantly more effective ideas to the last half of a list as compared to the first half. Maier and Hoffman (1964) also found that later generated solutions were superior to those ideas initially produced. Parnes and Meadow (1959) further found that subjects who produced more solutions to a problem also produced more high-quality ones.

Deferment-of-Judgment Principle

This principle states that more high-quality ideas can be produced if an individual defers critical evaluation of any particular alternative until an exhaustive list of possible solutions has been compiled. No evaluation or judgment should be made about any of the possible ideas during the process of generating alternatives. Consideration of the value, effectiveness, or moral acceptability of an alternative should be avoided completely, with the exception of the one requirement that the idea be relevant to the problem. Such brainstorming techniques have also proven effective in increasing the quality of idea production (Meadow & Parnes, 1959; Meadow, Parnes, & Reese, 1959).

Prematurely evaluating alternatives may permit development of only a restricted range of coping options. This decreases substantially the probability of ultimately identifying effective solutions. For example, Quentin B., a 29-year-old male, originally came to therapy due to feelings of depression and loneliness. One of his goals included meeting more women in general, and obtaining dates in particular. In attempts to generate potential alternatives to achieve these objectives, the therapist suggested the idea of going to a dating service. Quentin's initial reaction was to state that this alternative would be an impossibility and therefore should not even be listed. However, upon being reminded of the deferment principle, he was willing to entertain the idea in theory. Interestingly, during the decision-making phase, he actually decided to use this idea as one of several alternatives since upon analyzing the specific consequences of the solution, he decided it wasn't "as bad as I originally thought."

Strategies-Tactics Procedure

This approach suggests that individuals should initially conceptualize *general* means or strategies to solve a problem and subsequently produce various *tactics* or specific ways in which a strategy might be implemented. In this manner, a greater variety or range of ideas might be produced, which can also increase the generation of ideas (D'Zurilla, 1986). An example of a strategy for solving the problem of obtaining better grades in school might be "Study harder." Under this strategy, specific tactics might include "Increase the number of hours per night devoted to studying," "Take more notes in class," "Do extra readings in a subject in addition to the required ones," and "Prior to a class test, prepare sample test questions from which to study."

Using these general approaches to idea production also addresses the concern previously stated during the problem-orientation phase, namely, extreme approach behavior. Based on habits, convention, and impulsivity, individuals, in response to a stressful situation, may attempt to cope by engaging in previously successful solutions. Unless the current problem is exactly the same as the previous one, any impulsive attempt is likely to fail due to inattention to various problem parameters.

In addition to the preceding principles, training in this component emphasizes the use of concrete and unambiguous language when describing or delineating various alternative solutions. The problem solver can also increase the effectiveness of brainstorming by attempting to (1) generate combinations of ideas, (2) modify and improve upon certain alternatives, and/or (3) elaborate on previously generated ideas (D'Zurilla, 1986).

Research on Training in Generating Alternatives

A study by D'Zurilla and Nezu (1980) investigated the generation-of-alternatives principles. One hundred college students were divided randomly into four experimental groups and one control group. The first experimental condition involved training in the application of all three principles, whereas the second group received training in the deferment and quantity principles, but not the strategies approach. The third group was given instruction in quantity and strategies, but not deferment. The fourth group received instructions only in the quantity principle. The control group did not get instructions in any of the generation-of-alternatives principles. They were simply told to solve the problem. After initial training, all subjects were asked to solve two socially orientated test problems.

Results of this investigation indicated that the solutions produced by all four experimental groups were significantly more effective than those produced by the control subjects. However, no significant differences emerged among the experimental conditions. Because the quantity principle was common across all such conditions, the conclusion was that training in this particular principle accounted for the increased quality of the overall generated solutions. Neither the deferment principle nor the strategies procedure significantly enhanced these effects.

In spite of this finding, it may be premature to conclude that the deferment principle and the strategies procedure are of *no* value for facilitating the generation of alternatives. In this study, the design was such that only the quantity principle was independently assessed. Training in the other two operations was evaluated in *combination* with the quantity principle to determine whether they would add significantly to the effects of quantity instructions. However, the quantity training alone increased performance to nearly ceiling levels, so there would appear to be very little room left for any significant improvement by adding another component. If the effects of either the deferment principle or strategies procedure were assessed independently, it is possible that a significant effect might be found (D'Zurilla & Nezu, 1982).

The Nezu and D'Zurilla (1981b) study previously described, as well as an investigation conducted by Nezu and Ronan (1987) provide additional support for the efficacy of training in the quantity principle. One purpose of this latter study was to determine whether training depressed subjects in the quantity principle would increase the quality of solution alternatives generated in response to a socially oriented test problem. Results confirmed this hypothesis. Depressed subjects who received quantity instructions generated significantly more high-quality solutions than depressed individuals who did not receive such training.

Relation to Depression

Deficiencies in this problem-solving component can cause vulnerability to depression when an individual generates a restricted range of alternatives in response to a stressful situation, thus decreasing the likelihood of eventually identifying effective coping responses. The relation between this problem-solving process and depression is partially supported by the

Nezu and Ronan (1987) study, which found that depressed individuals generated both fewer alternatives and less effective responses to interpersonal problems relative to nondepressed controls (see Chapter 5).

DECISION MAKING

The goal of the decision-making process is to both evaluate the available solution possibilites and select the most effective alternative(s) for implementation. The major focus during this problem-solving process is the evaluation of a given alternative with regard to its consequences. Related to this process are both causal and consequential thinking (i.e., identifying cause-effect relations, anticipating the consequences of one's behavior).

Within the framework of the problem-solving model, this decision-making process draws upon *utility theory* (Churchman, 1961; Edwards, Lindman, & Phillips, 1965), which is an extension of research in the fields of economic game theory and statistics. This research has mostly dealt with the mathematical description of the processes involved in making choices and with the assignment of values to these choices (cf. von Neumann & Morgenstern, 1944; Luce, 1959). Utility theory itself represents a means-end conceptualization of decision theory, whereby the *expected utility* of a given alternative is a joint function of the consideration of both the *value* of each outcome and the *likelihood* of that alternative's achieving a given result. In essence, it provides for a costs/benefits analysis concerning the consequences of a particular solution (Payne, 1982).

In human decision making, this process is largely subjective, because it would be extremely difficult for individuals to predict with complete accuracy the consequences of their solutions in advance of their implementation. Edwards (1961) has described this process as the *subjective expected utility* model of human choice. Within this framework, to make the best decision possible, an individual must first assess the utility of various alternatives and then choose that one (or group) that has the greatest utility associated with it (i.e., the solution with the highest value and the greatest likelihood of achieving the desired outcome).

The decision-making aids used in the problem-solving therapy approach for depression constitute a *prescriptive* approach to decision theory, as compared to a *descriptive* approach. Prescriptive decision theory concerns itself with the choices that a person should make in a given situation. Descriptive decision theory deals with the choices that people *actually* make and not necessarily with what they should do (Becker & McClintock, 1967; Lee, 1971). In other words, a prescriptive model specifies certain rules or aids that people can follow to enhance the quality of decisions in specific situations, which may ultimately increase their decision-making ability in general.

Estimates of the likelihood that a particular alternative will have a particular effect is the first assessment that the problem solver should make. Essentially, this probability evaluation considers whether or not the alternative can actually meet the previously stated problem-solving goals. In other words, will it work? Of equal importance is the assessment of the *feasibility* or likelihood that the problem solver can actually implement the alternative in its optimal form. A given solution might theoretically be an excellent idea, but have practical limitations due to additional concerns. The individual in the situation must therefore undergo a personal assessment of his or her assets and liabilities to determine the feasibility of a given alternative.

For example, Jonathan G., in making a decision about career changes in response to frustrations with a current low-paying job, rated the alternative of "going back to school to obtain additional training" as quite high along the criteria of reaching his goal and various personal consequences. However, his current financial situation was such that any major additional expenditures would be unmanageable. Therefore, this alternative had to be rejected temporarily due to monetary limitations. However, upon this evaluation, Jonathan decided to return to school at a later date and concentrated on a newly formed *subgoal,* i.e., "How can I obtain sufficient finances to eventually go back to school?"

In making judgments about the *value* of an alternative, D'Zurilla and Nezu (1982) suggest that four categories of consequences should be considered: short-term or immediate consequences, long-term consequences, personal consequences (effects on oneself), and social consequences (effects on others). Personal consequences might involve the time and effort required to implement a particular alternative, personal and emotional costs versus gains, consistency with one's ethical and moral standards, and physical well-being. Within the social category, specific consequences may include effects on one's family, friends, or community.

In a slightly different manner, Wheeler and Janis (1980) recommend using a cost/benefit balance sheet divided into the following four categories to evaluate alternatives: (1) tangible or utilitarian considerations for the decision maker (i.e., gains or losses for self); (2) tangible considerations for the decision maker's family, friends, or associates who will be affected by the decision (i.e., gains or losses for others); (3) self-approval or disapproval including ethical considerations; and (4) approval or disapproval from others whose opinions are important to the decision maker.

Since individuals differ in their personal values, goals, and commitments, it is impossible to develop a standard set of consequences for each type of problematic situation. As such, it might be important for the individual to brainstorm all the potential effects of a given alternative along the guidelines already noted. In other words, "What are all the different consequences that might occur for myself if I carry out this solution?" "Who else would be affected?" and so forth.

In evaluating the costs and benefits of each alternative, the problem solver should use a rating system to indicate satisfaction with each solution (see Chapter 10 for an illustration of a rating system). After rating each alternative, the problem solver can then compare the different *overall* cost/benefit ratios associated with each potential solution. It is important to assess the total picture, rather than the valence of any specific outcome criterion. For example, a solution might be judged as extremely favorable concerning two criteria, but might be rejected because the overall expected costs outweigh the overall expected benefits (see Jonathan's problem, previously described).

Based on this comparison, the problem solver should then choose those alternatives for which the expected overall outcome most closely matches the problem-solving goals. If only a few ideas appear to be potentially satisfactory, then the problem solver must consider several questions— "Do I have enough information about the problem?" "Did I define the problem correctly?" "Are my goals too high?" "Did I generate enough options?" and so forth. At this point the individual may need to go back and engage again in the previous problem-solving tasks.

The individual who has identified a variety of satisfactory alternatives is encouraged to develop an overall *solution plan*, by combining potentially effective coping options for each subgoal in order to attack the problem from various perspectives. Further, it is often useful to have a contingency plan—a group of ideas to implement contingent upon the failure of previous ones (i.e., a backup plan).

To highlight the concept that the five major problem-solving components are interrelated, note that if the list of solution possibilities is of poor quality, then regardless of the effectiveness of one's decision-making skills, overall problem resolution is unlikely. Further, according to *prospect theory* of choice behavior (Kahneman & Tversky, 1979; Tversky & Kahneman, 1981), the manner in which the problem is initially "framed" (conceived and formulated), influences the nature of decision making. As such, the original definition of the problem becomes crucial for latter decision making. Moreover, Tversky and Kahneman suggest that people do not generally consider alternative frames for the same solution, or the frames' potential impact on the relative potential of the alternatives. This can lead to reduced decision-making effectiveness by causing a lack of commitment to implement a given solution (D'Zurilla, 1986). Finally, if the problem-solving goals are unrealistic, then the decision-making task becomes more difficult, if not impossible. Under these circumstances, the individual will have difficulty finding an alternative that can realistically be expected to produce the desired outcome.

Research on Training in Decision Making

Using real-life problem situations, Nezu & D'Zurilla (1979) investigated the efficacy of the prescriptive model of decision making with 53 college students. This study addressed the question of whether the use of specific decision-making criteria and guidelines would in fact increase the ability of an individual to effectively choose that alternative that has the most desirable outcome on a variety of levels for real-life problematic situations. The study utilized three conditions: (1) Guidelines and Specific Criteria (GSC), where the subjects received detailed instructions in the entire model; (2) Guidelines Only (GL), where subjects were given the global guidelines along which to direct their choices but did not get the specifics of these guidelines; and (3) No Systematic Training (NST), where subjects were told to simply decide which was the most effective solution.

All subjects in this investigation received a variety of possible solutions to a series of 12 problem situations and were asked to designate the best solutions according to their previous instructions. All solutions had been previously rated for their effectiveness. The results strongly supported the prediction that the GSC group would be the most effective decision makers and that the NSI group would score the lowest. Whereas the GSC group performed significantly better that both the other two conditions, the GL and NSI groups were not significantly different from each other in their performance. These overall findings suggest that specific training in this model does facilitate decision-making effectiveness.

The results from the Nezu and D'Zurilla (1979) study were later replicated in investigations by Nezu and D'Zurilla (1981a) and Nezu and Ronan (1987). The latter study found significant results for both depressed and nondepressed college students. Results also supportive of decision-making training for social problem solving were reported in the study by Cormier et al. (1986). These authors found that subjects who were trained in decision making performed significantly better on a problem-solving task at a one-month follow-up assessment than subjects who did not receive such training.

Relation to Depression

Although expected utility theory is not without its critics (cf. Pitz & Sachs, 1984), it has much to offer as a set of guidelines for prescriptive decision making (cf. Kunreuther & Schoemaker, 1981; Schoemaker, 1982; Wheeler & Janis, 1980). The major concern in its use as a decision aid is that individuals may show certain biases in estimating probabilities. For example, they may overestimate or underestimate the probability that a particular effect will follow a certain prior event or that a particular set of consequences will follow certain behaviors. Poor self-efficacy beliefs and inaccurate outcome expectations (Bandura, 1977) can influence the decision-making process. Errors of this type can lead to inaccurate assessment of the impact of a solution, which in turn can cause an ineffective decision. When such errors lead to an ineffective decision, depression can be activated as a function of the absence of problem resolution. If implemented, solutions judged inaccurately as effective, will probably lead to unsuccessful coping attempts. This will likely impact on one's motivation to continue to engage in the problem-solving process and may lead to feelings of uncontrollability and futility.

With regard to the consequences of a solution, Rehm (1977) postulates that depressed individuals selectively attend to negative versus positive events and to immediate versus long-term consequences. This selective attention to immediate consequences of behavior results in motivational deficits and precludes working toward long-term positive goals.

Further, in accord with a self-control conceptualization of depression, unrealistic goal setting and evaluative standards make individuals vulnerable to depression (Rehm, 1977). Since a depressed person sets overly stringent and perfectionistic standards, a mismatch between the actual outcome of a solution and the standard is inevitable. Thus, deficiencies in this aspect of decision making can lead to depressive reactions.

The relation between depression and decision-making deficiences is supported further in part by the Nezu and Ronan (1987) study that found depressed college students chose less effective alternatives to a series of interpersonal and social problems as compared to matched nondepressed controls. Further, a study by E. Costello (1983) indicated that depressed women were more conservative decisions makers (i.e, less willing to take a risk) than nondepressed women.

SOLUTION IMPLEMENTATION AND VERIFICATION

The major function of this last problem-solving component is the comparison between the anticipated and actual consequences that occur from solution implementation. Even though a problem may be solved symbolically, the effectiveness of a solution has not yet been established. By carrying out the coping response, it is possible to evaluate the outcome and verify its effectiveness.

Conceptually, this problem-solving component is based on aspects of *control* or *cybernetics* theory (Carver & Scheier, 1982; Miller, Galanter, & Pribram, 1960) and self-control theory (Bandura, 1971; Kanfer, 1970). The basic unit in control theory is a *negative feedback loop*. Within this loop, a *reference criterion* (i.e., problem-solving goal) and *perceptual input* (i.e., nature of the actual problem) are compared. Any difference between them constitutes an *error* (i.e., unresolved problem), which serves as a motivational factor for behavior (i.e., engaging in problem-solving attempts). The term negative is used to highlight the function of the loop, which is to reduce or negate this error. The selected behavior (i.e., solution) operates on one's environment, thereby influencing the perceptual input and reducing the error (i.e., problem resolution).

According to Miller et al. (1960), a person's activities are guided by the extent to which the behavior outcome is congruent or incongruent with a given standard. If attempts to reduce this discrepancy are successful (i.e., the outcome is congruent with the standard), the individual stops or "exits" from these activities. Conversely, if a match is incongruent, the individual continues to operate until achieving a successful match.

The manner in which this matching takes place is best articulated by self-control theory (Kanfer, 1970), which involves four components: (1) performance, (2) self-monitoring, (3) self-evaluation, and (4) self-reinforcement. Within a problem-solving framework, this procedure therefore encompasses: (1) implementation of a solution response; (2) observation of the actual consequences that occur after carrying out the solution; (3) evaluation of the effectiveness of the solution; and (4) self-reinforcement when the problem is resolved (D'Zurilla & Nezu, 1982).

The *performance step* of this process is the actual implementation of one's solution plan. As emphasized previously, problem-solving performance can be influenced by factors other than problem-solving ability, such as specific skill deficits, emotional inhibitions, and motivational (reinforcement) deficits. Although these types of obstacles should have been identified while engaging in the decision-making process (i.e., the likelihood that the individual within the problem can actually implement the chosen solution in its optimal form), at times it is impossible to anticipate such consequences. The individual who discovers immediately that such performance problems exist should engage in either of two approaches: (1) Return to the previous problem-solving operations such as generating alternatives and decision making in order to identify a different solution plan, or (2) reformulate the overall problem to include a subgoal for overcoming the obstacles related to effective coping performance.

The second step of this process, *self-monitoring*, involves observing the effects of the implemented solution. This entails measurement of the solution outcome at varying levels, not simply global attendance to the solution consequences. In order to obtain accurate information concerning the outcome, it is necessary to include an objective recording procedure. For example, consider the individual whose problem concerns obtaining a new job. Sending out resumes might be one possible alternative that is implemented (among an entire solution plan). Recording the number of companies that respond positively to the application would be one approach to self-recording.

Self-ratings may also be important to obtain, especially when frequency data is difficult to gather. For example, when emotional behavior is involved, such as sexual satisfaction, a couple might rate the degree of their sexual satisfaction after each encounter. The original definition and formulation of the problem determines the most appropriate measure of solution outcome. Under many circumstances, it may be important to develop several recording or rating systems to address each previously identified subgoal.

In the *evaluation* step, the individual compares the observed outcome with the desired outcome as specified during the problem-definition-and-formulation process (i.e., the problem-solving goal). According to control theory (Carver & Scheier, 1982), this includes matching the perceptual input and the reference criterion. If the error or control mismatch is low (i.e., the match is satisfactory), the individual moves to the last step, *self-reinforcement*. In other words, the individual should also reward problem resolution as a job well-done. This might include simple positive self-statements, tangible gifts, or rewards (i.e., dining at an expensive restaurant, buying a new article of clothing). The actual resolution of the problem in itself can be an important source of reinforcement, especially if it engenders additional social reinforcement, the reduction of aversive stimulation, the removal of an obstacle to a goal, or the resolution of a conflict. However, the self-reinforcement step is also crucial for overall problem solving for two reasons: (1) It reinforces effective problem-solving coping, and (2) it strengthens perceived self-control and self-efficacy expectations, which also impact on future problem-solving efforts.

If the match between the observed outcome and the problem-solving goal(s) is *not* satisfactory (i.e., the control mismatch is high), the individual must first attempt to discover the source of this discrepancy. The actual difficulties might involve either (1) the problem-solving process, (2) the performance of the solution response, or (3) both. If it involves (1), he or she should return to one or more of the previous problem-solving operations and attempt to discover another, more effective solution plan. If it is in (2), however, the individual faces the choice of either attempting to improve the performance or going through the problem-solving process once more to determine differing coping responses that may permit better implementation. Improving performance might require behavioral rehearsal of the skills used in the solution plan, reduction of the inhibitory effects of emotional arousal that impact on optimal coping performance, or provision of more self-incentives or self-reinforcement. Which avenue to take depends upon the actual factors interfering with the performance.

Ultimately, if these corrective procedures do not lead to effective problem resolution, seeking expert or professional help might be the best solution. Such help might be available from a friend or associate who has more experience or knowledge about a particular situation. It may also include the services of a mental health professional (i.e., psychologist, psychiatrist, clinical social worker, counselor). It is probably at this point that most outpatients seek psychotherapy for depression due to their overall unsuccessful attempts at coping.

Research on Solution Implementation and Verification

At the present time, there are no empirical studies that have specifically evaluated the importance of this component within the overall social problem-solving process. However, studies are not necessary to demonstrate that problem solving would be only an interesting symbolic exercise if solutions were not actually implemented and evaluated in a real-life context. Nor are studies needed to show that implementing a solution cannot establish or reinforce problem-solving effectiveness without incorporating the assessment and self-control procedures within the verification process (D'Zurilla & Nezu, 1982). Thus, evidence in support of the use of self-monitoring and evaluation procedures within a behavioral assessment framework (cf. Barlow, 1981; Nelson & Hayes, 1986), in addition to evidence in support of self-control and control theory (cf. Hyland, 1987; Kanfer, 1971) also support the importance of this set of problem-solving operations.

Relation to Depression

As noted earlier, the first step of this problem-solving component is the actual performance of a coping response. If the solution calls for overt behavior, then depression can be activated as a function of social skills deficits. For example, McLean (1981) posits that treatment for depression should address the remediation of social skills and performance deficits. Such depression-associated deficits might include difficulties in communication, assertiveness, and social interaction skills (cf. Coyne, 1976b; Lewinsohn, 1974). If an individual is unable to carry out a solution effectively, regardless of the hypothetical efficacy of the solution itself, the problem will likely remain unresolved. This would again likely impact negatively on one's outcome and efficacy expectations. According to Hyland (1987), a prolonged control mismatch (discrepancy between perceptual input and reference criterion), can lead to depression. Essentially, if the behaviors or activities selected to reduce this error continue to be ineffective, the continuation of the mismatch can lead to feelings of dysphoria, hopelessness, and depression.

To highlight the interplay among problem-solving components, remember that during the decision-making phase, alternatives that require a performance skill level beyond an individual's ability should have been identified as potentially ineffective choices. Thus, whereas a particular alternative may be effective for one individual, it does not follow automatically that it would be effective for another, given differences with regard to individuals' varying social skills, as well as the differing parameters of similar problems.

As noted previously, the next three steps of this component that focus on the verification aspect are consistent with a self-control model of behavior (Kanfer, 1970). Rehm's (1977; see Chapter 1, this volume) self-control theory of depression would appear applicable to this problem-solving component. Rehm suggests that depression can occur if individuals engage in the following six self-control deficiencies: (1) focusing on negative events to the exclusion of positive events; (2) attending to immediate consequences as opposed to long-term consequences; (3) setting stringent self-evaluative criteria; (4) engaging in self-blame errors consistent with expectations of a negative outcome; (5) administering insufficient self-reinforcement; and (6) self-administering excessive punishment. As can be seen, errors made along any of these six processes can result in ineffective problem solving. For example, inattention to long-term consequences may permit positive short-term effects but may ultimately result in future problems. Additionally, selective attention to negative consequences impedes on the accuracy of the evaluation or matching process. Moreover, excessively high standards create a sense of hopelessness and futility because no solution can achieve an unattainable goal.

This last verification error is particularly relevant for certain depressed individuals. Instead of being able to terminate the problem-solving process and engage in self-reinforcement, some people may continue to engage in the negative feedback loop (i.e., continue to engage in problem-solving attempts) but become lost in obsessive and compulsive problem-solving behaviors that go nowhere (D'Zurilla & Nezu, 1982). This can eventually lead to an increasingly large and prolonged control mismatch (Hyland, 1987). Rather than motivating this type of person to generate and evaluate additional alternatives, it is important to focus their efforts on reformulating goals (i.e., concentrating on emotion-focused goals, as well as more realistic goals).

General Summary and Implications of a Problem-Solving Formulation of Depression

It has been argued in this chapter that depression can result as a function of deficiencies, or decreased effectiveness, in any or all of the five major components of problem solving (problem orientation, problem definition and formulation, generation of alternatives, decision making, and solution implementation and verification). As noted in Chapter 4, the onset of depression can occur when an individual faces an actual problem situation. Such situations may eventuate as a function of the experience of major life events or may occur independent of such events. Not resolving these problems effectively may create a host of negative consequences, resulting in decreased personal and social reinforcement. On the other hand, effective resolution of the problem(s) will serve to decrease the likelihood of a depressive episode.

The more intense, pervasive, and long-lasting that these consequences are, the more likely that depression will also be severe and maintained over time. Moreover, the more problem-solving deficits that exist originally, as a function of faulty learning, the higher the probability that depression will be severe and long-lasting if such deficits continue to engender negative consequences associated with ineffective problem resolution over time. Deficits in problem solving are also likely to increase relapse rates, due to the high probability of problems occurring in the future.

It is also hypothesized that depression can remit spontaneously as a function of effective resolution of stressful situations through factors associated outside the individual (e.g., social support). For example, if an individual becomes depressed as a function of losing his or her job (and the occurrence of a wide range of associated negative consequences), depression might remit when a relative offers another source of employment or money. However, relapse is likely if ineffective problem-solving skills lead to ineffective coping on the new job.

Delineation of this third level of analysis within the overall problem-solving conceptualization is not an attempt simply to reinterpret current theories of depression into problem-solving terminology. Rather, it describes how the several causal variables posited by various cognitive-behavioral theories serve to interact with each other in a meaningful way (i.e., under the general rubric of problem-solving coping). As such, this model can account for the existence of both supportive and conflicting evidence with regard to any one theory, even though these theories may vary widely from each other in focus. In other words, not all depressed individuals have social skill deficits, negative attributional styles, distorted cognitive processes, and/or self-control deficiencies. Group comparisons between depressed and nondepressed persons often obscure individual differences among depressed persons (Craighead et al., 1984). This model is geared toward explaining how such individual differences exist in a dynamic fashion. More specifically, whereas it is posited here that depression occurs partially as a function of ineffective problem-solving coping, the actual deficits may vary across people. Thus, the amount of variance accounted for by each of the five problem-solving components in serving as a risk factor for depression varies as a function of individual differences.

Additionally, this model focuses on the dynamic interplay among causative factors, suggesting that deficiencies in one process can be compensated for by other factors. For example, as the Nezu, Kalmar, Ronan, and Clavijo (1986) study indicates, the probability of experiencing depression as a function of a particular attributional style can be moderated by another problem-solving process (i.e., ability to effectively cope with the negative consequences of a stressful event).

Inherent in this entire framework, therefore, is the notion that a *multitude* of biological and psychosocial factors can influence the onset and maintainence of clinical depression. As such, it is consistent with a pluralistic viewpoint of depression. More importantly, it attempts to provide a set of heuristic principles that can guide both assessment and therapy for depression. This model suggests that assessment be broad-based in scope with the goal of identifying specific problem-solving deficits that account idiosyncratically for depression in a given person. Thus, it provides for a nomothetic framework that guides an idiographic application. Therapy, then, should be geared toward remediation of the specific problem-solving deficits associated with the onset and maintenance of a depressive episode for a particular individual.

Several current therapies for depression, although not specifically based on problem-solving principles, may in fact actually increase patients' problem-solving skills either by including a truncated version of problem-solving therapy or by focusing on those variables that are related to problem-solving procedures. For example, behaviorally oriented treatment approaches often incorporate training in problem-solving skills as a part of the overall treatment package in order to help depressed individuals cope better with aversive events (cf. Lewinsohn, 1974; McLean, 1981). As indicated previously, several treatment goals within the self-control model of depression (Rehm, 1977) are related to problem-solving principles (e.g., goal setting). Providing social skills training to depressed patients (cf. Hersen, Bellack, & Himmelhoch, 1980) may also increase patients' problem solving by providing alternative methods of interacting with others. Lastly, cognitive techniques, as advocated by Beck (1967), may help depressed persons to better define and formulate problem situations, as well as decrease the cognitive distortions that might inhibit effective problem-solving attempts (e.g., a decrease in dichotomous thinking may increase ability to generate a wide range of alternative solutions).

CHAPTER 5

Problem Solving and Depression

Empirical Support for Model

This chapter presents research supportive of certain components of the problem-solving formulation of depression. These investigations are divided into studies that have (1) established the existence of a relation between problem-solving deficits and depression, (2) evaluated the moderating role that problem solving might serve in stress-related depression, and (3) assessed the effectiveness of treatment approaches for depression based on a problem-solving paradigm (Nezu, 1986c, 1987). Further, due to the pluralistic and integrative nature of the model, investigations that specifically provide support for the included cognitive-behavioral theories of depression (i.e., the association between depression and decreased levels of social reinforcement, causal attributions, negative cognitive distortions, irrational beliefs, self-control deficiencies, etc.) also can be viewed as consistent with this conceptualization (Nezu, 1987; see Chapter 1).

PROBLEM-SOLVING DEFICITS AND DEPRESSION

The relation between problem-solving deficits and depressive symptomatology is supported initially by several correlational studies that have incorporated different measures of the problem-solving construct (see Chapter 2 for descriptions of various measures of social problem solving). For example, using the Means-Ends Problem-Solving Procedure (MEPS; Platt & Spivack, 1975), Gotlib and Asarnow (1979) assessed potential differences in interpersonal problem solving between depressed and nondepressed college students. Depression in this study was determined psychometrically. Subjects designated as depressed had obtained a cutoff score of nine and above on the Beck Depression Inventory (BDI; Beck et al., 1961), whereas nondepressed subjects were defined by BDI scores of eight and below. In addition to these volunteers who were solicited from introductory classes, students in treatment for emotional problems at the university's campus counseling center also participated in this study.

Thus, the following four groups were compared: depressed and nonde-pressed college students, and depressed and nondepressed student coun-selees. In addition to the MEPS, all subjects were tested on an anagram task, which was conceived as a measure of impersonal problem-solving ability. Results indicated initially that a significant negative correlation existed between depression and MEPS scores, with differences between groups found only with regard to interpersonal problem-solving perform-ance. Nondepressed students performed significantly better than the other three groups; the depressed counselees obtained the lowest MEPS scores. No relation was evident between the performance on the anagram measure and the MEPS. Lastly, these depression-associated differences in problem solving were not a function of differences in intellectual functioning, as measured by the Vocabulary subscale of the Wechsler Adult Intelligence Test.

Consistent with the Gotlib and Asarnow (1979) study are two additional investigations that used the MEPS. Zemore and Dell (1983) also used university students as subjects and found the MEPS to be significantly correlated with both the BDI and a measure of depression-proneness. Specifically, university students with poor interpersonal problem-solving skills were found to be more depression-prone than students with good problem-solving skills. Additionally, Nezu and Kalmar (in press) found that within a group of nonreferred young adolescents (seventh graders), a strong negative relation did exist between MEPS scores and depressive symptoms.

Sacco and Graves (1984) used the Social Problem Situation Analysis Measure (SPSAM; Elias, Larcen, Zlotnow, & Chinsky, 1978) to compare depressed and nondepressed elementary school children. The SPSAM is a pictorial measure designed to assess a child's ability to understand and cognitively react to various problematic situations. This study designated as depressed those children who obtained a score of 11 or above on the Childhood Depression Inventory (CDI; Kovacs, 1980). The criterion for inclusion in the nondepressed group was a CDI score of 4 or below. Depressed subjects, in contrast to their nondepressed peers, showed poorer performance on the SPSAM, as well as lower self-ratings on questionnaire items assessing self-satisfaction with their interpersonal problem-solving performance.

Using measures that assessed two specific problem-solving tasks—generating alternative solutions and decision making—Nezu and Ronan (1987) compared depressed and nondepressed college students regarding these particular problem-solving skills. Depressed subjects were classified as those who reported a score of 12 and above on the BDI, whereas a score of 6 and below designated a subject as nondepressed. In the first of two studies reported, subjects were divided into four groups: depressed and nondepressed students who were asked to generate alternative solutions to an interpersonal problem, and depressed and nondepressed students who received specific training in this problem-solving skill. The assessment and training procedures had been developed in two previous studies (D'Zurilla & Nezu, 1980; Nezu & D'Zurilla, 1981b). Results indicated that depressed subjects as a whole produced significantly less effective solutions than nondepressed subjects, but that training in this skill did increase the effectiveness of their performance. A third finding revealed that depressed individuals generated significantly fewer alternatives in general than nondepressed subjects. This finding is consistent with a study by Dobson and Dobson (1981) that found both problem-solving deficits and a conservative problem-solving style characterized depressed individuals.

The second study by Nezu and Ronan (1987) reported similar results with regard to decision-making performance. Depressed subjects chose less effective alternatives for a series of eight interpersonal and social problems as compared to nondepressed persons. Again, training in this skill was found to be effective in facilitating better decision-making performance for both depressed and nondepressed subjects. This study used specific stimulus problems and alternative solutions that were derived and validated in two previous studies (Nezu & D'Zurilla, 1979; 1981a).

Other investigators have incorporated the PSI (Heppner & Petersen, 1982) as the measure of social problem solving. For example, using the PSI to distinguish between extreme groups among a college population, Nezu (1985) classified ineffective problem solvers and effective problem solvers as those subjects who scored one standard deviation above and below the sample mean (the PSI is structured such that higher scores indicate less effective problem solving). In addition to differences on a variety of measures of psychological distress, results indicated that effective problem solvers reported significantly lower BDI scores than ineffective problem solvers.

Three studies by Heppner and his associates incorporated a similar design to test various differences between effective and ineffective problem solvers among various populations of college students. With specific regard to depression, ineffective problem solvers reported significantly higher depression scores, as compared to effective problem solvers, as measured by (1) the MMPI Depression scale (Heppner & Anderson, 1985); (b) both the BDI and the Feelings and Concerns Survey, a measure of depressive mood experienced over the previous 4 years (Heppner et al., 1985); and (c) both the Cornell Medical Index and the Symptom Checklist (Heppner et al., 1987).

Because many of the above studies focused exclusively on depression-related deficits in problem solving among college students or subclinical populations, Nezu (1986a) conducted an investigation that involved clinically depressed individuals. The PSI served as the measure of problem solving in this study. Depressed individuals were identified as those subjects who had received a diagnosis of major depressive disorder according to critera outlined by DSM-III (American Psychiatric Association, 1980), as well as reported BDI scores of 16 and above and MMPI-D scores of $T > 70$. These individuals underwent a 90-minute semistructured interview based on guidelines suggested by the Schedule of Affective Disorders and Schizophrenia (SADS; Endicott & Spitzer, 1978). The mean BDI score for this group was 27.00, whereas the mean T-score for the MMPI-D scale was 82.82. Their mean age was 42.88 years (range of 29 to 69). Diagnoses of unipolar, major depressive disorder were made independently by two clinicians, where the resulting kappa value of agreement reached .98.

Results from multivariate analyses indicated that these depressed subjects reported significantly higher scores across all three PSI dimensions (problem-solving confidence, approach-avoidance style, personal control) as compared to nondepressed individuals who were matched according to various demographic variables. This finding suggests that the depression-related problem-solving deficits identified in previous studies with subclinical populations does extend to individuals experiencing depressive symptoms of clinical proportions.

Consistent with the above findings are two additional studies. Doerfler and Richards (1981) examined differences between adult women who were successful and unsuccessful in self-initiated attempts to cope with depressive episodes. Successful women were found to have engaged in more effective problem-solving attempts to overcome their depression. Beckham and Adams (1984) conducted a similar study with 164 clinically depressed individuals and found converging results. More specifically, subjects indicated that they perceived "taking action on problems" as one of the most helpful strategies for feeling better.

In summary, a substantial number of studies, using different measures of interpersonal problem solving, have identified a strong correlation between depression and problem-solving deficits. A major limitation of this research, however, is the heavy reliance on subclinical populations as subjects. Only the Nezu (1986a) and Beckham and Adams (1984) investigations involved individuals who had been reliably diagnosed as experiencing clinical depression. Whereas this criticism is applicable to the general literature regarding psychosocial aspects of depression (Gotlib, 1984; Nezu, Nezu, & Nezu, 1986), it is incumbent on future investigators in this area to focus on subject populations that include more clinically depressed individuals.

PROBLEM SOLVING AS A MODERATOR OF STRESS-RELATED DEPRESSION

Although the previously described research supports the existence of a strong relation between problem-solving deficits and depression, more relevant to the problem-solving model of depression is a group of studies that specifically evaluated the role of problem solving as a buffer or attenuator of the negative effects of stressful events. For example, Nezu, Nezu, Saraydarian, Kalmar, and Ronan (1986) found that problem solving, as measured by the PSI, served as a moderator between negative stressful life events and depressive symptoms among a university student population. Specifically, results from multiple regression analyses indicated that effective problem solvers under high levels of stress reported significantly lower BDI scores as compared to ineffective problem solvers under similar levels of high stress. A cross-validation of the regression analysis resulted in a minimal amount of shrinkage that could be due to sample-specific characteristics, thus increasing the validity of these findings.

A subsequent investigation conducted by Nezu, Perri, Nezu, and Mahoney (1987) sought to determine, among a population of clinically depressed individuals, if problem-solving skills also function as stress moderators. The 159 subjects included in this study were diagnosed as experiencing unipolar, major depressive disorder according to Research Diagnostic Criteria (RDC; Spitzer et al., 1978) after undergoing clinical interviews based on the SADS. Kappa values of agreement concerning diagnoses between pairs of interviewers ranged between .93 and .96. The mean age of these subjects was 45.62 years. Regression analyses again indicated that the stress × problem-solving interaction was significantly related to depression scores, as measured by the BDI. Follow-up analyses further demonstrated that, among this population, effective problem solvers under high levels of stress reported significantly lower BDI scores than ineffective problem solvers under similar levels of high stress.

However, since these two studies were cross-sectional in nature, it is not possible to rule out rival hypotheses regarding the effects of premorbid level of depression or biases related to depression-associated memory deficits about previous stressful life events. Therefore, Nezu and Ronan (1988) conducted a prospective study with 150 college students to determine whether problem-solving ability was an effective means of coping with stressful events concerning *consequent* depressive symptoms. Prior level of depression served as a covariate within the regression analyses to control for the influence of premorbid depressive level. This study was conducted at two different time periods. During the first testing, data was gathered concerning subjects' level of depressive symptoms, problem-solving ability, and occurrence of prior stressful events. Approximately three months later, subjects were contacted again to obtain information about current levels of depressive symptoms and the occurrence of stressful events subsequent to the first assessment point. In addition to using a prospective design to provide for a more rigorous test of the problem solving as stress-moderator hypothesis, both the MEPS and PSI were used as measures of problem solving in order to increase the construct validity of the findings.

Results from several multiple regression analyses indicated that, with regard to both measures of problem solving, all stress × problem-solving interactions were significant predictors of depressive symptoms assessed at Time 2, even after prior level of depression (i.e., BDI scores at Time 1) was statistically controlled. These findings suggest strongly that problem-solving effectiveness serves as an important moderator of stress-related depression. Put another way, ineffective problem-solving skills can create a potential vulnerability for depression under stressful conditions.

In an attempt to expand upon a simple stress-dysfunction paradigm, Nezu and Ronan (1985) proposed a model that incorporates negative life stress, current problems, problem-solving coping, and depressive symptomatology. Using path-analytic techniques, data from 205 college students were analyzed to test the following causal relations among these variables: (1) Negative stressful events often result in an increase in problematic situations; (2) the degree to which individuals effectively cope with these problems is a function of their problem-solving ability; and (3) effective resolution of these problems decreases the probability of depressive symptoms. In general, results from the path analysis supported this model. It was found that negative life stress was associated with depressive symptoms in both a direct fashion and an indirect manner via increases in the level of current problems. Further, current daily problems had a significant direct impact on depressive symptoms as well as an indirect influence via the quality of one's problem-solving skills. Finally, problem solving itself had a direct influence on the level of depressive symptoms. This model accounted for 42% of the variance associated with the prediction of depression scores.

In order to evaluate the validity and utility of this conceptualization for clinical depression, Nezu, Perri, and Nezu (1987) conducted a subsequent study that included 118 women who had been diagnosed as experiencing major depressive disorder (unipolar) according to RDC guidelines. In addition to using the BDI as a measure of depression, all subjects underwent a clinical interview with two clinicians who completed the Hamilton Rating Scale for Depression (HRSD; Hamilton, 1967). The overall resulting interrater reliability for the HRSD between the various pairs of interviewers was found to be $r = .92$.

Again path-analytic techniques were used to assess the interrelations among major stressful life events, current daily problems, problem solving, and depression. The results provided for both a direct replication of the Nezu and Ronan (1985) investigation and evidence of the validity and relevance of this model for depression as a clinical dysfunction.

PROBLEM-FOCUSED COPING AND DEPRESSION

Previously in this chapter, social problem solving was contrasted with the construct of problem-focused coping and defined to be more broad in scope. However, the degree to which problem-focused coping is subsumed under the process of problem solving suggests that research evaluating the stress-buffering nature of such coping attempts does affect the general understanding of the relation among problem solving, stress, and depression. This type of research has been growing over the past few years. In general, studies focusing on nondiagnosed community groups indicate that persons with little depressive symptomatology are more likely to engage in problem-focused coping responses, whereas avoidance and emotion-focused coping attempts characterize individuals with high depressive symptom levels (Billings & Moos, 1981; Folkman & Lazarus, 1980; Pearlin & Schooler, 1978). For example, Billings and Moos (1981) found that, among a group of 294 adult community residents, greater frequencies of problem-focused coping attempts in reaction to stressful life events attenuated the likelihood of depression occurring as a consequence of such events.

More importantly, a series of studies by Billings, Moos, and their colleagues provide evidence regarding the important relation between problem-focused coping and depression among various clinically depressed populations. For example, Mitchell, Cronkite, and Moos (1983) focused on a group of 157 depressed individuals and their spouses. This conjugal sample was drawn from a larger group of depressed patients who had begun treatment at one of five psychiatric facilities (both inpatient and outpatient). Subjects in the depressed group had a diagnosis of either major or minor depression according to RDC guidelines. These couples were compared with 157 control couples who had been matched along several sociodemographic criteria. Initial results indicated that depressed patients relied on more emotional-discharge coping and less on problem-focused coping in reaction to stressful situations than their spouses or control subjects. Further, spouses of patients under high levels of strain were less likely to exhibit depressive symptoms if they used higher proportions of problem-focused coping.

In another study, Billings, Cronkite, and Moos (1983) examined the influence of stressful events and coping on depression by comparing 409 men and women entering psychiatric treatment for unipolar depression with a sociodemographically matched control group of 409 nondepressed men and women. Treatment facilities included both community outpatient centers and hospital-based inpatient units. All subjects in the clinical group had been diagnosed as experiencing major or minor depression according to RDC guidelines. Results indicated that depressed individuals, as compared to their control peers, reported significantly more stressful events, and experienced more severe life strains associated with both their own and their family members' physical illness, their family relationships, and their home and work situations. Further, depressed subjects were less likely to use problem solving and more likely to use emotion-focused coping responses than control subjects. These results were consistent with a third report by Billings and Moos (1984), which found that among a group of 424 men and women entering treatment for depression, coping responses directed toward problem solving were associated with less severe dysfunction. Further, emotional-discharge coping responses (i.e., verbal and behavioral expressions of unpleasant emotions and indirect attempts at reducing tension, for example, by increased eating or drinking), more frequently used by women, were linked with more dysfunctional symptom patterns.

In order to evaluate the relation between coping and unipolar depression during the posttreatment phase, Billings and Moos (1985) conducted a 12-month follow-up of 380 of the depressed sample originally described in the preceding study (Billings, Cronkite, & Moos, 1983). Using conservative guidelines, three patient groups were identified with regard to the severity of depressive symptoms and whether they were in a treatment episode at follow-up. These included remitted patients (34.9% of the sample), partially remitted patients (31.4% of the sample), and nonremitted patients (33.7% of the sample). These three patient groups were compared to each other as well as with 370 subjects of the original community comparison sample. In order to prevent confounding patient-control comparisons, those controls who exhibited significant depressive features at follow-up were eliminated from the data analyses.

Relevant to the present discussion, results from analyses concerning follow-up data indicated that remitted and partially remitted patients were similar to the control subjects with regard to the use of problem-solving coping responses. However, in comparison to controls, nonremitted patients engaged in more emotional-discharge coping and less problem-solving coping. Analyses focusing on differences between intake and follow-up indicated that at intake, remitted patients reported significantly more emotional-discharge and less problem-solving coping reactions than the control subjects. However, remitted patients' coping patterns became more similar to those of the controls at follow-up. Changes occurring between intake and follow-up for remitted patients reached significance concerning increased problem-solving coping and reduced emotional-discharge coping. Similar analyses indicated no significant changes between intake and follow-up for the control sample.

As a means of identifying various risk factors for failure to recover from depression, Billings and Moos (1985) focused on their nonremitted patient subsample. Results from a multiple regression analysis, which included various risk factors assessed at treatment intake, indicated that lack of problem-solving coping was an important predictor of nonremission versus remission status at the follow-up. Other risk factors included initial severity of depressive symptomatology, higher age, lower education level, few acute stressors, and few close social relationships.

In summary, in a variety of studies, social problem solving and problem-focused coping have been shown to be important moderators of the likelihood that individuals may experience depression as a consequence of stress. In other words, problem-solving deficits may serve as a vulnerability factor that predisposes one to depression under stressful conditions. Further, it is important to note that several studies described in this section included subjects who had been reliably diagnosed as experiencing major depressive disorder according to either DSM III or RDC criteria, thereby increasing the clinical relevance and validity of the findings.

PROBLEM-SOLVING THERAPY FOR DEPRESSION

If problem-solving deficits have been found to be related to depression, therapy based on overcoming such deficits should therefore lead to decreases in depressive symptomatology. Testing this hypothesis has been the goal of several investigations.

In a single-case study reported by Caple and Blechman (1976), problem-solving training was one of several components used to treat a depressed female outpatient. Whereas the patient's depression level was reduced significantly, the specific contribution of problem solving was not evaluated. Shipley and Fazio (1973) reported two studies that partially involved the teaching of various problem-solving skills to psychometrically identified depressed college students. Results of both investigations indicated that problem-solving training was superior to various control conditions. However, problem solving was also embedded among a variety of cognitive-behavioral techniques, making an assessment of the unique contributions of such training difficult.

The first study to isolate problem-solving therapy as a means of evaluating its unique effectiveness as a treatment procedure for depression was conducted by Hussian and Lawrence (1981). These authors included 36 depressed nursing-home patients over 60 years of age in a study that tested the relative efficacy of social problem-solving (PS) and social-reinforcement (SR) approaches to treatment. A waiting-list control (WLC) condition was also included. Both treatment groups met for five 30-minute training sessions during a 1-week period. During a second treatment week, subjects in each condition were then assigned randomly to either continue in the same therapy or to participate in the other treatment approach. Thus, one PS subgroup continued to receive problem-solving training (PS-PS), whereas a second PS group received the SR condition (PS-SR). The initial SR group was also divided to produce two groups: SR-SR and SR-PS. Finally, one half of the WLC continued in this condition, whereas the other half participated in an informational control group.

Results of the study indicated a significant reduction in depression, as measured by the BDI, for only those groups that received problem-solving training (i.e., the difference between the SR-SR and control groups was nonsignificant). Additionally the superiority of the PS condition was maintained at a 2-week follow-up assessment.

In the first problem-solving outcome study to include reliably diagnosed depressed individuals, Nezu (1986c) assigned randomly 26 subjects to one of the following groups: Problem-Solving Therapy (PST), Problem-Focused Therapy (PFT), and a Waiting-List Control (WLC). These individuals were community residents diagnosed as experiencing nonpsychotic, unipolar depression, according to RDC guidelines. The mean age of the participants was 41.73 years, whereas the mean number of years of formal education was 15.96.

In addition to meeting RDC criteria for a current episode of unipolar depression, treatment participants had also to report scores of 16 and above on the BDI and MMPI-D scores of $T > 70$. Exclusion criteria included bipolar disorders, the presence of mental retardation, psychotic symptomatology, active substance abuse, or current involvement in any form of psychological or pharmacological treatment for depression. Diagnoses of major depressive disorder were made independently by two clinicians where the resulting kappa value of agreement reached .96.

The PST condition was based on a systematic model of social problem solving as delineated by D'Zurilla and Nezu (1982) and included training in all five components (problem orientation, problem definition and formulation, generation of alternatives, decision making, solution implementation and verification). Subjects in the PFT group were provided with a similar treatment rationale as that of the PST condition, that is, resolution of problematic situations and other sources of stress would lead to a decrease in depression. However, members of this group were not provided with a systematic model for problem resolution. Instead, they were encouraged to use the sessions to discuss problems with other group members. Essentially, this treatment condition resembled a group psychotherapy program that emphasized the influence of current difficulties and crises in maintaining and/or causing depression. It was included as a reasonable treatment alternative providing an appropriate methodological contrast to the PST condition but would also be viewed by its members as a legitimate treatment modality. Both treatment programs were conducted over eight 90-minute sessions.

Members of the WLC condition were told that the program was unable to accommodate any further members, but that at the end of the 8 weeks, they would be able to receive treatment if still desired.

Results of pre-post analyses indicated that PST subjects reported a significant decrease in their depressive symptoms, as measured by both the BDI (change of means from 23.91 to 9.82) and MMPI-D (change of means from 81.36 to 54.27) scales, which was also found to covary with concurrent increases in problem-solving effectiveness, as measured by the PSI, and the adoption of an internal locus of control orientation. This improvement was maintained at a 6-month follow-up assessment (mean BDI = 9.50; mean MMPI-D = 52.50). Moreover, PST subjects reported significantly lower posttreatment depression scores than either the PFT (mean BDI = 18.00; MMPI-D = 67.32) or WLC groups (mean BDI = 21.00; mean MMPI-D = 76.33). Additional analyses indicated these changes to be clinically meaningful. For example, using BDI scores as the measure of depression, analyses indicated that 90.9% of the PST subjects showed clinically meaningful improvement, as compared to rates of 22.2% for PFT subjects and 16.7% for the WLC condition.

The purpose of a subsequent study by Nezu and Perri (1987) was twofold: (1) to provide for a partial replication of the Nezu (1986c) study, and (2) to assess the relative contribution of the problem-orientation component in treating depressed individuals. A dismantling strategy was used to address these goals by assigning randomly 39 individuals who had been reliably diagnosed, according to RDC criteria, as experiencing major depressive disorder to one of three conditions: (1) Problem-Solving Therapy

(PST); (2) Abbreviated Problem-Solving Therapy (APST); and (3) Waiting-List Control (WLC).

In addition to the BDI, the Hamilton Rating Scale for Depression (Hamilton, 1967), a measure of clinician ratings, was used to assess changes in depression. Estimates of interrater reliability (kappa values of agreement) between pairs of clinicians completing the HRSD were found to be .96 at pretreatment and .94 at the posttreatment assessment. Both treatment conditions included ten 2-hour therapy sessions conducted in groups by various pairs of advanced clinical psychology graduate students (counterbalanced by condition).

Members of the PST condition received training in all five components of the social problem-solving model. APST participants were provided with a similar package, with the exception of training in the problem-orientation component. As noted in Chapter 4, problem orientation can be described as a set of orienting responses that consists of the immediate cognitive-affective-behavioral reactions of a person when first confronted with a problematic situation. These orienting responses include a particular type of attentional set (i.e., a sensitivity to problems) and a set of general and relatively stable beliefs, assumptions, appraisals, and expectations concerning life's problems and one's own general problem-solving ability. Therefore, training in this component is geared to facilitate an individual's adoption of a problem-solving set that contains the following aspects: (1) the identification or recognition of a problem when one occurs; (2) acceptance of the view that problems in living are normal and inevitable and that problem solving is a viable means of coping with them; (3) the expectation that one is capable of solving a particular problem effectively (i.e., perceived control), and (4) the set to stop and think when confronted with a problem instead of responding automatically with habits based on previous experiences in similar situations (D'Zurilla & Nezu, 1982).

Subjects in the WLC condition were requested to wait until the program was able to accommodate them at a later date.

Pretest analyses indicated that all three conditions were equivalent initially concerning both mean BDI (PST = 26.00; APST = 27.71; WLC = 27.27) and mean HRSD (PST = 24.07; APST = 25.29; WLC = 25.91) scores. Pre-post analyses indicated that subjects in the PST condition displayed significantly lower levels of depressive symptoms at posttreatment (mean BDI = 6.57; mean HRSD = 7.71) as compared to both the APST (mean BDI = 13.00; mean HRSD = 13.07) and WLC (mean BDI = 24.73; mean HRSD = 21.00) subjects. Further, APST subjects reported significantly lower posttreatment depression scores than WLC participants. Decreases in depressive symptoms were also significantly correlated with increases in problem-solving ability, as measured by the PSI, and these results were clinically significant.

A 6-month follow-up assessment revealed no significant differences between posttreatment and follow-up scores for either treatment condition. In other words, the therapeutic benefits obtained by subjects in both treatment conditions were maintained 6 months after completing treatment. These results provide further support for problem-solving therapy as an effective treatment approach for unipolar depression. Moreover, this study suggests that whereas a version of problem-solving therapy without the problem-orientation component (APST) is significantly more effective than no treatment (WLC), the inclusion of this training within the full problem-solving therapy (PST) adds significantly to the overall effectiveness of such an approach. The importance of the problem-orientation component was believed to involve its facilitative effects on motivation to actually engage in the other four problem-solving stages. In other words, whereas subjects in the APST acquired skills to define problems better, establish more concrete and realistic goals, make more effective decisions, and monitor the consequences of their implemented solutions, the inhibitive effects of depression on motivation may have minimized the impact of such skills on reducing their affective reactions to stressful problems.

Although only three studies thus far have been conducted to evaluate the specific efficacy of a problem-solving treatment approach for depression, they provide strong initial support for its effectiveness in reducing depressive symptomatology. More importantly, these studies suggest that decreases in depression were associated with increases in overall problem-solving ability.

SUMMARY

The research cited provides support for (1) the existence of a strong relation between problem-solving deficits and depression; (2) the moderating role that problem solving plays in naturalistic settings concerning the likelihood that individuals will experience depressive symptoms under stressful conditions; and (3) the initial efficacy of a problem-solving therapy approach for unipolar depression.

As indicated previously, certain aspects of the overall model are speculative in nature, particularly with regard to the relation between the problem-solving formulation and biological correlates of depression. Future research efforts need to focus on investigations that address the validity of the building blocks that constitute these hypothesized integrative bridges. It is hoped that the present explication of this theoretical model will engender such empirical attempts.

PART TWO

Problem-Solving Therapy for Depression

Clinical Guidelines

CHAPTER 6

General Clinical Considerations

If life gives you lemons, make lemonade.

ANONYMOUS

Whatever you can do, or dream you can, begin it . . .
Boldness has genius, power, and magic in it.

GOETHE

Beginning with this chapter, the remainder of this volume will focus on the *application* of a problem-solving therapy approach to unipolar depression. It will first address various general clinical issues, such as structure, the therapist-patient relationship, assessment guidelines, and the use of certain adjunctive therapeutic strategies throughout problem-solving therapy. The next five chapters will focus on a detailed description of training in each of the five major problem-solving component processes. Within these chapters, a variety of therapeutic strategies that address specific depression associated problem-solving deficits will be presented. Additionally, various therapist-patient dialogues will illustrate important aspects of treatment.

GENERAL CHARACTERISTICS OF PROBLEM-SOLVING THERAPY

Treatment Goals

Overall, the goals of problem-solving therapy are to (1) help depressed individuals identify previous and current life situations (major life events and current daily problems) that are antecedents of a depressive episode; (2) minimize the extent to which their depressive symptoms impact negatively on current and future attempts at coping; (3) increase the effectiveness of their problem-solving attempts at coping with current problem

113

situations; and (4) teach general skills that will enable them to deal more effectively with future problems in order to prevent depressive reactions. Depending upon the patient's life circumstances and the specific characteristics of the stressful situations being experienced, treatment can focus on changing the problematic nature of these situations, the maladaptive response to these events (i.e., the depression per se), or both. In most clinical cases, it is important to address both aspects.

Structure of Therapy Approach

Problem-solving therapy can be applied in a highly structured, time-limited format, similar to our research program (cf. Nezu, 1986c; Nezu & Perri, 1987), or within a broader, open-ended therapy format. It can be undertaken with groups or on a one-to-one basis. Problem-solving therapy can be viewed as the sole treatment program, as part of a larger therapy package, or as a form of maintenance and generalization training.

If conducted in a group format, a version of problem-solving therapy as implemented within our structured research project can be used. Table 6.1 describes the overall format of a 10-week intervention program where problem solving is the primary treatment component (see Appendix A for a detailed list of the essential aspects covered in each session).

A group approach can be especially helpful to facilitate both adoption of certain positive problem-orientation beliefs (e.g., "Problems are a common part of living") and the success of training in various problem-solving skills (e.g., group brainstorming of alternatives). In undertaking a group program, it is extremely important to consider the particular constellation of a group as a significant variable in implementing problem-solving or any cognitive-behavioral therapy (Flowers, 1979; Sansbury, 1979). For example, more talkative group members may tend to overshadow less assertive participants. Group therapists need to encourage the less talk-

TABLE 6.1.   Overview of 10-Week Problem-Solving Group Program

Session Number	Topic
1	Introduction and Rationale
2	Problem Orientation
3	Problem Definition and Formulation
4	Generation of Alternatives
5	Decision Making
6	Solution Implementation and Verification
7–9	Maintenance and Generalization
10	Wrap-up and Termination

ative members to participate fully. A further recommendation is that each group be led by a team of two cotherapists experienced in both problem-solving strategies and general group therapy techniques. A group of six to eight members is an optimal size.

Using a problem-solving approach on an individual basis greatly enhances the ability to specifically tailor the intervention to the particular needs of the patient. In clinical practice, there are some individuals who are particularly concerned with the ability of group members to be confidential outside the group. In such a case, individual treatment should be implemented. To date, no empirical evidence suggests the relative efficacy of group versus individual problem-solving treatment. In the absence of such information, it is appropriate for the therapist to use clinical judgment in reaching a decision.

If problem-solving therapy is used in conjunction with other treatment strategies, the overall therapy should take place within a larger *general problem-solving framework* (D'Zurilla, 1986), where the additional techniques are incorporated to facilitate training in various problem-solving skills. For example, the use of cognitive restructuring techniques would be highly appropriate during problem-definition-and-formulation training in order to minimize the extent to which various cognitive distortions prevent depressed individuals from accurately defining a problem. Use of relaxation exercises during the generation-of-alternatives process can also facilitate creativity by decreasing possible interference associated with emotional reactivity (Nezu & Nezu, in press).

Overview of the Process of Problem-Solving Therapy

In general, problem-solving therapy can be divided into three major stages: (1) assessment, (2) intervention, and (3) maintenance and generalization training.

ASSESSMENT.   Upon diagnosis of a nonpsychotic depressive disorder, one of the first decisions that a therapist needs to make in conjunction with this approach concerns its appropriateness for a particular patient. The identification of various problem-solving deficits associated with depression is likely to underscore the potential utility for such a person. However, even in the absence of specific identified problem-solving deficits, this treatment approach is likely to be helpful in treating depression because it can increase one's overall sense of control and social competence (Nezu, 1987; Nezu, Nezu, & Perri, in press).

Parenthetically, decisions regarding the appropriateness and potential utility of problem-solving therapy should be made subsequent to intake sessions addressing issues of differential diagnosis and need for medication referrals. For example, the presence of severe neurovegetative symptoms, often indicative of melancholic depression, may require some form of psychopharmacological intervention and a psychiatric referral as an adjunct to problem-solving treatment.

Pretreatment assessment should be geared toward identification of specific problem-solving and coping skills deficits associated with depression. Use of various self-report and observational procedures are useful in conducting such an evaluation (see Chapter 2 and section on Pretreatment Assessment in this chapter). Additionally, assessment should also be conducted throughout treatment in order to provide a continuous evaluation of the feasibility and efficacy of treatment with a particular individual. This entails process measures of the severity of current depressive symptoms (see Chapter 1), as well as changes in the performance of various problem-solving skills (see section on Process Assessment in this chapter).

INTERVENTION.   Problem-solving treatment itself focuses primarily on training in the five major problem-solving component processes (problem orientation, problem definition and formulation, generation of alternatives, decision making, solution implementation and verification). In such skills training, the incorporation of various teaching or training procedures throughout treatment enhances effective learning. These include (1) instruction, (2) prompting, (3) modeling, (4) behavioral rehearsal, (5) homework assignments, (6) shaping, (7) reinforcement, and (8) feedback.

The earlier aspects of problem-solving treatment deal primarily with *instructions* concerning the purpose, rationale, goals, application, and relevance to depression of each of the five major problem-solving operations. The rationale of each skill should be presented with special care. Often the misapplication of a problem-solving operation may be caused by the therapist's inattention to the need for providing the information to the patient in a clear, concise, and understandable manner. This material can be presented didactically, as well as in the form of handouts (see Appendix B for an example of a patient handout describing the overall problem-solving approach). In either format, it is important to use language that is concrete and unambiguous (in keeping with the philosophy of this approach), as well as on the reading level of a particular patient population.

Prompting is a procedure in which a cue is provided that helps lead an individual to a correct response. The problem-solving therapist should offer continuous prompts during training in the specific problem-solving skills. For example, a prompt during brainstorming sessions might require the therapist to begin generating alternative solutions. This helps facilitate the patient's skill acquisition. Prompts can be particularly useful also when discussing potential consequences of a specific alternative during the decision-making phase.

Modeling is a very powerful and important teaching procedure. Within this treatment approach, modeling of all problem-solving operations is especially important. This can be done in vivo, through filmed or pictorial presentation, or through role-playing. When illustrating the application of a problem-solving skill, example problems should be relevant to the particular patient. For instance, situations about meeting new people or making friends would be used during modeling procedures for a depressed person who is experiencing difficulties with loneliness.

To facilitate learning and to help individuals discriminate more effectively, it is important to model both correct *and* incorrect ways of applying various problem-solving skills. Consider the following therapist-patient dialogue that focuses on demonstrating the *failure* to use the deferment-of-judgment principle of brainstorming ideas.

THERAPIST (TH): John, we've already discussed the notion that thinking of a large number of alternatives is important when attempting to identify effective solutions. In using this quantity principle, it is also important not to judge or evaluate any of these ideas until later. In other words, we should defer judgment until we have generated as many possible ideas as we can.

PATIENT (P): I'm not sure what you mean. Shouldn't I try to evaluate how good they are when I'm thinking of ideas?

TH: Not at this point. Later on, during the decision-making phase. Right now, it is generally a good idea to try to think of as many ideas as possible. Deferring judgment helps you to accomplish this more easily. Let me show you what I mean. First, I am going to demonstrate what *not* to do.

P: OK, that would be helpful to me.

TH: OK, let's start with the problem that we have been discussing the last couple of sessions. We have already stated the goal—"How can I increase the chances of getting a raise and promotion in my company?" (Therapist begins pretending that he or she is the actual problem solver within the situation.) OK, let me think of several alternatives. Maybe I should try to talk to my boss more often. No, that's not a good idea. He never listens to anybody, anyhow! Maybe I should stay later at work to show that I am really committed to this job. No, that's not a good idea either. The later I stay, the more angry I get at my job because I'm unappreciated! So what can I do?

This problem-solving method really doesn't help me at all! I can't come up with any ideas! (Therapist stops demonstration.) OK, John, what do you think about this method?

P: Well, I see what you mean. I used to get angry and frustrated with my son, Ron, when he used to do the same thing with his schoolwork. If you continue to judge each alternative, then maybe you might never come up with any solutions at all.

Th: Exactly! That's a very good point. Also, it tends to make someone give up and become easily discouraged.

P: That's when I start getting down on myself and feel depressed.

Th: That's also a good self-observation. Why don't you try to generate some ideas now for the same problem, and remember to use *both* the quantity *and* deferment principles.

P: OK, I'll give it a try.

At this point, the therapist may use prompts to help facilitate John's attempts at generating alternative ideas.

Behavioral rehearsal or practice of the various problem-solving operations is extremely important in order to maximize learning. Various analogies about driving a car are clinically useful as a means of illustrating this fact. For example, the following statement highlights the importance of practice.

Remember when you were first learning how to drive a car. The various dials on the dashboard were difficult to understand. The wheel seemed awkward. You were not sure when to put your foot on the brake. You may not have felt comfortable. "How much should I turn the wheel when I make a turn? When should I put on the turn signal lights? How can I ever drive on the highway?" These may have been questions you initially asked yourself the first time you tried to drive. Now you drive almost every day of your life. You no longer ask these questions because driving has become a habit. The more you initially practiced, the more comfortable you probably felt. Practice was the key! The more often you drive, the more of a habit it becomes. It is the same with these problem-solving skills. The more that you practice, the more it may become second nature to you. However, I am sure it feels somewhat awkward at this point. But remember, driving felt the same way at first. Therefore, it is extremely important to practice these skills as much as possible.

If a particular patient is known to have acquired certain skills in other areas of life, such as playing a musical instrument or mastering a foreign language, it is particularly relevant to use these examples as illustrations.

Practice or rehearsal should occur both during sessions and between them. To accomplish the extrasession practice, *homework assignments* are an important feature of the treatment approach. It is clinically useful to characterize the importance of homework by pointing out that a 1- or 2-hour session amounts to only 1/168 or 1/84 of a week's time. In order to have a major impact on life situations, problem-solving therapy needs to be continued by patients on their own in between sessions.

Homework assignments are given at the end of each session and usually correspond to the particular problem-solving operation that was discussed during that session. During the latter segments of treatment, much emphasis is given to practicing the application of the entire model in real-life situations. In vivo treatment applications are an extremely important component of any cognitive-behavioral intervention. There are examples of problem-solving homework assignments and worksheets throughout the next five chapters.

Shaping is the process by which a response is gradually changed in quality. As a general strategy, it is useful to develop a hierarchy of a patient's problems, based on the dimensions of severity and complexity. Less intense or difficult problems can then be used as relevant examples earlier during problem-solving training. Once the patient has mastered certain prerequisite skills, more difficult problems can be addressed. Not only does this procedure minimize the likelihood of emotional distress interfering with the learning process, but it also increases the probability of early success. The effective application of a problem-solving operation then can be used to strengthen the patient's positive orientation in general, and his or her self-efficacy beliefs in particular.

The problem-solving therapist should also provide *reinforcement* to patients for active attempts to simply engage in any problem-solving operation, as well as successful problem resolution. Reinforcement is part of a larger *feedback* system that should be incorporated throughout treatment. In addition to instructions concerning the use of various problem-solving skills, the therapist should provide corrective feedback to the patient who is applying the skills incorrectly. By also eliciting continuous feedback from the patient through probes and questions the therapist can evaluate understanding of each operation's rationale, as well as its acceptability to the individual. As part of the feedback process, the therapist should often summarize the major points of treatment in order to underscore their importance. This should not only occur at the end of a session, but throughout treatment.

MAINTENANCE AND GENERALIZATION TRAINING.   The third overall phase of problem-solving treatment is training in maintenance and generalization. Because the overall thrust of this approach is to train individuals in a set of problem-solving skills, generalization is built into the philosophy of the model. However, as noted previously, substantial practice in these skills is paramount. Therefore, the third stage entails helping the patient to apply the entire model across a wide range of problematic situations. For each new problematic situation addressed, no matter how minor, patients are encouraged to use the five major problem-solving components to aid in its resolution. Continuous feedback by the therapist facilitates appropriate application of these skills.

During this phase the therapist may also teach the patient additional coping skills that have previously been identified as particular skill deficits during either the decision-making or solution implementation process. For example, during the evaluation of alternatives in the decision-making process, the therapist and patient together may identify a deficit in assertiveness skills. Alternatives that relate to the general construct of assertiveness may therefore have been initially evaluated as poor, because of the particular person's difficulties or inability to optimally implement such alternatives. If the therapist and patient agree that becoming more assertive is a reasonable treatment goal, such training may be added within the overall problem-solving approach. Training in other social (e.g., communication skills) or self-control (e.g., relaxation training) skills may also be appropriate targets depending on the nature of the patient's overall strengths and weaknesses.

TERMINATION OF TREATMENT.   The latter sessions should also address issues of termination and patient independence. Again, because the overall philosophy of this approach focuses on teaching skills that individuals can apply by themselves in future problematic situations, a major theme throughout intervention encourages independence. Providing patients with handouts throughout treatment helps them to feel less apprehensive in ending therapy. Encouraging patients to refer back to these handouts regularly can also aid in maximizing future utilization of their training. Occasionally, a patient's distress concerning termination can represent a final problem requiring use of the model.

Booster or maintenance problem-solving sessions facilitate generalization and prevent relapse. Such sessions are especially appropriate during long-term follow-up of the patient's progress. These sessions should be geared particularly toward analyzing the patient's actual application of the skills learned during treatment. Further, gradually tapering off the frequency of sessions toward the end of treatment helps to minimize difficulties with termination and relapse (i.e., scheduling sessions every 2 weeks).

THERAPIST-PATIENT RELATIONSHIP

As in other forms of psychotherapy, the therapist-patient relationship is important within a problem-solving approach. Although problem-solving therapy consists of various training modules, minimization of the therapist-patient relationship can have a severe impact on the overall effectiveness of treatment. Goldstein (1975) suggests that without a favorable therapist-patient relationship, client change rarely occurs.

Therapist Characteristics

As a general strategy, it is important for the problem-solving therapist to display *warmth, empathy, trust,* and a sense of *genuineness.* These non-specific factors, as identified by other therapists (cf. Rogers, 1957; Truax & Carkhuff, 1967), by themselves are not sufficient treatment strategies to effectively help the depressed patient. However, if they are displayed judiciously, the patient will probably be more receptive to the therapist's judgment and overall rationale of treatment.

For example, at times a patient's initial reaction to the problem-solving approach includes statements such as "It's too simple—I must be depressed for some other reason," or "This problem-solving approach appears too *cold*—I can't think so logically all the time!" The general manner in which the therapist is perceived can minimize much of this early resistance. If the problem-solving therapist conveys a sense of empathy and trust, it is more likely that the patient will begin treatment with at least a wait-and-see attitude.

Additionally, it is important for a therapist using this approach to be well versed in the areas of depression, stress, coping, and social problem solving. Being able to answer specific questions about depression considerably advances a sense of trust and professionalism in a therapist.

Further, the best therapists for this approach are the ones who tend to use problem-solving strategies in their own lives as a means of coping with stressful situations. This is especially valid if the stressful situation involves conducting problem-solving therapy for the first time. For example, beginning therapists, psychology students, interns, and psychiatric residents, frequently demonstrate a predictable naïveté in their initial approach to training in certain problem-orientation variables. Armed with a plethora of information concerning the types of selective thinking processess and negative appraisals and attributions often associated with depression, student therapists often report surprise and frustration when patients resist changing these beliefs. Made aware of the consequences of these maladaptive perceptions and provided with alternative, more adaptive beliefs, how can certain patients be so stubborn? These students, however, are often wrestling with their own perceptual sets and self-evaluations concerning performance as new problem-solving therapists! They experience dissonance between constructive coping thoughts and their actual negative emotions (e.g., "I know that performing poorly as a new therapist does not mean the end of my training and failure as a clinician, but I feel like such a failure"). Supervision of student therapists, therefore, should entail an examination of their own competing self-evaluations and expectancies, which ultimately may help them respect the difficulties in changing their patients' habituated emotionally laden cognitive schemas.

Moreover, the problem-solving therapist should be able to use these strategies to help with clinical decision making and judgment. A model of clinical decision making based upon a problem-solving formulation has been presented elsewhere (Nezu & Nezu, in press; Nezu, Petronko, & Nezu, 1982). Essentially, this approach suggests that the therapist needs to be flexible in thinking about development of individualized patient treatment programs and to be aware of various errors and biases inherent in human judgment. Use of problem-solving operations, such as brainstorming all possible solutions (i.e., treatment strategies) for a particular individual with a given set of symptoms maximizes the likelihood that treatment will be both effective and individualized.

Another important therapist characteristic is the ability to present information in a clear, concise, and understandable manner. Within this model, the therapist continuously provides explanations and rationales for each problem-solving operation and its relevance to coping with depression and stressful circumstances. The patient who is unable to understand the reasons underlying these skills will have added difficulty in applying them to real-life situations.

Of equal importance is the therapist's ability to strike a balance between being an active, directive practitioner and conveying a sense of collaboration with the patient. In line with the philosophy of this approach, the therapist needs to be active throughout treatment, presenting rationales and instructions, modeling the application of various skills, and providing corrective feedback and reinforcement. However, he or she must also join with the patient in a collaborative relationship that emphasizes trust, openness, and concern for the client. This collaboration comes into play especially when the patient and therapist mutually make decisions concerning treatment goals, problems to address, and treatment evaluation (i.e., progress of symptom reduction and increase in problem-solving skills).

Clinically, analogies such as becoming a team of "investigative reporters," "detectives," or "personal scientists," are useful in characterizing this collaborative relationship. They help convey (1) a sense of mutual exploration into the nature of the patient's problems and experience of depression, and (2) the perspective of active members on a team working toward a mutual goal of either "getting at the bottom of the story," "solving the mystery," or "testing various experimental hypotheses." Persuasion, coercion, or cold, logical refutation of dysfunctional thoughts or maladaptive coping patterns are not characteristic of an effective problem-solving approach. Rather, explanation, demonstration, guided instruction, corrective feedback, and teaching are more appropriate for helping the depressed person to learn how to cope more effectively with stressful situations.

Patient Characteristics

To date, there is no empirical evidence to help determine various patient characteristics that might be related to either treatment success or failure. Clinical experience does suggest, however, that as the major treatment modality, problem-solving therapy is appropriate for a wide range of nonpsychotic affective disorders, including major depressive disorder and dysthymic disorder. The patients who have participated either clinically or within the research program span a wide range of ages (14–74), socioeconomic status, educational levels, ethnic backgrounds, and history of previous depressive episodes and psychotherapy contacts. In keeping with this idiographic philosophy, it is important to apply problem-solving therapy on an individualized basis. The unique history and personal learning experiences that a patient brings to treatment should be meaningfully incorporated into the overall intervention plan.

The presence of severe melancholia, psychotic symptomatology, below normal intelligence, and antisocial personality features may be contraindicative of this approach. Individuals with a history of melancholic or psychotic disturbance whose symptoms have become somewhat stabilized through medication need not, however, be ruled out as candidates for problem-solving treatment. Persons exhibiting severe characterological difficulties, such as borderline personality features, may require adjunct treatments that initially provide greater external structure and support (e.g., day treatment milieu or individualized therapy sessions). Until further investigations are conducted, caution should be used in applying this approach with these populations. The efficacy of a combined medication and problem-solving approach for an in-patient depressed population is currently being tested, as well as a combined group and individual approach for borderline patients.

PREPARING THE PATIENT

Pretreatment Assessment

DIAGNOSIS OF DEPRESSION.   One of the most important ways to gather initial information concerning differential diagnosis is a semistructured interview. If the person is depressed, it is likely that this interview will be difficult to conduct at times, because of the symptoms of lethargy, sad mood, and problems in concentration. The interviewer needs to be sensitive to both the patient's overall sad demeanor (both verbal and nonverbal) and hesitancies in answering questions. Rapid-fire questions are unlikely to produce an atmosphere of trust and openness. Especially if conducted as part of individual therapy, the interview is a crucial time to create an environment of trust and open communication that will be especially important during treatment. Although the interviewer at times needs to be directive and to take the major responsibility for leading the interview, it is often helpful in capturing a comprehensive clinical picture to allow the patient to direct the flow of information.

The interviewer should also be well versed in the content area of depression in order to determine whether the symptom picture being observed is reflective of a depressive disorder. Knowledge of DSM III-R is particularly useful with regard to a *differential* diagnosis. In addition to collecting information about the person's experience of depression, it is necessary to gather a comprehensive history including data about previous depressive episodes, hospitalizations, medical complications, usage of prescription and nonprescription drugs, educational, social, and family background, and current level of functioning. Of crucial importance are inquiries about the patient's potential for suicide. It is essential to ask questions concerning both previous and current suicide ideation, intent, and actual plans. Clinically, it is recommended to ask such questions directly. Inexperienced therapists often believe that by asking questions about suicide, they are "planting a seed" that did not exist previously. A conservative approach should be taken, where the therapist not only asks such questions but also continuously evaluates them throughout treatment. If a strong sense of suicide ideation is present, then further inquiries concerning whether the patient has an active suicide plan become important.

In assessing the actual symptoms of depression, a semistructured interview should be used, such as the SADS or HRSD (see Chapter 1). Table 6.2 contains the general areas of depressive symptomatology that represent the targets of inquiry. In addition to the semistructured inter-

TABLE 6.2.   Symptoms of Major Depressive and Dysthymic Disorder:
Areas of Inquiry

Depressed mood, sad affect
Markedly diminished interest in previously pleasurable activities
Significant weight loss *or* gain
Insomnia *or* hypersomnia
Psychomotor retardation *or* agitation
General fatigue and loss of energy
Feelings of worthlessness, excessive or inappropriate guilt
Difficulties in concentration, indecisiveness
Recurrent thoughts of death, suicidal ideation

view, the patient should complete the BDI, which also provides useful
information during an item analysis.

PROBLEM-SOLVING ASSESSMENT.   During the initial interviews, the
therapist also conducts a comprehensive assessment of the patient's current level of functioning. Within the model, this assessment focuses heavily on the various stressful life events that the patient is currently experiencing, as well as the ones he or she has experienced within the past
few years. Additionally, it is important to evaluate the actual coping
attempts that the patient has tried as a means of dealing with stressful
situations. Such questions should be couched in terms of information
gathering with a view to minimizing the possibility that the patient hears
them as reprimands of poor coping ability. Interview assessment should
entail inquiries regarding all facets of the problem-solving model, including
initial perceptions of the events, how the goals were defined, what actual
alternatives were considered, which solutions were actually implemented,
and how the individual felt about the outcome. The following is an example
of the beginning of such an interview with a patient after the diagnosis of
major depressive disorder.

THERAPIST (TH): It appears that the recent breakup with your boyfriend
    has upset you quite a bit.
PATIENT (P): Yes, it has. I really can't sleep at nights anymore. I can't
    stop thinking about Jason. He was everything to me.
TH: Do you feel that it is possible to get back together with him? Would
    this be something that you would want?
P: Absolutely! As I told you before, this is supposed to be a trial sepa-
    ration for us. We haven't broken up forever. But I feel that if he

wanted to separate now, then he probably will be leaving me in the future. I'm afraid that this is his way of letting me down gently.

TH: So you believe that instead of Jason telling you the truth about needing to be apart for awhile, he actually plans to leave you? What exactly makes you think this?

P: Nothing, really. I have no reason to believe that he is lying to me. He never has before. In fact, it was initially my idea to date other people, not his. My parents' divorce has always made me feel real nervous about not finding the right mate for life. But I'm afraid that I have screwed everything up!

TH: What would you actually like to see happen in this situation?

P: I'm not sure. I hope that this separation makes us get closer together in the future.

TH: Have you had the chance to think of any ways that could help you reach this goal?

P: Not really. I've been so worried and depressed about what might go wrong that I haven't thought about anything else!

TH: Dorothy, I can appreciate that. It seems that your worries and fears have taken over all your thoughts.

P: I guess so. It's so hard to think about anything else.

TH: I understand. One of the things that I would like to do is talk more about possible ways that you could reach that goal, whether or not that goal is in your best interests, how to evaluate the different possible solutions to this problem, and so on. How does that sound for now?

P: OK. But what I also want to talk about is whether my fears are realistic. I'm getting so depressed just thinking about losing Jason.

TH: I agree with you, Dorothy. The way in which you understand, perceive, and think about this situation can also have a large impact on your feelings. I think it would be important to talk about both of these areas. Of crucial importance, however, is to discuss ways that you can use to solve problems or difficult life situations in general. Basically, I think it might be a good idea to focus on learning new strategies to help you make better decisions that are in your best interests.

P: That sounds good to me.

In addition to an interview that focuses on current life problems and coping attempts, administration of various self-report measures can help complete a comprehensive picture. As described in Chapter 2, the PSI and SPSI can provide for an overall assessment of general problem-solving abilities. The PSI can be especially useful in determining the patient's self-appraisal of his or her problem-solving skills. The SPSI is helpful in developing a profile of the specific problem-solving skill deficits characteristic of a particular patient. More specifically, as noted previously, not all depressed individuals have deficits across the five major problem-solving components. Rather, individuals may differ in the types of problem-solving deficits that exist. Although overall training should focus on the entire model (cf. Nezu & Perri, 1987), a greater emphasis may be placed during treatment on ameliorating specifically identified deficits.

D'Zurilla's (1986) PSSM method (see Chapter 2) can also serve as a useful pretreatment assessment of actual attempts to solve real-life problems. Lastly, Figure 6.1 depicts the Record of Coping Attempts used in our research program. This record requests individuals to describe a recently experienced problem situation, to list their thoughts, feelings, and coping behavior within the situation, and to rate their overall satisfaction with their general coping response. The record is generally administered not only at pretreatment but also provides for an initial homework assignment at the beginning of treatment. The completed form supplies valuable clinical information concerning the types of problems that the patient experiences, as well as overall coping reactions.

Several additional inventories exist that provide information concerning the types of recently experienced stressful events. The use of the Life Experiences Survey (LES; Sarason, Johnson, & Siegel, 1978) is recommended as a measure of major life changes. The LES is a 47-item self-report measure that allows subjects to indicate the incidence of various important life change events (e.g., death of a family member, leaving home for the first time) experienced during the past year. Individuals can indicate also the occurrence of significant events not specified on the LES list. Further, a supplemental list of 10 events relevant to a university student population is included (e.g., beginning a new school experience). The LES requests individuals to rate the perceived stressful impact of each of these events on a 7-point scale, ranging from -3 to $+3$. Scores can thus be differentiated between events that were perceived as having a positive, neutral, or negative impact. For example, depending upon varying life circumstances, two individuals experiencing a divorce might rate this event quite differently. One person may perceive this event to be quite negative and devastating, whereas the second may rate the divorce as quite positive.

The Mooney Problem Checklist (Mooney & Gordon, 1950) or the Personal Problems Checklist (Schinka, 1986) is also useful to assess self-

Name: _____ Date: _____

Description of problem situation:

Thoughts (before, during, or after situation):

Feelings (before, during, or after situation):

Actual coping behavior:

How pleased were you with your general reaction to the problem? (circle one)

1	2	3	4	5
Not at All		Somewhat		Very Much

Figure 6.1. Record of Coping Attempts.

defined problematic situations. Both checklists contain a comprehensive list of possible problems across a wide range of life categories (e.g., religion, sex, relationship with family, finances, etc.). Completion of these checklists can aid the assessment process substantially. Both checklists are also available in varying forms depending on age levels. For example, the Personal Problems Checklist has adult, adolescent, and child versions.

RELATED MEASURES OF DEPRESSION-ASSOCIATED PSYCHOLOGICAL VARIABLES. As delineated within Chapter 4, a problem-solving formulation of depression can be viewed as the umbrella subsuming several contemporary cognitive-behavior theories. As such, it may be advisable to include some inventories often used to measure these specific depression-related variables. This evaluation again might be helpful to assess specific deficits within a particular problem-solving component (see Chapter 4).

Based on either their widespread use or demonstrated psychometric properties, the following self-report measures are recommended:

1. *The Attributional Style Questionnaire* (ASQ; Peterson, Semmel, von Baeyer, Abramson, Metalsky, & Seligman, 1982). The ASQ assesses a person's attributional style along the dimensions of internality, stability, and globality. It contains 12 hypothetical situations for which respondents indicate their perceptions concerning the cause of the problem situation. Six of the 12 situations have positive outcomes, whereas the remaining six have negative outcomes. The ASQ can be helpful to determine the presence of a strong attributional bias concerning the cause of stressful events within the context of the problem-orientation component.

2. *Automatic Thoughts Questionnaire* (ATQ; Hollon & Kendall, 1980). Originally developed to facilitate research addressing a cognitive model of depression, the ATQ contains a list of 30 specific thoughts (e.g., "I feel worthless") that have been empirically shown to reliably discriminate between depressed and nondepressed persons. Each cognition is rated for frequency of occurrence on a 1-to-5 scale. The ATQ can be used as a measure of dysfunctional thoughts related to feelings of depression.

3. *Self-Control Schedule* (SCS; Rosenbaum, 1980). The SCS contains 36 items that provide information concerning the (a) use of cognitions to control emotional and physical reactivity; (b) application of active coping attempts in reaction to common problems; (c) ability to delay gratification; and (d) perceptions of one's self-efficacy. This inventory can aid the assessment procedure by providing information concerning various self-control deficits within the context of a problem-solving conceptualization.

4. *Pleasant Events Schedule* (PES; MacPhillamy & Lewinsohn, 1982)

and the *Unpleasant Events Schedule* (UES: Lewinsohn & Talkington, 1979). The PES was developed to assess self-reported frequency and enjoyability of a wide variety of common pleasurable activities (320 items). Scores are indicative of the level of one's overall social reinforcement. The UES, also consisting of 320 items, measures the level of aversive stimuli present in one's social environment. Items reflect a wide range of stressful life events, chronic strains, and daily problems. Both measures are useful to assess the quality of one's overall level of activity. The use of the UES, in particular, is consistent with assessing the frequency and types of current problems.

These inventories are also useful as posttreatment measures to help evaluate the effectiveness of treatment and determine the desirability of its termination or the need for follow-up booster sessions. However, depending upon the overall therapist-patient relationship, the motivation of the client, and the actual necessity for obtaining such information, the problem-solving therapist need not require completion of all the previously mentioned inventories and questionnaires. These inventories can be quite helpful during the assessment and evaluation phases of treatment. Yet, for certain patients, the entire battery may prove too taxing; for others, it may "turn them off" to this therapy approach. Therefore, therapists need to be judicious in the assignment of assessment materials.

Process Assessment

In keeping with the philosophy of continuous monitoring and evaluation, various assessment measures should be administered throughout the course of treatment. In addition to the various homework assignments, these include the BDI (every two sessions), PSSM, and Record of Coping Attempts. The BDI helps determine the progress of therapy as defined by reduction in depressive symptomatology. The PSSM and Record of Coping Attempts address the progress made concerning facilitation of problem-solving skills.

Presenting the Rationale of Problem-Solving Treatment

Before actual training in the various problem-solving skills begins, it is important to present the patient with a clear explanation of the overall model. This rationale establishes a common framework within which both the therapist and patient collaborate. Without such an explanation, the client will not be able to comprehend the reasons underlying training in the problem-solving operations. In providing this rationale, it is essential to use language and terms that are easily understood by a given individual. Additionally, incorporating as many examples particularly salient to the patient at hand is important in order to make problem-solving therapy as relevant as possible. The following is an example of such a rationale.

The basic treatment approach that I am recommending is called "problem-solving therapy." According to this approach, people can become depressed if they have difficulties coping with stressful life problems. Some people have difficulty coping because they never learned how. Others have difficulty because of the overwhelming severity of the problems themselves. At times, the way that we think about these problems can also make us depressed. For example, if we believe that we can't do anything to change a problem—that no matter what we try, nothing ever works—we probably won't feel like solving the problem. This in turn may lead to more problems and stress. The general upshot of this vicious cycle may be depression, especially if the consequences of not solving the problem are severe. Becoming depressed can increase our feelings of being out of control, which then reinforce feelings of depression. Another difficulty people may experience relates to poor or ineffective problem-solving skills. For example, in trying to solve a problem, we might fail if our goals are too high, or if we don't think of enough options, or if our decisions about which solutions might be effective are poor. According to this treatment approach, a wide variety of skills are involved in effective problem solving. Basically, the purpose of this approach is to help you to learn these skills in order to cope better with stressful situations. We will be focusing on five major skills: what we think about problems in general; how we define problems and set goals; how we think of various solutions to real-life problems; how we make decisions; and how to evaluate the success of our attempts. Throughout our sessions together, we will be focusing on learning more effective ways of coping with difficult and stressful current and future problems.

In addition to providing an overall rationale for the general treatment approach, such explanations should continue throughout training. Moreover, it is important to elicit feedback from the patient regarding his or her initial and subsequent reactions to these rationales. Unless the patient has a minimal amount of acceptance of the rationale, any treatment is doomed to fail. Therefore, further explanations and encouragement to "take a risk" may be important. More specifically, it is appropriate to recommend to a patient who indicates initial skepticism with this model, "Give it a chance over the next one or two sessions." In general, such patients readily adopt the approach within this time period. However, highly resistent clients should also be offered either a different therapy strategy or another referral. Continuing a patient in this treatment in light of nonacceptance is unwise.

The following are some challenging questions and comments that are often heard upon presentation of the rationale and more importantly, some possible answers as guidelines for the problem-solving therapist.

1. *Isn't depression biologically determined? How can this problem-solving approach help me if this is true?* Yes, there is much research to indicate that certain biochemical factors are involved in depression. However, this does not mean that psychotherapy cannot be helpful. More importantly, research indicates that some of these depression-related biological factors involve one's reaction to stressful situations. If one is able to effectively cope with stress, it may be possible to prevent the adverse biochemical factors that result in depression. Teaching you various problem-solving skills specifically is aimed at helping you to cope better.

2. *I agree with your approach, but only when I am not depressed! How can I think so logically and rationally when I get so upset and low?* It may appear now that it is very difficult to think of solving a problem when you are experiencing intense emotions. Part of the training involves using these emotions to your advantage in helping to eventually overcome them. Also, a major part of this treatment involves practicing these skills until they become second nature to you. In this manner, you will be able to forestall the more intense feelings of depression.

3. *Can this approach help me to never become depressed again?* Not really. My goal is not to rid you forever of any feelings of sadness. In essence, that would be similar to stripping you of your humanness and making you into an unfeeling robot. My goal is to help you not to allow such feelings to affect your overall coping attempts, which might lead to more intense feelings of depression. Feeling sadness or grief is normal; feeling extremely depressed is something we can try to prevent.

4. *I don't have any difficulties solving my problems! I do everything that you are talking about!* I am glad that you have some general understanding of this approach. It is very possible that you use some of the techniques that we will be discussing. However, sometimes people use these skills only in certain parts of their life, usually work. They tend not to use them for problems in other areas of living, for example, their relationships. Also, sometimes a certain type of problem becomes extremely difficult to solve. By focusing on these skills, I hope to capitalize on your own previous experience.

5. *I have so many problems, how can I solve all of them?* Right now you are probably feeling very overwhelmed by the multitude of stressful situations that you are experiencing. We will try to take one problem at

a time. Often many of the problems you are faced with are similar in nature or related to a more general problem. Most importantly, this approach is geared toward teaching you the skills required to cope more effectively. In this manner, you will be able to handle the problems more readily as they occur.

6. *What you are talking about sounds as if it will take forever to solve a problem. Sometimes a decision needs to be made in a hurry!* Sometimes impulsive actions may make problems even worse. But there are times when decisions need to be made more quickly. Since a major thrust of our sessions will involve practicing these skills, they will hopefully become second nature to you over time. As such, you will be able to use this approach in a more rapid fashion.

7. *What happens if I can figure out what to do, but I can't do it? For example, sometimes I know what I should do, but I'm afraid that it won't work.* One of the areas that we will discuss involves an assessment of your overall strengths and weaknesses. In general, a good solution is one that not only solves the problems in theory, but one that you can actually carry out. If you cannot implement a solution, then it obviously will be ineffective, no matter how good it sounds on paper. However, one focus of therapy can also be geared to help overcome some of your limitations in other skill areas that might be important.

PITFALLS TO AVOID

Regardless of how effective a particular psychotherapy approach appears to be as a result of research support, the actual *implementation* of the approach may not always proceed smoothly. Below are a list of technical problems that can severely impact on the effectiveness of a problem-solving approach if not avoided.

1. *Training Is Presented in a Mechanistic Manner.* The clinician needs to create an environment that is therapeutic in nature. Conducting problem-solving therapy in a cold, rotelike manner is likely to result in premature termination by the patient. Beginning therapists should be careful not to rely too heavily on the training modules. Whereas the *content* of this approach is important, the *process* of its implementation is also crucial.

2. *Therapy Is Not Relevant to a Particular Patient.* The therapist should endeavor to individualize treatment depending on a particular patient. Examples used to illustrate various problem-solving operations need to

be relevant to the specific individual's life. Unique learning histories and previous learning experiences are valuable sources of clinical data to aid in applying these nomothetic principles in an idiographic manner.

3. *Homework Is Not Incorporated into Treatment.* At some point during each session, the previous week's homework assignment should be discussed. In vivo practice of the problem-solving components is crucial in attaining initial skill acquisition, generalization, and maintenance. Forgetting to cover the homework also takes away a valuable opportunity to provide corrective feedback and reinforcement to the client. Further, it tends to provide the patient with the message, "Homework really isn't important to complete."

4. *Therapist Focuses More on Treatment Implementation Than the Patient's Feelings.* Minimizing the importance of the therapist-patient relationship can influence the effectiveness of treatment, even if correctly implemented. As noted previously, client change is unlikely to occur if the patient feels that the therapist is uncaring or insensitive to pain or sadness.

5. *Therapist Uses Humor Injudiciously.* Humor, if used wisely, can be an effective therapeutic tool (Salameh, 1983). It is also an effective coping strategy in dealing with stressful circumstances (Nezu & Nezu, 1987a; Nezu, Nezu, & Blisset, 1988). Utilizing humor correctly can help distance a person from an emotionally laden situation and provide alternative perspectives from which to understand the nature of the problem. However, if used by the therapist injudiciously, the patient may take offense, believing himself or herself the source of the joke. This may destroy the therapist-patient relationship.

6. *Treatment Focuses Only on Superficial Problems.* The therapist's own problem-solving and clinical decision-making abilities must be relied upon to help assess the nature of the patient's real problems. If only superficial or unimportant problems are discussed during treatment, relapse is likely to occur. This is particularly important when dealing with a patient who externalizes most problems as "Things other people do to me." The therapist needs to continuously engage in his or her own problem definition and formulation to ensure that an accurate assessment has occurred (Nezu & Nezu, in press).

7. *Focus on Solution Implementation Is Minimal.* The therapist should endeavor to encourage the patient to implement as many solutions as possible during treatment. If therapy is mainly focused on training in the other problem-solving skills, to the exclusion of actual solution implementation, then any reduction in depressive symptoms is only temporary at best. The goal of training is not only skill acquisition, but successful

resolution of many of the patient's problems. In fact, it is unlikely that any accurate assessment of the client's overall change in problem-solving abilities can occur in the absence of attempts to implement a solution.

8. *Assessment of Suicide Potential Is Inadequate.* Since recent research has found a strong association between social problem-solving deficits and suicidal ideation (cf. Schotte & Clum, 1982, 1987), a problem-solving approach would appear to be particularly appropriate for this potentially lethal problem. However, the therapist needs to be extremely careful in assessing suicide intent, especially with regard to the severity of hopelessness feelings, the other alternatives considered, the concreteness of one's plans, and the urgency of the desire. If the patient's suicidal wishes are serious and/or the patient appears to be in a state of crisis, the therapist should initially act as the problem solver *for* the patient, providing goals, alternatives, and potential consequences to consider. In other words, a supportive, structured environment needs to be provided, in which the patient may begin to become aware of his or her own resources. Only when the suicide potential is lessened can the therapist begin to conduct problem-solving training proper. Further, continuous evaluation of changes in suicidal intent throughout treatment is imperative.

9. *Evaluation of Patient's Assests and Limitations Is Inadequate.* During the decision-making phase, one of the most important criteria to use for determining the overall quality of a solution alternative is the problem solver's ability to implement it in its optimal form. At times, a solution requires various important performance skills (i.e., social or self-control skills). The therapist needs to be careful to aid the patient during initial problem-solving attempts in this evaluation. Attempts at problem resolution via implemented solutions that are unsuccessful because of these skill deficits can lead to actual increases in depression. As noted previously, problem-solving treatment may entail training in other social or self-control skills (e.g., assertiveness, communication, and relaxation skills).

Moreover, the problem-solving therapist should help the patient to determine the extent to which he or she actually has control over certain aspects of the problem situation. This becomes especially important when applying this approach with an adolescent population. Even though certain identified alternatives can be effective hypothetically, adolescents typically have less control over their environment as compared to adults (cf. Nezu & Kalmar, in press). As such, care needs to be taken to accurately assess the overall problem situation before encouraging the adolescent to implement certain solutions.

10. *Therapist Equates Problem-Solving Coping With Problem-Focused Coping.* As underscored in Chapter 3, *problem-solving* is defined as a general coping process by which a person attempts to identify, discover, or invent a solution or adaptive coping response. On the other hand, *problem-focused coping* is described as specific attempts to change the problematic nature of the situation itself. This concept is further distinguished from *emotion-focused coping,* which is characterized by attempts to manage the emotional distress associated with a stressful problem. Therapists should not convey the premise that all problems can be solved by problem-focused attempts. Emotion-focused coping strategies may be extremely important to consider, especially when the situation is realistically appraised as unchangeable. For example, the loss of a loved one engenders significant grief and depressive reactions. To suggest that the problem can be solved by replacing the loved one misses far from the appropriate therapeutic mark.

CHAPTER 7

Training in Problem Orientation

Nothing is either good or bad, but thinking makes it so.

SHAKESPEARE

The problem-orientation component reflects the general set of beliefs and perceptions that influence an individual's understanding of and reaction to stressful problems in living. As noted in Chapter 4, this entails five specific variables: problem perception, problem attribution, problem appraisal, personal control beliefs, and approach/avoidance style. Training in this stage is geared to provide the client with a rational, positive, and constructive orientation to problems in living and problem solving as a means of coping with them. The therapist's basic goal is to change those dysfunctional perceptions, core beliefs, and attitudes that may inhibit or interfere with attempts to engage in the remaining problem-solving operations.

The direction of treatment is toward facilitating adoption of the type of problem-solving orientation described in the following pages. Therapeutic techniques aimed at collaborating with the client to develop and own these beliefs comprise the remainder of this chapter.

COMPONENTS OF A CONSTRUCTIVE PROBLEM ORIENTATION

1. *Acceptance of Problems as a Normal, Predictable Part of Living.* Adoption of this cognitive set helps individuals to reject the belief that their problems in life are proof that they are crazy, abnormal, or personally deficient. They develop a tendency to discriminate between external aspects and internal, emotional factors that contribute to the problem, rather than to make overgeneralized negative attributions and ascriptions toward themselves. This belief also minimizes the emotional

reactivity persons experience when actually confronted with a problem. Problems are placed within the perspective of predictable aspects in everyone's life.

2. *Belief in One's Ability to Solve Life's Problems Effectively.* This set facilitates perceptions of competency and self-efficacy despite the experience of transient emotional distress. Individuals can believe that although there are no perfect solutions, there are many effective alternatives that they are capable of developing and implementing on their own.

3. *Labeling of Discomfort, Distress, and Physiological Symptoms as Cues to Identify the Existence of a Problem.* Rather than fearing and attempting to further avoid the experience of affective, cognitive, and physiological symptoms (e.g., worry, sad mood, self-deprecating thoughts, apprehension, digestive upset, autonomic arousal), individuals identify them as indicators or "red alerts" that a challenging problem exists. This labeling process facilitates anticipation of the problem-solving process as an opportunity for a corrective learning experience, or as a way to improve the quality of life.

4. *Inhibition of the Natural Tendency to Respond Emotionally to Problems and Instead to Utilize the "Stop and Think" Technique in Problem Situations.* Upon using initial negative emotions as cues that a problem exists, effective problem solvers then attempt to embark upon the problem-solving process, rather than allowing the emotionality to intensify or become prolonged. This orientation is extremely important for individuals with a history of unique vulnerability to emotional arousal and heightened autonomic sensitivity to threatening situations and cognitions.

5. *Adoption of Realistic Expectations Concerning the Problem-Solving Process and Recognition that Effort and Time Are Involved in Identifying and Implementing Effective Solutions.* This set enables individuals to respect the need to analyze a situation carefully, tolerate the discomfort of the lack of immediate solutions, and withhold judgment until the process is complete.

Therapeutic intervention from a problem-solving perspective initially facilitates the patient's adoption of these five important attitudinal sets. The remaining components of treatment (i.e., problem definition and formulation, generation of alternatives, decision making, solution implementation and verification) provide for a heuristic set of guidelines that the patient can use to help mobilize strengths and transform these attitudes into action.

During problem-orientation training, the therapist needs to be sensitive to the strength of the patient's habituated maladaptive cognitive and emotional reactivity and the difficulty the patient may sometimes experience in owning new beliefs and perceptions. As future stages of treatment focus on more overt behavioral goals, these initial perspectives will require continual reinforcement. The focus of this chapter is to describe various strategies that are used to help individuals become more aware of their maladaptive problem orientations and to learn ways to prevent such beliefs from influencing their actual problem-solving coping attempts. Treatment strategies within this problem-solving component involve (1) use of the reversed advocate role-play technique; (2) helping the patient to "cast a problem horoscope"; (3) teaching the client to use his or her feelings as cues that a problem exists; and (4) training the depressed individual to use the "Stop and Think" technique.

REVERSED ADVOCATE ROLE-PLAY STRATEGY

One continuing and pervasive theme underlying all cognitive restructuring techniques is the focus on helping clients to analyze their thoughts and beliefs, as well as to test the validity and utility of these beliefs in their everyday lives. The various schools of cognitive therapy, as exemplified by noted practitioners such as Beck (1976), Mahoney and Thoresen (1974), and Ellis (1985), all aim at working with patients to change their irrational beliefs and distorted perceptions of external stimuli. Problem-solving therapy is grounded with a similar theoretical philosophy in that an individual's unrealistic and maladaptive perceptions of problems in living represent a target for change.

Therapeutic Principle

As any therapist who has worked with depressed individuals will testify, such patients do not easily change their beliefs, particularly when negative emotions are aroused. Whereas the concept that problems are a normal part of living may make logical and intuitive sense to a particular patient, specific problems may still trigger a sense of fear, hopelessness, and impending catastrophe. In other words, although this belief may gain intellectual acceptance, certain patients require a significant degree of convincing before actually maintaining such a belief.

For example, a statement often heard during initial treatment exemplifies this point: "I know it's sensible and logical to think this way, but my intelligence tells me one thing, yet my emotions want to throw reason out the window!" Indeed, patients may experience concern that it is

abnormal to continue to react as if they still hold a belief that they intel-
lectually recognize as incorrect. At such a point in time, depressive symptoms of hopelessness and critical self-evaluation can be exacerbated.
Therefore, an initial step frequently involves developing a patient's ability
to recognize that the experience of both positive and negative emotions
is a precious human phenomenon, whereas a majority of depressive symptoms may be reactions to certain beliefs that are rooted in early social
learning. The patient must view changing the inevitability of a hopeless
outcome as a product of personal relearning, objective evaluation, and
practice, rather than the result of a therapist's "magic wand." For this
reason, it is important to collaboratively develop an individual's constructive orientation to problems.

Clinical experience suggests that it is essential for both the patient and
therapist to respect the strength of habituated cognitive-emotional associations and to predict resistance to change as part of the therapeutic
process. Rather than simply describing the set of beliefs listed previously
hoping that the patient adopts them at face value (a gross irrational expectancy), the therapist can use *reversed advocacy role-plays* as a strategy
for the patient's relearning process. It is helpful to begin with this strategy
because the therapist assumes an understanding role toward the client's
maladaptive beliefs.

Particularly at the start of treatment, when the client may be experiencing evaluative concerns regarding the therapist's perceptions of him
or her, this technique may meet with less resistance than other strategies.
During many reversed advocacy role-play procedures, patients have reported a sense of relief that others experience the same private thoughts
as their own, or they have stated, "The therapist really understands how
I feel."

Procedure

In this exercise, any or all of the maladaptive or irrational attitudes toward
problems in the following list are temporarily adopted by the therapist
through a role-play format. These attitudes reflect various aspects of a
maladaptive problem-orientation set. The role of the patient is to attempt
to provide reasons or arguments for the statement or belief being incorrect
or dysfunctional. In this manner, the patient begins to actually verbalize
those aspects of a positive orientation. The process of identifying a more
appropriate set of beliefs toward problems and providing justification for
the validity of these attitudes, helps the client to begin to actually adopt
or own them.

1. Problems are NOT common to everyone—if I have problems or encounter a problematic situation, this means that I am abnormal.
2. Most people do NOT have similar kinds of problems—no one has problems like mine (unless they are sick or pathetic).
3. It is absolutely AWFUL and CATASTROPHIC when things in my life do not go right!
4. ALL of my problems are ALWAYS caused by me.
5. ALL my problems are ALWAYS caused by others and this rotten world!
6. It is best to avoid facing problems or making decisions when they occur, no matter how small or large. I should avoid making decisions no matter what the consequences.
7. The FIRST solution that comes to mind is usually the best. I should operate on instincts.
8. There is a RIGHT and PERFECT solution to most problems.
9. Only someone who is experiecing the exact same problem can be helpful to me—NO one else can understand.
10. People can't change. This is the way I am and the way I'll ALWAYS be!
11. Average people CANNOT solve most of life's problems on their own.
12. If I am a good person, I am ENTITLED to a life without problems.

Clinical Example

In the following dialogue, the reversed advocate role-play strategy focuses on Statements 1 and 10 in the preceding list. The depicted patient was a 38-year-old high school teacher, Eric, who had entered treatment following several months of depression that included loss of energy, significant weight gain, strong feelings of loneliness, and suicidal ideation. He had recently separated from his girlfriend and was expressing feelings of hopelessness and worthlessness regarding both his overall life and himself.

THERAPIST (TH): Eric, it seems as if at times the way that you think tends to affect your feelings. I would like to try a role-play exercise where I'll take the part of a friend of yours at the school where you work. Just go along with me for now because I'd like to make a certain point. Try your best to make a valid, realistic case against any irrational, illogical, or incorrect statements that you hear, OK?

PATIENT (P): OK, I'll give it a try.

TH: (Beginning the role-play) I know I seem really down lately. I wouldn't blame you for not wanting to see me anymore. Who wants a real jerk for a friend?

P: I don't think you're a jerk, but it does sound like something is bugging you, what's wrong?

TH: Something bugging me! That's an understatement—nothing in my life goes right! Just when I thought things were getting a little better in my life, I get a call from the principal telling me that two kids in my class are complaining that they can't understand my teaching— I'm unfair and unreasonable. He wants to come in and observe my class! Boy, when I can't even teach after 10 years, I might as well pack it in. I feel like going to bed and giving up.

P: Why give up? You're a good teacher. It must be a pain in the neck to have to go through an evaluation, though.

TH: Pain in the neck? My teaching career is over! To have this problem after 10 years in the classroom, I must be a bad teacher.

P: That's not true! A lot of teachers have problems with kids from time to time. I know I have.

TH: But not like this. Don't you realize that if he's coming to evaluate me, the principal probably believes those two? That means I've failed and lost my professional respect.

P: No, it doesn't! It's just that you have a pain-in-the-neck problem with a few kids.

TH: But if I was any good, I wouldn't!

P: Then you're saying that we're all no good, because all of us have problems from time to time.

TH: But it's different with me—I never thought this would happen.

P: That doesn't mean you can't get through the evaluation and go on teaching and do a good job just because this happened. We all have problems sometimes. You're no worse or different than any of us.

TH: I don't know. When I have a problem with a kid accusing me of bad teaching, I take it personally. That's just the way I am. I can't change that.

P: Yes, you can. You better change or you're going to be miserable. That's part of teaching. You can't be perfect.

TH: I feel like I should be perfect. You know how I am. I want to be really good.

P: It's impossible to be perfect and never have any problems with the kids.

TH: Are you sure about that?

P: Of course I'm sure. Be realistic for heaven's sake!

Clinical Comment

In the above sequence, the therapist presented a situation relevant to the patient's own life experience but focused on a situation which the patient could objectively appraise. The therapist's aim was to strengthen the rational attitude that this individual already held concerning work-related difficulties. Later, when the therapist used a reversed advocate role-play situation concerning interpersonal relationships (an emotionally charged topic for this patient), Eric's ability to develop a counterattitude to the therapist's distorted thinking had already been practiced, and thus became more easily facilitated regarding the salient problem of loneliness. Also note that the therapist, rather than suggesting that Eric argue with the "professional clinician," assumed the role of a hypothetical friend or colleague. This strategy minimizes the likelihood that the patient may feel inhibited toward disagreeing with the therapist.

The following dialogue is an example of a reversed advocate role-play with the same patient that focuses on Statement 12 ("I am entitled to a life without problems"). This time the therapist (a female) is attempting to impact upon a set of cognitive distortions more salient for this particular patient.

THERAPIST (TH): Eric, let's try another role-play. Once again I'll take the role of another one of your colleagues.

PATIENT (P): And you want me to argue your points again?

TH: Good, you're really getting the idea. Just try to refute what I'm saying with an argument based on a more realistic and sensible set of beliefs. OK, let's begin. (Therapist begins role-play at this point.) My life is over. All I ever wanted was to be happy. I thought when I was an adult, I would be happy. I worked hard, tried to be a good wife and mother, and a good daughter to my parents, but it's just not working out.

P: I know exactly how you feel (Recognizing these complaints as similar to his own). I don't know if I can argue with this person (Laughs a little). OK, I'll cooperate. How come you're not happy?

TH: Oh, I know that sometimes I seem like I'm enjoying myself, but deep down there's this emptiness, wondering what life is about. How come I'm not really happy? My kids have an attitude, my husband and I argue, and teaching isn't the constant challenge I thought it would be. I feel like I deserve more than this. I should be happier. There's nothing I can do. I don't deserve this kind of life.

P: What kind of life? You have a steady job, you have a family to go home to, and lots of friends.

TH: Yeah, but so many problems too, and that seems so unfair. I expected so much more.

P: What did you expect?

TH: That if I was a good person and tried hard, I wouldn't have any problems and I would be happy. I would feel good all the time.

P: Nobody feels good all the time. At least you have a family! Even when you're basically happy, you still get sick, see people die, or have arguments. You're actually lucky to have someone to share your hassles with.

TH: I thought it would be different. That life would be like my daydreams when I was a kid. Happy marriage, beautiful kids, good job—lots of appreciation for my hard work.

P: You have some of those things, but life is not daydreams—you can't be happy all the time!

TH: But I deserve to be happy all the time—I'm different than other people. I'd like to be like you. Single, footloose, no worries!

P: Footloose! Are you crazy? Sometimes I get so lonely, I want to die!

TH: You mean you get sad sometimes? I don't know. I feel like at this stage of my life I should be happy and content all the time.

P: Well, who do you think you are! What makes you think you deserve to be happy more than anyone else?

TH: But I'm smart, and nice, and I work hard.

P: So do a lot of people.

TH: Then I guess those of us should be happy all the time—we're entitled to it!

P: That's ridiculous! No one is entitled to perfect happiness all the time.

TH: Why not?

P: Because that's not life. It's a stupid setup to expect it.

TH: What do you mean setup? I deserve it!

P: Where did you ever get that idea?

TH: From the movies.

P: (Laughs out loud) Well, the movies are fake. Life is not Hollywood!

Clinical Comment

As in the previous example, the therapist ends the role-play when the patient is advocating actively for a more rational approach to life's problems. In this particular sequence, the therapist hypothesized that the patient's overt emotional expression (laughter) indicated heightened emotional sensitivity and awareness that the "happily ever after" theme of the dialogue was more closely striking upon the patient's own self-evaluations.

Additional Considerations

In using this strategy, it is important for the therapist to couch the exercise within the framework of concern for the patient. The patient should not perceive the clinician as attempting to sarcastically mimic his or her beliefs. Rather, the therapist explains that these beliefs at times may engender feelings of depression or distress, which in turn may inhibit or interfere with later attempts to cope with a stressful problem. As such, the clinician indicates that the purpose of this procedure is to facilitate the patient's adoption of a more positive orientation towards problems in living.

It is also therapeutically important to avoid conveying that the patient has crazy beliefs or that the feelings of depression are the sole product of distorted thinking. This latter point is particularly salient for individuals who have recently experienced a major crisis. For example, a patient who has just lost his or her job will probably resist the idea that the depression is related to distorted thinking patterns, as compared to the plethora of negative consequences associated with unwanted unemployment.

As stated throughout this volume, not all depressed individuals are characterized by maladaptive thinking or negative orientations. However, at a minimum, the reversed advocate role-play strategy should be used concerning several major themes in order to reinforce the constructive aspects of the patient's general set. For those depressed individuals who appear to maintain a strong negative orientation, it is particularly important to focus heavily on this component. Additional cognitive restructuring techniques (cf. Beck, 1976; Goldfried & Davison, 1976) may be useful as adjuncts to this basic strategy.

Although the patient's orientation is addressed via this problem-solving component early during treatment, it is important to emphasize continuous evaluation and attention throughout intervention. The therapist can refer to the success of these exercises when a patient periodically displays a reversion back to a negative orientation during latter stages of training.

To facilitate adoption of a constructive orientation, the patient is encouraged to complete several Problem Orientation Worksheets (see Figure 7.1) during this training phase. As a homework assignment, the individual briefly describes a recent problem, indicates the initial reaction to the problem, and compares this reaction to the included description of a

Name: _____ Date: _____

Briefly describe the problem situation.

Briefly describe your initial reaction to this problem.

How does this compare with a POSITIVE ORIENTATION as described below?

Positive problem orientation:

Problems are a common part of life; many people have similar kinds of problems.
It is better to face or confront a problem when it occurs, rather than avoid it.
I can solve this problem effectively!
I should use my feelings as a *cue* that a problem exists.
I should "STOP and THINK" before I act impulsively!

Figure 7.1. Problem Orientation Worksheet.

healthy, positive problem orientation. In this comparison, the patient has the opportunity to identify those dysfunctional beliefs that are still being maintained. The therapist can then remind the client of the more constructive set of attitudes already discussed during previous treatment sessions.

CASTING A PROBLEM "HOROSCOPE"

Therapeutic Principle

This therapeutic strategy trains the patient to better recognize the occurrence of problem situations in his or her life (problem perception). Accurate appraisal and labeling of problem situations is a necessary prerequisite to future problem-solving activity. Labeling a situation as a problem functions as a cue that can help to inhibit the tendency to react *automatically*. In other words, accurate identification of a personal problem becomes a metaphoric "red light," that can be followed by self-instruction to "STOP and THINK" before reacting. The individual is then alerted to a needed shift in set that will require cognitive and emotional energy. This is a skill that is required repeatedly throughout life, and it can ultimately promote the orientation towards challenge and growth.

This strategy includes two therapeutic exercises. The first exercise requires constructing a list of various areas of life in which potential problems frequently can occur. This technique reinforces the set to accept problems as a normal part of life. Secondly, it helps facilitate the patient's problem perception skills. The therapist and patient then collaboratively predict the specific areas from the list in which that particular patient is either currently, or in the future, most likely to experience problems. Whereas the first list alerts the patient to potential life stress areas that exist with significant frequency for most people, the second list provides a sphere of prediction unique to the individual patient.

Procedure

In the first exercise, the depressed patient identifies and lists areas of life in which problems occur. The therapist may add to the list in order to cover the general areas of problems that occur in many people's lives. Additionally, the patient is requested to generate specific examples of problems within each life category. A general list of different life areas follows.

1. Job
2. Friendships

3. Relationships with opposite sex; spouse
4. Religion; moral values
5. Recreation
6. Finances
7. Career
8. Children
9. Parents
10. Sex
11. Self-image
12. Education
13. Fears; anxieties
14. Aging
15. Community
16. Environment
17. Loneliness

After completion of a general list, the patient and therapist develop a more specific list. It is constructed with attention to both an assessment of current life problems and the prediction of particular areas of vulnerability unique to the patient. Use of the Personal Problems Checklist (Schinka, 1986), Mooney Problem Checklist (Mooney & Gordon, 1950), and/or the Life Experiences Survey (Sarason et al., 1978) can facilitate this process (see Chapter 6).

Clinical Example

The following dialogue demonstrates development of a predictive list of specific areas for a 57-year-old patient, Elsa. She had been referred for individual treatment following a hospitalization for severe unipolar depression. Upon entering outpatient treatment, she reported continuation of depressive symptoms that included suicidal ideation and severe dysphoric mood, as well as distress associated with uncontrolled incidents of excessive gambling. Elsa's risk of suicide had been assessed during several initial interviews and was determined to be minimal at the time of this session. Additionally, Elsa had agreed to a contract with her therapist requiring her to immediately indicate any increase in suicidal ideation or intention.

THERAPIST (TH): Well, we have here a rather thorough list of potential areas in which people are likely to experience problems. The next step for us is to focus on areas that will allow us to predict unique areas of vulnerability for you.

PATIENT (P): That makes sense. As we were listing these general problems, I got to thinking about how my family, community, and some friends, like my landlord, don't give me any problems. In fact, I do pretty well in the finance department, too, when I don't blow my whole paycheck on gambling. But when I saw you write down aging, I didn't even want to think about it—yet I do think about it all the time. I guess I really believe that even with the antidepressant medication, I still think about things very negatively.

TH: And from the time we've spent during discussions about your problem orientation, when we analyzed the distortions depressed people often make in their reactions to problems, would you say that your fears of aging and thoughts about growing older are problems that you find particularly distressing?

P: Even as you say it, I don't want to discuss it. It feels better to avoid the subject, or I'll get depressed. I guess that means we better list it as one of my more difficult problems.

TH: Congratulations, Elsa, it takes courage to confront a tough problem!

P: And my job, we should list that too—but I honestly think my problems with work are there because of my stroke last year. God, sometimes I think about getting old and sick and not being able to do my work. I'd really feel like killing myself then! My work is all I have, except for the gambling, but that's another problem in and of itself. I don't feel good after I gamble.

TH: Let's review the list now, including the areas you've just included in the last few moments. You mentioned aging again, so we know that this is a predictable problem area. From what you're saying, we should probably add your job, experiencing suicidal thoughts, gambling, and lack of activities or interests that help you to feel good. As you look at the list can you think of anything else?

P: Well, it's probably the age thing again, but I've always liked men . . . and sex. I get depressed when I think about not having a man in my life.

TH: From the description of your life that you have given me, loneliness seems to be a rather new problem area.

P: I never was lonely. I was always a very independent woman! And I always did things that other women were afraid of doing. That's why morals and religion don't bother me. I did what I wanted to do. But when you get older, you're not attractive to men anymore. I know, there goes my negative thinking again. But I get so mad about getting old sometimes. It's a real problem!

TH: I'm glad you caught that first statement as an example of extreme and negative thinking. It sounds as if your feelings are telling you to add self-image, loneliness, and lack of enjoyable activities to the list as well.

P: Yes. That really has become a problem for me. I guess some people would have problems for all areas on this list!

TH: If you remember, we generated the original list in the first place because we wanted to predict the most frequent areas that people experience difficulties.

P: My list has some areas, but not all of them. Did we make this list on purpose, so that I'd start to feel normal (Laughs)?

TH: Your humor is a great asset, Elsa! But if you're starting to think of experiencing problems as normal, you're not only accurate, you're thinking realistically and productively!

Clinical Comment

Although Elsa was originally referred for her gambling problem, continued dysphoria, and suicidal thinking, this exercise reveals that her hopeless evaluations of her life were associated, to a large extent, with the overwhelming losses she perceived as part of the aging process. It became important for Elsa to identify the other areas of her life in which she experienced problems. This problem perception skill provided her with the ability to discontinue her covert labeling of all distressful experiences as hopelessly predictable concomitants of aging and to identify problems that were not related to her age. During subsequent sessions, treatment was aimed at applying the problem-solving model toward the wide range of separate problem areas identified during this exercise, only some of which were directly related to aging.

USING FEELINGS AS CUES TO THE EXISTENCE OF A PROBLEM

Therapeutic Principle

Emotional arousal represents one of the three major spheres in which to implement therapeutic change. Although cognitive and behavioral spheres of assessment and therapeutic intervention represent the two other major areas of impact, patients most frequently seek treatment fueled by emotions. Common presenting complaints include profound experiences of sadness, fear, hopelessness, embarrassment, helplessness, worthlessness, confusion, anger, and pain. Usually, an individual has attempted to relieve emotional discomfort through previously conditioned means of coping prior to seeking help.

It is not uncommon to discover emotional numbness at the end of a patient's unsuccessful coping responses—a "shutting down" of those feelings that have become intolerable. When individuals begin to experience depression as inevitable fact and either continue to engage in dysfunctional thinking patterns or impulsively act in order to avoid distressful emotion (rather than constructively act toward alleviating it), negative feelings become exacerbated to an intolerable level. Perceptions, cognitions, and attributions become negatively selective, and further negative emotions result. Individual energy becomes so focused upon relief from emotional distress that the patient feels defeated, exhausted, and defenseless. It is not surprising that when problem-solving therapy is initially presented to depressed patients, they react with criticism that it involves too much work or that it is "OK for people who don't have the kind of [or as severe] problems that I have." In fact, many patients come to treatment feeling so completely incompetent at coping with feelings that their expectancy is to place themselves in someone else's care and to rely on the therapist's judgment and decision making rather than their own.

Creating a sufficient shift in set, so as to motivate the patient to invest any additional energy, requires therapeutic skill and creativity. Therapist support and reinforcement for any independent steps, especially in the initial stages of treatment, becomes crucial. Emphasizing the structure of the problem-solving model when initially presenting the treatment rationale provides patients during the early stages of therapy with a defined coping schema that may be used with confidence because it is sanctioned by the therapist.

Part of this strategy is to orient the patient toward adopting the belief that the experienced feelings can be useful cues to attend to, rather than painful experiences to avoid at all cost. The strategy requires empathic understanding by the therapist that negative emotions *are* unpleasant and distressful. The goal for the patient is to embrace the concept that emotions, painful as they may be, are normal, not lethal, and in fact, can provide insightful subjective cues for personal problem identification.

Procedure

In this exercise, the patient and therapist review examples of feelings (and often subsequent thoughts) that may function as cues for recognition of a problem. The therapist may generate a few examples to model the way in which feelings can serve this purpose.

Clinical Example

In the following dialogue, the previously described patient, Elsa, is taught how feelings can be cues to facilitate both problem perception and later personal problem-solving attempts.

THERAPIST (TH): Some examples of the ways people have found feelings helpful in identifying the existence of a problem include feeling frustrated, as though nothing you can do would change anything; feeling fearful, as though your life is unpredictable and you have no control over what happens to you; feeling angry that you have to put up with certain people or things; experiencing a sick stomach or a racing heart; or feeling hopeless and worthless, similar to the way you felt when we first talked about learning to cope with and reduce your depression through problem solving.

PATIENT (P): That's just it! It all seems like so much thinking. I get tired of thinking all the time. I'm tired. Sometimes I just want to run away—that's when I take off and gamble.

TH: Sometimes feelings can be real painful, Elsa. You just want to get away from them and get some relief.

P: Relief . . . yes that's exactly the word! My problems are too complicated, I can't go back in time, make myself younger, so I do whatever my impulses tell me. Sometimes I think it's better that way—I don't have to think.

TH: How long does gambling successfully remove the painful feelings?

P: It's no good. When I blow the money and come home, I'm depressed again. Maybe even worse than before.

TH: Sounds like kind of a "short-acting mood fix."

P: Yes, it is! Sometimes I feel like an addict who needs to feel OK for a couple of hours. But you know, at the moment I leave for the casino, it's such a relief! That's why relief is such a good way to describe why I gamble. It works better than the antidepressants I previously tried because I still had to think.

TH: Elsa, when you're at work, and you're experiencing a problem, how do you know it's a problem?

P: I guess you could say when things aren't running smoothly. Maybe one of the people I supervise tells me something is wrong, or someone's work is going downhill, or there could be a problem with the computers or something like that.

TH: Sounds like a lot of responsibility. Ever feel like just leaving the office and forgetting everything?

P: Sure!

TH: Why don't you?

P: Because it's my job to take care of it. Besides, I feel good when I've finally helped one of the employees, or when things are going smoothly in the office again.

TH: Even if you know that in the near future, you will be cued to the presence of still another office problem?

P: Better I should know about it, then I can do something to make it better.

TH: Feelings can serve as useful cues as well, Elsa.

P: Except that when I'm in the middle of feeling disgusted and hopeless, I just feel that way. Like yesterday, when my friend asked me to go to the office cocktail party—it was like "Why go? I'll feel too self-conscious to talk to anyone" . . . I just wanted to run. I couldn't stand to be humiliated.

TH: Do you feel like running at this moment?

P: Now? No.

TH: Would you explain that?

P: Because you are someone who I'm coming to for help. I don't think you're going to insult me or make me feel terrible. It's different here than at a cocktail party.

TH: So your feelings are different today at this moment than they were yesterday.

P: Sure . . . and they may be different later on today.

TH: Good point, Elsa! Feelings change, depending upon the situation and our interpretation of the situation. In fact, feelings can be a cue or signal to change either the situation in some way, or what we are saying to ourselves about the situation. The tough job comes with tolerating unpleasant feelings long enough to figure out what they are trying to tell us.

P: I never thought of it that way. It seems like using your head to solve things is good for work, but not for personal things because of feelings. I never thought of taking feelings into account to solve the problem. I just wanted to feel better.

TH: Feel better . . . or not feel at all?

P: That's what the gambling does . . . it numbs me . . . for awhile.

TH: Now think of all the information your feelings may be giving you about working on these problems that you may be missing when you numb yourself. No wonder you feel confused at times. It would be like trying to solve a problem at work without any information as to what the problem is, except to know that something, somewhere, is wrong.

P: You know, sometimes when I've come in here and started to cry or argue with you, I actually felt better when I left. Maybe I've been too scared to feel before.

Clinical Comment

Elsa's realization that emotions are not lethal, but in fact, are adaptive cues or alerts to either perceived loss or danger, was an important insight. Since confrontation of her fears of aging and associated losses was obviously painful for her, she had begun during this session to develop the necessary tolerance of negative affect required to more carefully define her intrapersonal problems with aging. Further, she was able to develop an important attitudinal orientation to accurately label feelings and use the experience as part of her personal data base for future decision making.

In training depressed persons to use their feelings as cues, idiosyncratic ways that an individual experiences emotional distress can be identified and used as cues. This may entail specific thoughts an individual might have in reaction to a stressful problem (e.g., "I think I screwed up again, like always"), physiological or somatic sensations (e.g., "I feel so tired," "I feel butterflies in my stomach"), or mood states (e.g., "I feel so lousy and alone"). The person can then utilize these individualistic reactions as salient cues. The metaphor of a bright red traffic light or a large traffic stop sign is a means of providing a visual image to "STOP and THINK." In other words, patients are taught to use feelings, thoughts, or somatic responses as cues that a problem exists, then to visualize a red traffic light that signals to the person, "Stop and Think". The cue *stop* aids in minimizing the likelihood of acting impulsively or of actually escalating the initial affective response. The cue *think* refers to the need to reiterate previously practiced positive orientation statements, as well as to engage in the remainder of the problem-solving operations (e.g., problem definition and formulation).

SUMMARY

This chapter presented the therapeutic goals and strategies associated with the orientation component of problem-solving therapy for depression. Goals included facilitating adoption, by the patient, of the following aspects of a positive and realistic orientation: (1) acceptance of problems as a normal part of living; (2) belief in one's ability to solve problems effectively; (3) labeling of one's experience of distress as a cue that a problem exists; (4) inhibiting the tendency to respond automatically; and (5) recognizing that problem resolution often entails considerable time and effort. Therapeutic strategies for problem-orientation training include: (1) the reversed advocate role-play strategy; (2) casting a problem horoscope; (3) teaching the patient to use feelings as cues; and (4) training the depressed individual to use the "Stop and Think" technique. Examples taken from therapy session transcripts were presented with the hope of translating previously delineated theoretical concepts into active clinical dialogue.

Since the motivational sets developed during this stage of treatment significantly impact upon the effectiveness of later problem-solving success, a careful assessment of therapeutic progress concerning changes in the patient's problem orientation should be conducted before continuing training in the next phases of the treatment model.

CHAPTER 8

Training in Problem Definition and Formulation

The worst, the most corrupting lies, are problems poorly stated.

GEORGES BERNANOS, FRENCH THEOLOGIAN

In the therapeutic setting, problems stated as the reason for self-referral are usually vague statements (e.g., "I feel as though I'm losing my grip," "Everything is hopeless," "I need some help," "I'm in a crisis"), a formulation of the individual's own symptoms ("I'm so depressed," "I'm so nervous," "I'm about to give up"), or a description of some external incident or impetus for coming to seek help (e.g., "My priest said I should come," "I'm going crazy," "My family is so screwed up," "My job is too stressful"). Individuals never approach clinical treatment with the referral complaint of "I have a problem-solving deficit and need to learn new strategies for coping with major and minor life events" (although this would make the task of therapists significantly less tedious). Initial phases of most therapeutic work involve sorting out important historical information, clarifying situational contexts, and examining the individual's social learning history, emotional idiosyncrasies, and recent significant life events. Additionally, the therapist needs to understand the patient's current beliefs, attributions, and expectations of the environment.

The second component of problem-solving therapy, problem definition and formulation, provides a set of guidelines by which the patient can learn to get beyond the immediately obvious referral problem and define stressful situations so as to maximize problem resolution. The purpose of this component of training is to teach individuals to define and formulate problems in a way that increases the effectiveness of the remaining problem-solving operations.

These problem-definition tasks represent some of the most difficult and complex activities in the entire problem-solving process. It remains crucial that the patient master such skills with a certain degree of competence

156

in order to facilitate further problem-solving effectiveness. Through training in the problem-definition process, the individual learns how to organize and prioritize a personal assessment of his or her own problematic life circumstances, as well as how thoughts, emotions, and behavioral deficits may be exacerbating their current distress.

A patient who recently terminated a successful treatment process expressed the importance of accurate problem definition during a final session, while also providing feedback concerning her overall therapy experience. Ethel, a 57-year-old widow, had come to treatment for obesity and chronic dysphoria after many unsuccessful experiences with a variety of weight reduction programs, as well as 8 years of traditional psychoanalytic therapy. An articulate woman, with a master's degree in art education, she had frequently complained, during the initial sessions, of her past interpersonal failures and lack of self-control and self-discipline. After completing several posttreatment measures, she remembered that when she had completed the SPSI as an initial assessment measure, the experience had caused her some distress. "I had such difficulty filling this form out," she stated. "It seems now that my trouble with feeling so down and tired, and my weight, as well as so many other things in my life had been so vague. I realize now that my own attitude was the problem that had to change—never taking responsibility for thinking anything through." She continued to review how, for many years, she conceptualized all of her problems in terms of her weight, which had obscured her investigation of the real intrapersonal or attitude problems she needed to solve in order to improve her quality of life.

The following list itemizes the five specific problem-definition-and-formulation tasks that are the goals of training in this problem-solving component. The therapeutic strategies that are helpful in facilitating the patient's learning of this process are also provided. It is important to note that these component processes are not distinct skills and categories to be focused upon in therapeutic isolation. Instead, these problem-definition-and-formulation operations represent an important set of overlapping skills that collectively reflect the most optimal means of setting personal goals.

PROBLEM-DEFINITION-AND-FORMULATION TASKS

1. Seek all available facts and information concerning the problem.
2. Describe the facts in clear and unambiguous terms.
3. Identify those factors that actually make the situation a problem.

4. Differentiate relevant from irrelevant information and objective facts from unverified inferences, assumptions, and interpretations.

5. Set realistic problem-solving goals.

GATHERING ALL RELEVANT INFORMATION

Therapeutic Principle

The first step in the process of problem definition is the gathering of *all* available information. The therapist may need to focus initially on reversing the patient's habituated pattern of selectively searching for discriminating negative facts that support his or her feelings of hopelessness. Certainly there may be information available that suggests a reasonable explanation for the patient's sadness or anxiety. One example is the individual who has experienced an actual loss. Part of an attempt to elicit all information concerning this patient's depression might engender a statement such as, "My mother and I were close; she died of cancer 2 years ago." In such a case, further reports of loneliness, sadness, and loss associated with the event seem predictable. However, in addition to further information that supports a rationale for emotional distress, descriptions of various "as if" feelings are often reported that become confused with actual fact.

Examples of such descriptions for the preceding situation might include these thoughts: "I feel as if things have never been the same for me since," or "I'll never have that kind of closeness again." Additionally, there is usually a plethora of available information or facts that have been selectively avoided by the depressed patient (e.g., how the patient's own behavior has changed over the last 2 years; how the mother's death has had an impact on other parts of the patient's life; how the patient has avoided intimacy with persons other than the mother because of concerns about security; how the patient lacks the social skills to develop a larger support system; or how recent problems with the patient's employment have exacerbated feelings of loneliness, making the absence of the patient's mother especially salient).

It thus becomes important to teach the patient to gather *all* available data, including information that carries both a negative *and* positive valence. Additionally, there may be facts concerning the problem that carry no particular emotional valence for the individual, but simply supply needed information. For instance, perhaps the patient in the previous example lacked basic information concerning the availability of local bereavement groups for relatives of cancer victims.

It is often helpful to emphasize with patients that it is easy to confuse an *opinion* about what is being experienced with a *fact*. It should be pointed out to the preceding patient that feelings of hopelessness are symptoms of depression, which is a fact concerning the way he or she is currently experiencing the world, and not a fact of the actual conditions of the world.

This patient also needs to ascertain which factors about this situation actually contribute to the feelings of hopelessness. It may be useful to provide the patient with the empathic message that feeling hopeless is recognized as a true experience—he or she need not argue its existence. However, the patient will derive optimal benefit from investigating and gathering, with the therapist, other available information to best understand these feelings and begin to alleviate them.

Searching for and gathering all information and facts about the problem avoids the mistake of making an inferential leap that could lead to further problems and confusion. This faulty inferential leap may frequently be due to the assumption that an "as if" feeling is a true and unchangeable fact. Further confusion arises when these faulty beliefs contradict and obscure positive information that would be helpful in setting realistic goals and solving the problem. In beginning this process, the strategy of "Becoming an Investigative Reporter" can be helpful.

Procedure

Any investigative reporter is aware of the necessary components for a well-covered story. Essential features include answering questions such as "Who"? "What"? "When"? "Where"? "Why"? and "How"? Providing this information to readers enables them to objectively view the various contexts and viewpoints in the story. More importantly, it helps them to understand what has actually happened. Conclusions that are based only on partial information may be extremely misleading. A patient engaging in this strategy should be reminded that an ethical reporter gathers *all* the facts and uses reliable sources. Additionally, particularly where personal evaluations and interpersonal relationships are concerned, a reporter nearly always seeks corroboration among sources of information.

Clinical Example

Jay was a 34-year-old, single male who came to treatment following a recent break-up of a 2-year relationship. This resulted in a move from another part of the country. Until very recently, he was living with various extended family and friends who provided him with a place to stay. Upon entering treatment, he complained of poor self-esteem, frequent crying spells, feelings of being a failure, and perceptions of himself as boring and unattractive. He had come to treatment when his friends had stopped calling and spoke to him less frequently. A married friend, Rob, had recently asked Jay to expedite his own living arrangements after he had stayed with him for more than two months. Jay stated feeling abandoned by his friends and family and hopeless because "No one understands or cares." In the transcript provided below, Jay was engaged to work with the therapist as an investigative reporter in order to gather all the facts and seek additional information to evaluate the reasons for a recent decrease in the frequency of contact by his friends.

THERAPIST (TH): So, how did it go this past weekend?

PATIENT (P): I interviewed my friends over the weekend as you asked. I'll admit, when I wrote down what they were saying and kind of tried to pretend I was a reporter, just getting the facts, not reacting, it was pretty interesting, but hard. I really wanted to defend myself.

TH: Sounds like it was tough—you must have really had to work at it. What additional information did you get concerning your friends?

P: Well, I began by asking Rob (the friend with whom the patient had been recently staying) why it was important for me to move out. I wanted to tell him how hurt I was that he could throw me out like that, but I didn't.

TH: You will find it more helpful at this point to stick to the facts. By saying, even to yourself, that Rob is uncaring and throwing you out, you make assumptions that may or may not be true.

P: Well, that's what I figured after the way you had explained the purpose of the homework. Anyway, Rob was kind of scared to tell me the truth, because he said I seemed so sensitive lately, and that I turn everything he says around—kind of into an insult. I don't mean to do that, it's just that I feel so bad all the time, I really don't want to be a burden to my friends.

TH: Is that the kind of thinking you were referring to when you said before it was hard not to defend yourself, Jay?

P: Yes . . . Anyway, after I told Rob that I would try not to act badly toward him, if he told me the truth, he was a little more willing to talk.

TH: Good!

P: Rob said that it has been really difficult for him since I came back. At first he was glad that I was coming to visit, because he thought about the fun we used to have—playing cards, joking around, things like that. He and Debbie (Rob's wife) had actually looked forward to my staying with them—if you can believe it. But Rob said that when I actually came, that I was real down all the time, and argumentative. Then he said something really wild—that he and Debbie started to feel guilty when they were happy, and that they started to fight because Debbie was mad when Rob didn't ask me to leave! What a bitch!

TH: Sounds like you had some impact on the household.

P: Yeah, I was a real gift!

TH: Yet you say Debbie, as well as Rob, had originally looked foward to your visit?

P: Apparently. He told me that she had been excited because she was happy for Rob to have his friend around again, and that she had several friends she would like to introduce me to. Also, Debbie told him she always really liked my sense of humor. I guess she's not really a bitch, it just makes me mad that she doesn't understand.

TH: What actually happened when you came to stay?

P: I guess my staying with them was really different than what she and Rob expected.

TH: What facts do you have to support this?

P: Well, I can see what they mean when they talk about the good parts of my coming to stay with them. I used to be more like what they expected. But when I came to stay, I argued with them when they tried to make me feel good, I insulted some of Debbie's friends, but only because I felt they thought they're better than me. I walked around pretty pissed off—they always seemed so happy with each other. I hate to admit it, but I'm really jealous of Rob and Debbie. I wasn't any great person to be with, but I'm going through a bad time now, and if they were really my friends, they would understand.

TH: Would you say that it's a fact that a friend always understands all problems, all the time, and always acts in a sympathetic manner?

P: No, of course not. Friends are human. In fact, I think even though I'm going through a bad time, that I'm still Rob's friend, and I don't always understand what he goes through. I would like to have been a better friend and made it easier for them while I was staying there. I start getting mad at them, and feeling proud, like I don't need their charity, and should be able to do things on my own.

Clinical Comment

This transcript reveals that when Jay started to investigate facts, his problem began taking on a different definition from the one originally stated as a result of inferential leaps. In other words, rather than stating his problem as "Rob and Debbie not caring and throwing me out on the street," Jay began to examine the ways in which his recent difficulties have affected the manner in which he relates to others. Particularly during the last few moments of dialogue, we can observe the irrational and dysfunctional assumptions that underlie some of Jay's actions. Although distorted beliefs such as "I must solve all problems completely on my own with no help from anyone, at any time, otherwise I am a failure" will require future therapeutic focus, his new perspective on the definition of the problem is more likely to eventually produce accurate and realistic goals for change. Future areas of investigation might involve an examination of the specific ways that Jay might improve his relationship with people like Rob and Debbie, who provide him with both support and social networking opportunities.

DESCRIBING FACTS IN UNAMBIGUOUS TERMS

Therapeutic Principle

This problem-definition skill, that of developing operational definitions for both overt and covert behavioral targets for change, rests at the core of behavioral assessment. This is particularly important when a patient is experiencing overwhelming emotions, such as sadness, anger, or hopelessness. In many instances, an individual will approach treatment with the belief that the experience of these feelings is the problem. Many patients express a degree of relief when told that the experience of these feelings in and of itself is not the problem. Rather, feelings may be useful guides in defining the real problems they are facing.

Defining problems that involve painful emotions reflects a more comprehensive use of the *personal investigative reporter strategy* whereby the individual continues to look for facts related to the experience of these emotions. The patient is taught to continue to ask questions concerning the who, what, where, when, why, and how of their experienced distress. Ambiguous terms are to be avoided. Instead, a reporter is responsible for using clear and concise language to minimize the potential for misinterpretation.

These investigative questions often lead to a discrimination of the type of problem or problems involved. Common variations of problem types include the presence of a deficit (e.g., lack of vocational training), a mismatch of personal expectancies (e.g., "I thought I would get more satisfaction from this job"), cognitive distortions (e.g., "I have failed as a woman because my child has a behavior problem"), or sustained confusion over conflicting goals (e.g., finding intrinsic satisfaction with work that has limited financial reward while also requiring a certain income in order to see oneself as a success).

Using clear terms to both define a problem and identify specific goals also provides a means to better evaluate the actual outcome of a solution when it is later implemented. This aspect of problem definition is particularly important with depressed individuals, because attaining goals is one important way to define success and competency, an experience that depressed individuals may not readily recognize if vaguely stated.

Procedure

When explaining to the patient the rationale of the investigative reporter strategy for using unambiguous terms, an analogy may be drawn that describes a reporter as needing to look for concrete and specific information to substantiate his or her points. Otherwise, the newspaper would be at risk for accusations of making arbitrary inferences and biased, unfounded conclusions. The purpose of asking the questions who, what, where, when, why, and how in this strategy is to encourage the patient to use language that is both concrete and unambiguous. Moreover, it aids the patient to distinguish between relevant and irrelevant information, differentiate between objective facts and subjective assumptions, and avoid distorted interpretations of current life experiences.

Clinical Example

Carol was a successful, attractive, 35-year-old attorney and mother of two. She had recently completed law school and had obtained her first position in a prestigious law firm. The problems that she described upon entering treatment began with the discovery of a brief sexual liaison between her husband, also an attorney, and a paralegal in his office 2 years earlier. These problems were stated with both agonized hopelessness and vague terms: "Alan never loved me," "I knew I would never be happy," "My marriage is over," "I will never be able to trust anyone again."

To all the world, Carol and her husband had maintained a perfect relationship since they had met 10 years ago in law school. After dropping out of school in order to raise their children, Carol was finally accomplishing her long-term goal of a legal career, and yet she felt as though all of her dreams had been shattered by her husband, whom she had previously believed to be her best friend. Despite the fact that a significant degree of information was available to her to begin to define the problem more objectively, she had focused on her feelings of anger, humiliation, and shock for several weeks prior to seeking treatment. Her husband, Alan, who eventually attended treatment with the patient, had stated in an equally hopeless manner that he would never be able to undo this hurt of "the only person who is truly important to me." Further, he was becoming increasingly absorbed in his own guilt and self-admonishment. His very admission and sharing of what he viewed as a serious mistake and immature reaction to his wife's recent success had represented for Alan an attempt to clear the air, and reestablish the most important aspect of his life.

Although Carol initially sought individual treatment for depressive symptoms of hopelessness, anhedonia, pervasive feelings of sadness, and suicidal thoughts, her therapist had suggested joint sessions with her husband in order to aid in improved problem definition. The following transcript is an illustration of how the investigative reporter strategy previously described may begin to clarify problems more objectively.

CAROL (C): I just never thought this could ever happen. All the wonderful and close experiences Alan and I shared have been ruined! It's something I can't face.

ALAN (A): That's not true! I do love you—I was afraid I wouldn't be enough for you, only I didn't see it back then. I never wanted to hurt you, you're my whole life!

C: Liar! How can you say that, after what you did?

THERAPIST (TH): Carol, you say that the problem existing is that your marriage is ruined. Let's assume that to be true for a moment. I'd like you to picture yourself, for a moment, as kind of an investigative reporter who is attempting to get all the facts to this story. Realizing this is not easy for you, let's give it a try. Suppose you were covering "The Story of Alan and Carol's Ruined Marriage," you might ask the typical reporter's questions of who, how, why, when, where, and what, in order to get at the facts. Remembering that you want to separate out hearsay from facts, let's proceed. Alan, please feel free to join in this exercise. How would you begin?

C: I guess with what happened. That's easy. Alan slept with someone else and lied to me.

TH: Alan, would you agree this is what happened?

A: Yes. I wish to God it didn't, but yes. I would add that I acted like a jerk in a lot of ways. I was feeling kind of crazy. Like I was jealous of Carol's success, yet wanting her to have it all at the same time.

TH: What would you ask next, Carol?

C: When did you start feeling this way?

TH: And?

C: Two years ago, on two occasions, when I was away for a couple of weekends staying with my friend and study partner, Judy, craming for exams, Alan went to Susan's house and ended up sleeping with her. That answers "Who," as well.

TH: Alan?

A: That's when I acted like a selfish ass—but I always felt that Carol would one day finish law school and find out she didn't need me anymore. I thought—how could she? She's beautiful, intelligent, and she can do anything she sets her mind to!

C: Why did you always act so self-assured? Why didn't you tell me this? How could you let this happen to us?

TH: What other *how* questions would you ask, Carol, if you were attempting to get to the bottom of this story?

C: How did this happen? How long did it last? How come only twice? There were plenty of opportunities. And why? What did he want in her that I couldn't give him?

TH: What information can we use to begin to answer these questions factually?

A: It happened because I was feeling worried Carol wouldn't love me anymore—that she wouldn't need me. I didn't understand it at the time, but I guess having someone look up to me so much made me feel stronger. I stopped it because I didn't have any real relationship with Sue and I knew it was very wrong. It was empty and meaningless. I felt like I was being crazy and stupid and immature—pathetic. It was like I woke up one day and said, what are you doing? I didn't care a bit about Susan. It was then I stopped the whole thing.

TH: Do you have any difficulty seeing Alan's answers as facts? Are there other facts that don't make sense?

C: I believe what he says. He's told me this a million times, and adding everything up, I can believe that's true. But I'm so disappointed in the way he handled this whole thing. I've been afraid of losing him too sometimes. As a matter of fact, my worst fear has always been exactly what happened! I never would have done what he did. How am I supposed to deal with the humiliation? How could he hurt me that way? How can I trust him ever again? How can I respect him, when he behaved so childishly and so selfishly?

A: I don't blame her for feeling that way. For me, how can I show her that I love her? How can I show her I learned something from all this? How can I ever get over the guilt of hurting someone I love? I didn't just degrade myself, I screwed up a beautiful marriage. Now I really do believe that I don't deserve her. How can I convince Carol that I'm different?

TH: These are extremely important *how* questions. And I'm struck by the fact that we are back to the original problem stated as—"The marriage is screwed up." What would both of you say are the facts that we currently have investigated that support this 9-year-marriage as now being screwed up.

C: If this didn't happen, our marriage wouldn't be screwed up—we would have everything we wanted!

A: We always had everything we wanted—each other. I was so afraid of losing it. I hate what I did and I hate the hurt it caused, but I do feel relieved to know how deeply Carol loved me and that I'm not holding in any lies any more.

C: That's a hell of a way to feel relieved that I love you! You could have found that out without being so deceitful.

A: I agree Carol, but . . .

TH: So do I, but distasteful as it is, this does help answer the question, "Why?" Carol, you said before that your marriage had "everything." What specifically did you mean by everything?

C: Each other to count on, to support, to understand. For me, a wonderful person as a husband. Also great kids, a good career, someone to share it with . . . someone I truly loved and respected . . . before this. But I need my husband to be a best friend I can count on— honesty, I guess. Someone who'll protect me, not destroy me.

TH: What is it about Alan now, that makes you assess him as different than that?

C: Nothing now . . . but it's like he's two different people—the one who loves me and the creep who hurt me, even if it was because he was afraid.

A: I still feel terrible about it. I don't know if I can ever make it up to her.

C: I don't want him to make it up—I want him to have not let this happen! I guess our marriage isn't all screwed up, but it feels like it! I'm so angry at him for putting us through this! How can I not be angry? How can I ever trust him again (Cries)?

TH: Those are some of the many *how* questions both of you have asked before, probably the few questions we couldn't answer directly with facts. Maybe those troublesome questions provide us with a clearer picture of what the problem really is, since there doesn't seem to be an immediate or easy answer to these questions. By definition, that's exactly what makes a problem, a problem.

C: You mean like how can I deal with what happened and how can I respect or trust Alan? How can I get over feeling so humiliated?

A: Or how can I communicate to Carol how much I love her and would never do anything so stupid again? Or how can I make our marriage happy again?

C: That feels right. I didn't really believe it was a fact my marriage was over or I never would have sought help. If this didn't happen, I guess I would say the marriage is better than ever. I just don't know how to cope with it all.

TH: You're referring to all those *how's* you both stated before?

C: Right.

Clinical Comment

Despite the fact that initially it seemed to both Carol and Alan that their prolonged emotional distress would last forever, their hopeless expectations were related to the belief that their marriage was indeed "screwed up" and irreparably damaged. This ambiguous assumption exacerbated feelings of futility and loss, since they thought that nothing could be done, regardless of how caring, creative, or noble, to save it. The investigative reporter strategy was helpful in clarifying that the problem involved each partner's ability to cope with a negative and destructive event, as well as to reduce the likelihood of similar, future events, rather than to accept the inaccurate conclusion that the marriage was "ruined" (another vague and ambiguous term). Such terms as "screwed up" and "ruined" tended to create more guilt and distress in Alan because of the connotative meanings that he ascribed to these phrases. Learning to use concrete language helped both Carol and Alan to communicate their feelings more accurately, which led to an overall improvement in their ability to understand each other.

Subsequent sessions focusing on problem definition addressed intrapersonal obstacles and subproblems particular to each spouse that investigated the how, what, where, and why of this situation as exceeding their capabilities to adequately cope 2 years after a significantly stressful event. Both spouses focused their efforts on more emotion-focused goals, because their objectives entailed minimizing the impact of distress associated with a problem previously experienced. These goals included Carol's investigation of cognitive distortions she was continuing to make regarding her own attractiveness, as well as her arbitrary inferences concerning the presence of this type of marital difficulty. Alan, who asked to remain in active treatment with Carol, focused on emotional goals of reduced guilt, as well as on improvement of his ability to communicate his own fears of competency to Carol. After several months of treatment, emotion-and problem-focused goals were combined as Carol and Alan decided that they should view their love, work, and commitment to each other as a new beginning. Their process of problem solving resulted in the decision to plan a honeymoon in Paris.

MINIMIZING COGNITIVE DISTORTIONS

Therapeutic Principle

After gathering as much information about the problem as possible and using concrete and unambiguous terms to describe this information, the next step in the problem-definition-and-formulation process is to identify those factors that actually make the situation a problem. However, in defining a problem, depressed individuals often may use information that is based on idiosyncratic judgments, inferences, valuations, assumptions, and interpretations. As such, it is important to help patients to discriminate between facts and assumptions.

This trimming down of the available information into facts versus assumptions and focusing on those facts that actually contribute to the problem is analogous to using a funnel approach in the selection of clinical targets for intervention. In essence, after initially gathering and considering all available data, only that which is relevant, factual, and useful becomes the focus of strategic attention. The following treatment rationale provided to patients by the therapist illustrates this point.

> We may consider an event a fact if it is something that actually happened or is true and has been observed to be so. An assumption is a belief not based on certainty or actual observation, but which seems to be true or probable. In other words, the assumption is an inference that takes for granted certain events but has not been proven or observed. By looking for all the facts rather than forming a hasty conclusion based on arbitrary inferences or assumptions, we are better prepared to solve the problem. However, after gaining all the facts to the best of our ability, we now will need to select the facts that are most salient or important in forming a more educated conclusion.

Procedure

The purpose of this intervention is to provide moments during the process of problem definition that allow the patient to pause, sum up information gathered thus far in the process, and decide the focus or direction of further problem definition and formulation. The strategy involves listing the facts and information gathered concerning the particular problem under investigation. The various facts and information are reviewed, assessing whether the information is fact or fiction (suggesting a possible faulty assumption), and further, whether the information is important enough to use while developing realistic goals.

Clinical Example

In the transcript provided below, Evelyn, a 30-year-old female, discusses problems concerning her current feelings of distress. Evelyn had only recently moved out of the town she had lived in all her life. She had frequently described her relationship with her mother and father as very close. Her symptoms of depression focused on her feelings of being trapped and conflicted between the demands of a new relationship with a male friend, a new job and apartment, and her continued habit of visiting her parents frequently (holidays, every weekend, and several evenings after work). Over the last several months, she had been fighting more often with her male friend, felt a sense of emptiness at work, and experienced frequent crying spells and feelings of anger and sadness.

THERAPIST (TH): Let's review the facts you have gathered so far in your attempts to define the main problems you are currently experiencing. Let's look for the information that's most important. Let's also attempt to distinguish between facts and assumptions.

PATIENT (P): I know I feel really stressed out. A lot of times I know I said that my boyfriend and I have a lot of disagreements, but there are so many good qualities in him. I think there are a lot of reasons why I feel this way. I sometimes start fights, even when I don't have to when I feel depressed. It hasn't been easy moving to a whole new place, and meeting new people, and my parents have really put a lot more pressure on me than I had realized! I think sometimes I'm carrying their problems with my moving out and feeling responsible for them. You know, as we gather facts about my job, my boyfriend, and my finances with the new place, I begin to feel a little excited! I realize when we talk about my parents, I start to feel angry and depressed. I think I feel really guilty about leaving them, especially if I need them again.

TH: If you need them again?

P: I guess . . . if things don't work out . . . if I have to go back home . . . if . . .

TH: If there's no one else and you're alone.

P: Yes.

TH: What is the likelihood that this will happen?

P: Truth is, I don't know . . . I've never been really on my own . . . in many ways . . . I feel like I'm more like 21 and leaving home for the first time. I would feel better if they agreed with my decisions—more secure. But they don't like my boyfriend and they criticize my apartment. It's like they're always waiting to say "I told you so."

TH: Why not just go home, and reduce the stress on yourself?

P: Because, like I told you, I'm happy when I'm with my boyfriend, unless we're arguing about seeing my parents . . . and I would feel successful being in my own place if I didn't have this gnawing feeling like I'm betraying my mother and father.

TH: Let's examine some of those gnawing feelings concerning the facts.

P: You remember . . . whenever I call my parents, there are all these sarcastic comments I get making it sound like I don't care about them anymore.

TH: Is this a fact? That you no longer care or love them? Or is this fictional?

P: Of course not! I love them! That is a fact. What is also a fact is that they don't see it that way. I wish I could make them see that I still love them even if my life is different and I don't see them as much. I'd also like to tell them how it affects me when they act that way.

TH: Why don't you?

P: I think I feel too afraid of hurting them . . . of them saying I'm ungrateful. I wish I could. I wish I was more . . . more . . .

TH: Assertive?

P: Yes. As a matter of fact, being more assertive would probably help a lot . . . I wouldn't feel so bottled up all the time.

Clinical Comment

Although Evelyn originally gathered facts concerning all the areas in her life in which she experienced problems, she had begun to focus on areas that were appearing most salient. These included her difficulty in separating from her parents, her own doubts of self-efficacy, and lack of assertiveness. This process became especially important, since focusing on the more salient reasons for experiencing distress (i.e., problems) would probably maximize the likelihood of some generalized improvement to other related areas. For example, decisions to visit her parents made as a result of irrational guilt appeared to be the basis of at least some arguments with her current boyfriend. Conversely, some of the problems encountered with both her boyfriend and work associates might be improved through more assertive behavior.

UNDERSTANDING THE NATURE OF A PROBLEM

Therapeutic Principle

Throughout the process of problem definition, patients are encouraged to gather all available information, use concrete and unambiguous language, and minimize the likelihood of confusion and distortions of information as a means of better understanding the nature of a problem. Although the personal investigative reporter strategy is particularly helpful in this regard, additional strategies may be useful to aid in identifying those factors that make a situation a problem. Through the personal investigative reporter strategy previously presented, individuals learned to ask a variety of fact-finding questions (who, what, when, where, why, and how) as a means of providing initial relevant information about the problem. Through the next strategy, the how questions that may have been previously stated may now begin to be more specifically and carefully delineated in order to obtain a more accurate formulation of the problem. For example, the how question, "How can I ever have the kind of relationship I want?" may now begin to be more specifically developed. Through the use of imagery and fantasy these goals may become more specific and detailed. Using imagery to articulate goals helps the individual to identify the specific nature of the *discrepancy* between the demand of the situation and the desired outcome. Identifying this discrepancy can lead to a better description of the obstacles to overcome or the conflicts to resolve in order to best cope with the stressful problem.

Additionally, the labeling of goals as fantasy often serves to avoid the negative evaluation so often expressed by depressed individuals concerning their abilities to meet these goals. Encouraging active imagery and fantasy also permits an initial assessment of the types of criteria that a given patient may use when evaluating alternative solutions. Although these descriptions may be somewhat unrealistic at this point, this strategy is a helpful means of motivating the patient to continue the problem-solving process.

Procedure

Depressed individuals, in their predictions of hopelessness and futility of the future, rarely will spontaneously describe fantasies of happiness, success, contentment, and problem resolution. Yet patients frequently describe fantasies that are preceeded by the two words "if only" (e.g., "If only I hadn't been so stupid, I might have had a great job and been making big money"). The strategy of using fantasy imagery during problem definition reinforces the concept that there is, even if only in fantasy, a set of conditions in which the problem can be significantly improved. The use of this strategy helps individuals to begin to shift from the set of "But I'll never be able to _____, so what is the use of setting goals?"

Additionally, the use of positive fantasies and imagery supplies a better definition of idiosyncratic characteristics reflecting a given patient's conceptualization of success. This helps to further clarify the specific nature of the problem as experienced by different individuals. For example, for two different patients, both of whom describe lack of employment as a chief target area, one's fantasy of being successfully employed may be focused on doing something enjoyable, whereas the second person may visualize having more money to purchase expensive items. Such information can provide a more comprehensive understanding of a person's unique definition of problem resolution. According to this strategy, the therapist asks the patient to vividly describe a positive image of the future in which the major problems are resolved. Details are requested to obtain a comprehensive overall picture of what this image entails.

Clinical Example

Anna, a 62-year-old grandmother, entered treatment following a recommendation from her family priest that her symptoms of depression required professional intervention. She initially appeared hostile, withholding, sarcastic, and hopeless. During the first session, she complained that her 40-year-old son had recently moved to take a new job, resulting in decreased family contact. Moreover, she had also experienced a severe arthritic inflammation, resulting in her loss of ability to take long walks with her husband, an activity they both had enjoyed. From the first therapeutic session, the patient had created the picture of a person who was attending treatment with the goal of proving to her priest that he was wrong to recommend therapy and insensitive in not realizing that nothing would help.

Anna's decision to return for the first few sessions was probably due to the nonevaluative way in which the therapist responded, since she appeared to elicit both anger and frustration from friends who began to shy away from her. Several weeks of treatment were characterized by Anna venting reactionary feelings of anger. She also continued to voice frequent misconceptions and overgeneralizations concerning issues of both aging and problem-solving therapy (e.g., "If I have to be taught how to solve problems at my age, I might as well throw in the towel," "So if my thinking is causing all these problems, you're saying I'm stupid, right?").

During problem-definition training, Anna focused on facts that indicated that the parts of her life she had always enjoyed the most were gone—children had moved away, her physical attractiveness was waning, her physical strength and abilities as a sportswoman had significantly decreased, and her own depressive symptoms were having a negative impact upon her marital relationship and other friendships. In fact, her priest's recommendation for treatment was made following her decision to stop participating in church-related activities (which she previously attended with enthusiasm), stating to him, "God is probably punishing me for something I did by making me so miserable." Indeed, this was one of many arbitrary inferences that were assessed as assumptions during one of the previous sessions. Following is a transcript where Anna was encouraged to use fantasy imagery as a means of both generating positive images of the future and better defining the real problem.

THERAPIST (TH): Let's assume for a moment, Anna, that we had a magic wand, and by waving it, right now, your life could be just the way you want it to be. Describe the fantasy that comes to mind.

PATIENT (P): I'd be forty again, I'd have my youth, my strength, and my health. I'd be feeling good and not so miserable . . . but since you can't give me 20 years back . . .

TH: Just stick with the fantasy for a moment—get a picture of it in your mind. Describe to me what you're doing.

P: Everything I did when I was forty. Raising my children, busy with their lives, swimming, playing tennis, shopping for clothes . . . I had some figure then!

TH: Since this is a magic fantasy, is there anything you see yourself doing that you didn't actually do when you were 40?

P: Not much, except I would be getting an education. I didn't think it was important then. Women were made to believe raising kids was all that was important, but now I know I would have liked to have gotten a college degree.

TH: What are you studying in your fantasy?

P: Physical education of course, or physical therapy, health, things related to exercise and sports—I was always very interested in things like that. I would have something to fall back on now, something of importance. No one can ever take away your education!

TH: Sounds like one advantage of the age you are at now is being able to know that there are certain interests which seem to have been important over a long period of time. That's important knowledge to have.

P: Except that I never got that degree, and I gave up doing it for my kids . . . and I don't have them anymore. Maybe I would feel a little better if I was in better physical shape or had done something for myself, like get that degree.

TH: Sounds like you might be starting to develop some goals which may improve the way you feel.

P: Oh sure, start to go to college now at my age. How can I do something for myself now, like go to college, or involve myself in sports, without feeling like I'm too old?

TH: Does that sound totally and completely impossible?

P: Right now I want to say that it does, but I guess it is not totally impossible.

TH: In fact, there's a little part of you that might be willing to try to figure out an answer to the question you just asked.

P: I guess there is.

TH: Anna, we're off and running!

Clinical Comment

It is not surprising that Anna's depressive symptoms had become a source of frustration to the significant people in her life. Previous attempts by friends and family to help her were met with sarcasm and anger. They began to fear her anger and avoided discussions about aging. Unfortunately, Anna's anger was largely invested in expressing to her friends the resentments she had toward having given up earlier valued personal goals for those she had assumed were important to her family. With little reinforcement available to her at present, she had begun to blame others for the demands made upon her throughout her life. These feelings were stressful, and Anna believed she should be punished for harboring angry feelings toward those she loved, as well as toward her family priest, who frequently would emphasize the heavenly rewards for those who were self-sacrificing. The use of fantasy was helpful in eliciting changes she could have made in her earlier years, as well as ways she might be reinforced in the present, without having to directly confront the resentment she felt toward significant others in her life. As Anna became more instrumental in seeking ways to meet personal goals, she was pleased and surprised to see that her attempts received support and encouragement from her family. She became more active in the church again but with a different activity focus—she organized the parish's Special Olympics program!

SETTING REALISTIC PROBLEM-SOLVING GOALS

Therapeutic Principle

This final component in the problem-definition-and-formulation process involves setting concrete goals that can realistically approximate the criteria delineated during previous therapeutic exercises (i.e., the fantasy and imagery strategy described previously). If the patient has begun to adopt a more rationally based orientation to problem solving, this may require no more than two or three sessions focused on evaluating the general goals involved (problem-focused vs. emotion-focused objectives), a list of subgoals that may be involved, and an investigation of current obstacles.

The patient, however, may still be reacting to habituated cognitive distortions and double standards concerning self-competency. It is then necessary to focus on reducing overly perfectionistic goals. For example, with reference to the clinical example previously presented, Anna might have chosen the problem-focused goal of obtaining a degree from the best possible school (while achieving only perfect grades) in order to compensate for her age, believing that the better school could make her appear less of a foolish old woman. This objective would be likely to provide her with little opportunity for alternatives and unnecessarily high expectations in consideration of her current needs. As such, success is less likely to occur. Therefore, it seems more reasonable to separate her goals into the two areas of problem-focused goals (e.g., getting a college education through a local college with special curriculums designed for senior citizens), and emotion-focused goals (e.g., learning to be more accepting of the aging process).

Procedure

In setting realistic goals, the patient is encouraged to delineate a set of concrete obstacles that currently prevent attainment of desired goals.

These obstacles may involve a skill deficit, lack of resources, uncertainty, fears, or interpersonal conflicts. It is important to consider and predict which obstacles exist, since the processing of future alternatives will be focused directly on overcoming these obstacles in order to meet the stated goals. Often goals can be stated beginning with the phrase "How can I . . .?" In listing these obstacles, it often becomes apparent that several subgoals or objectives (both problem-focused and emotion-focused) will be necessary to consider as a means of addressing the overall problem from a number of perspectives.

Clinical Example

During subsequent sessions, Anna had in fact decided to focus on the goals described above—to obtain a college education (problem-focused) and to learn to cope more effectively with the process of aging (emotion-focused). Further, she realized that these goals were not completely independent, in that her fears of appearing foolish and looking like "an old dog trying to learn new tricks" represented a major obstacle to seeking the college education. On the other hand, she realized that getting the education might help her form new opinions toward aging. Since obtaining a college education appeared the most tangible and concrete objective, she decided to focus on this goal initially. However, it was mutually agreed that treatment would also simultaneously focus on developing more effective emotion-focused coping strategies regarding aging. The transcript below provides an example of how she began to list current obstacles during a session.

THERAPIST (TH): Let's focus on the goal of getting a college degree, Anna. What obstacles do you see as immediately present?

PATIENT (P): Well, I would have said before that I had no idea about how to go about it, but I called the community college here in the county and found that they have these special degree counseling programs for senior citizens. I could use some more information, though, about other programs. There's one at another university nearby also. Should I write these down?

TH: Good idea.

P: Luckily, money doesn't seem to be much of a problem—we're pretty comfortable. However, there are many obstacles I see with my age. I know that I'm afraid I won't do well and the people at the university will think, "Who are you trying to kid?" . . . There are some good reasons for me feeling this way. I don't have as much energy or self-discipline to study as I used to, and I'm concerned that my memory may not be as good.

TH: So we should list fears concerning your ability to complete the work, and possibly needing to arrange study times when you would have the most energy as obstacles.

P: You know, I never thought of arranging special time for me as necessary. Time itself is another problem. You know that my husband is semiretired. We like to travel to Florida in the winter for extended periods of time. It seems like it's too long to miss any classes, yet not long enough to get involved with any training down there.

TH: Another obstacle is finding a way to travel to Florida during the winter, yet still enroll in classes?

P: Yes . . . that's really a big one!

TH: Anything else?

P: Just little things . . . nothing much really.

TH: Let's list them—remember that the more we anticipate, even the little obstacles, the better prepared we will be in meeting the goals.

P: Well, I don't know how my husband will react. He always said I should do what makes me happy . . . but I've been there just for him for a long time. He may feel like he's getting old too and that I don't want to take care of him anymore.

TH: That's very important—your concern over your husband's feelings is another possible obstacle in meeting these goals.

Clinical Comment

At this point in the process of problem definition and formulation, Anna is almost prepared to begin to generate alternative solutions (and combinations of solutions) that address attainment of her goals. In identifying these obstacles, it is evident that some of the problem parameters existing for this patient include novelty (e.g. going back to school again), specific behavioral deficits (e.g., lack of study skills, possible memory deficits), and conflicting stimulus demands (e.g., traveling with her husband during the winter months, the marital relationship). Accurate identification of these obstacles can aid her to better understand that her difficulties are complex, which eventually can result in her perception that the presence of varied obstacles is an indication that all her difficulties were not solely a result of aging.

Name: _____ Date: _____

In describing a recent problem, try to answer the following questions: WHO? WHAT? WHEN? WHERE? WHY? and HOW? Remember to use CONCRETE terms.

Briefly state your goal(s). Remember to be SPECIFIC and REALISTIC.

List the important obstacles to these goals. Be SPECIFIC.

Figure 8.1. Problem Definition and Formulation Worksheet.

SUMMARY

The ultimate objectives of the problem-definition-and-formulation process are to assess the nature of the problem situation as accurately as possible and to identify a set of realistic goals or objectives. Through the five tasks presented, the patient gradually learns to relabel emotional distress as a valuable source of information. Combined with an understanding of those factors and circumstances that contribute to the problem, the patient begins to develop a comprehensive assessment of the nature of the stressful situation that can facilitate the effectiveness of later problem-solving operations. The five tasks involved in the process have been described separately and sequentially for the purpose of illustration. However, these therapeutic tasks may be developed simultaneously or in an order decided upon by the therapist as optimal for any given individual. Further, Figure 8.1 provides an example of a Problem Definition and Formulation Worksheet that can be used during the treatment sessions and as homework assignments in order to facilitate skill acquisition.

During a day treatment group therapy training session a patient announced, "The problem that I have is that I can't define my problem!" This comment drew empathetic laughter from the other participants who were wrestling with the same difficulty. The statement, however, exemplifies both the importance and complexity of providing patients with adequate training in the five problem-definition-and-formulation tasks provided in this chapter. The strategies presented have been used with patients in order to facilitate a sense of challenge by creating a way for them to observe, as well as experience, the circumstances and factors concerning their current depressive symptoms.

CHAPTER 9

Training in Generation of Alternatives

> *Nothing is more dangerous than an idea,*
> *When it's the only one you have.*
>
> EMILE AUGUSTE CHARTIER

During the generation-of-alternatives phase of problem solving, the therapist assists the patient in developing a wide range of potential solutions for each identified problem. Training patients to develop a range of coping options is based on the premise that the availability of a large number of alternative actions will increase the chances of eventually identifying an effective solution. Often patients expect that there is one right answer for each problem and that therapy, or the therapist, will provide it for them. Moreover, in trying to find the right solution to a problem, patients sometimes believe that the first idea that comes to mind is the best one. Therefore, in order to maximize problem-solving effectiveness, the therapist needs to convey to patients the necessity of generating as many different options as possible.

BRAINSTORMING

At the outset of the generation-of-alternatives process, the therapist may wish to provide an overview by conceptualizing the procedure as an exercise in productive thinking and by introducing the technique of brainstorming. An opening statement such as the following one may be helpful.

> Now that we have identified some of the key problems facing you, it is important that we move onto the next step in the problem-solving process. It's called the "generation of alternatives," and I consider it to be an important tool for increasing our ability to think productively. Often, when people face problems, particularly when they confront difficult problems, their thinking is ruled by their emotions. As a result, they tend to worry a lot and the worrying usually centers their thoughts on the negative things

in their lives. Sometimes the more they think about it, the worse they feel; and a vicious cycle of negative thinking and negative feelings gets started. Often, the person feels helpless about changing either the problem or their feelings. This type of thinking, that is dominated by worrying and ruminating, can be thought of as "nonproductive thinking." Nonproductive thinking usually leads to an accumulation of more negative feelings, and it doesn't help to resolve the problem. What I'd like for us to do in today's session is to learn how to avoid negative thinking by developing those skills that lead to productive thinking. Productive thinking involves confronting your problems head-on by creatively developing a long list of possible ways to resolve the problems facing you. What we will be doing in today's session is learning a set of skills called "brainstorming." Brainstorming will help you to break out of the cycle of negative thinking and negative feelings. Brainstorming will improve your productive thinking abilities and will help you to cope more effectively with the problems that are facing you.

The Therapeutic Principle

The key procedure for developing an exhaustive list of solution possibilities is *brainstorming*. In teaching patients the techniques of brainstorming, it is helpful to describe the process in terms of three guiding principles. They are (1) the quantity principle, (2) the deferment-of-judgment principle, and (3) the strategy-tactics procedure. It is crucial that the therapist convey to the patient that the most effective way to learn about brainstorming is to experience it through practice in generating coping options for real-life problems.

In using brainstorming to generate alternative solutions, the therapist should guide the patient in developing solution ideas that are both *relevant* and *specific*. Relevant options are oriented toward accomplishing the objective(s) necessary to resolve the identified problem. Specific options are stated in concrete and unambiguous terms so that the patient can later evaluate how effective they were in meeting the goal and resolving the problem. The following sections describe in detail how to implement the procedures of brainstorming during the course of therapy with depressed patients.

The Quantity Principle

From the start, the therapist should instill in the patient the importance of generating a quantity of ideas. The quantity principle suggests that the more solution alternatives a person produces, the more high-quality ideas he or she will come up with, thereby increasing the likelihood that an effective solution will ultimately be developed.

Two basic rules govern the application of the quantity principle. The first rule is to have the patient *generate as many responses as possible*; the second is to *combine and improve responses to make additional new solution responses* (D'Zurilla & Nezu, 1982). By increasing the number of alternative solutions, the patient will improve the selection of high-quality possibilities. The therapist should facilitate the generation of alternatives by occasionally offering solution ideas, particularly concerning differing strategies or classes of ideas. It is helpful at times to begin such training with an exercise that emphasizes the use of list-making in solving a simple, impersonal problem, derived from the literature on creativity training.

List making is a simple and direct method to help the patient improve both the quantity and quality of thinking. Two distinct positive features are inherent in making a list of alternatives. First, it helps to focus the patient's attention and concentration on productive thinking, and second, it results in a written record of output. The use of an initial problem that is impersonal in nature helps to relax the patient's defensiveness by providing a neutral task, unencumbered by emotional factors. The following two-part exercise can be used to illustrate the quantity principle.

Quantity Exercise (Part 1): "Let me give you an exercise based on the Brick Test originally developed by the well-known psychologist, J. P. Guilford. A corporate executive whose company manufactures red building bricks is concerned about a drop in sales. He has hired you to assist him in developing new uses for his products. Here's what I would like you to do. Spend the next few minutes thinking about this problem. After three minutes, I will ask you to tell me what you have come up with." (After 3 minutes have elapsed, the therapist asks the patient to describe his or her ideas.)

Quantity Exercise (Part 2): "Now what I would like you to do is to use the next three minutes making a list of all the possible uses for bricks. This time, however, I would like you to take this piece of paper and make a *written list* keeping in mind two rules. First, you should generate as many responses as possible, and second, you should combine and improve responses to develop new possibilities."

When the quantity exercise is effective, patients typically are more productive using the "quantity-listing" instructions than the suggestion to "spend a few minutes." Part 1 typically results in five or fewer responses, whereas Part 2 increases productivity to the range of 10 to 20 responses.

Quantity training should involve substantial practice, especially with regard to personally identified stressful situations. The use of impersonal examples facilitates practice in creativity and flexible thinking. However, it is also important to focus heavily on the depressed individual's real-life problems to avoid the perception of this approach as being personally irrelevant. For example, one therapist who used this technique asked a patient to generate novel ways to use a single concrete brick. On a list of creative ideas, the patient noted, "I could use the brick to hit you on the head for thinking of such a stupid exercise!"

In developing responses to personal problem situations, patients should be encouraged to produce as many ideas as possible for each identified goal or subgoal. This ensures identification of a variety of effective solutions that can ultimately be implemented to attack the problem from a number of perspectives.

The Deferment-of-Judgment Principle

According to the deferment-of-judgment principle, productive thinking will be enhanced if the problem solver suspends critical evaluation of potential solutions during the generation-of-alternatives phase. The rationale for this principle suggests that if one analyzes or judges solution ideas too early in the problem-solving process, many potentially effective ideas may be rejected prematurely. Moreover, a judgmental stance may cause the patient to be overly concerned about producing the right answers, thereby inhibiting productive and creative thinking. In applying this principle, the therapist should instruct the patient to suspend judgment and to avoid criticism when generating alternatives. Instead, patients should be encouraged to be creative by letting go of their imagination.

Getting depressed individuals to delay self-criticism of their thinking is often a difficult task. It is not unusual during the generation-of-alternatives to have a depressed patient claim to be "drawing a blank"—unable to think of a single possibility. In such situations it is helpful to tell the patient, "It is OK to make up an answer." The process of making up something is virtually identical to creatively generating a potential solution. A key distinction, however, rests in the extra degree of permission granted by the instruction, "Make up a response." For many patients, this instruction enables them to establish some distance from their responses. They are less inhibited in generating made-up responses because such responses are not expected to be perfect. In effect, the instruction to make up something gives the patient the freedom to generate alternatives without responsibility for coming up with good solutions (cf. Baugh, 1981).

The Strategies-Tactics Principle

In generating alternative solutions, it is helpful to distinguish between two categories of solution possibilities, strategies and tactics. *Strategies* represent general courses of action that an individual plans to take in order to resolve an identified problem. *Tactics* represent the specific steps that detail how the person plans to implement the strategy in a particular situation. According to the strategy-tactics principle, a greater number of high-quality solution alternatives will be generated when the problem solver generates a wide variety of both strategies and tactics. Therefore, the therapist should assist the patient in developing a range of different general approaches (i.e., strategies) to the problem as well as a variety of specific, concrete actions (i.e., tactics) to implement the general courses of action. Using the strategy-tactics principle, the therapist encourages the patient to think of a wide range of possible solutions across a variety of strategies or classes of approaches rather than to focus on one or two narrow tactics. For example, in completing the brick exercise, some individuals think only in terms of one common strategy, namely, using a brick as a construction material. Often the potential solutions that they generate are simply multiple tactics representing one general strategy (e.g., constructing a fireplace or patio, or building a wall or garage). In such an instance, the individual may generate a quantity of tactics, including some novel ones, but overall problem-solving effectiveness is likely to be limited by the use of only one strategy. A more effective approach to generating alternatives includes several strategies along with multiple tactics for implementing those strategies. For instance, Adams (1976) has suggested that alternative strategies for the brick exercise might include their use as recreational objects (e.g., playground blocks for children), artistic substances (e.g., raw material for sculptures), heating elements (e.g., to warm sheets on cold nights), or athletic equipment (e.g., the "brick shot put").

Clinical Example

Lisa B. was a 27-year-old divorced woman whose identified problems included dissatisfaction with her appearance. She was unhappy with the way she looked in general and with her weight in particular. She reported that she had gradually gained weight over the past few years. At the initial session, she weighed 161 lb, 30 lb over her ideal weight. She reported that she felt trapped; she saw her weight as a major contributor to her depression. Yet when feeling depressed, she often used food to make herself "feel good." Often she engaged in nighttime eating episodes in which she consumed excessive amounts of calories. The following day she would not only feel depressed, but she would also feel guilty about her overeating. In generating alternatives to deal with her unhappiness about her appearance, Lisa came up with the following possible solutions:

Join Weight Watchers
Go on a total fast for 2 to 3 days
Try the Stillman Diet
Go to a diet doctor to get reducing pills
Stop eating breakfast and lunch
Become a vegetarian
Try the Cambridge Diet
Join a weight loss group at the local YWCA
Eliminate all sweets from my diet

On first inspection, it would appear that Lisa had generated a quantity of reasonable solution ideas for dealing with the identified problem. In reviewing her list of alternatives, Lisa and the therapist attempted to group her coping options into classes of strategies that reflected a common theme. They found that all her responses were related to dieting, and they were concerned that she had selected only *one* general strategy for coping with the problem. The strategies and tactics principle suggests that the greater the number of different approaches to the problem, the greater the chances of success. Moreover, in this case, the particular strategy that Lisa chose was one that was unlikely to be effective (i.e., excessive dietary restraint is likely to prompt overeating and an eventual weight gain; cf. Polivy & Herman, 1985).

After reviewing the strategy-tactics principle, Lisa and her therapist attempted to generate a variety of strategies in addition to dieting. Furthermore, Lisa used the first two brainstorming techniques (i.e., the quantity and deferment-of-judgment principles) to generate several specific tactics for each new strategy that she devised. Below is her revised list of strategies and tactics:

Strategy 1: Improve my physical appearance.
Tactics: Get a new hair style; color my hair; get a haircut; go to an expensive beauty parlor; get a facial; get a makeup consultation; learn how to use makeup to play down my fat cheeks; get plastic surgery; have liposuction; get a manicure; get a pedicure; go to a tanning salon; get a color analysis.

Strategy 2:   Use exercise to improve my body.

Tactics: Take up jogging; sign up for a tennis class; join a bowling league; buy a Jane Fonda videotape; buy an exercise bike; buy a 10-speed bike; join a bicycle club; walk 2 miles a day; run 2 miles a day; do calisthenics; learn isometrics; join a health club; do stretching exercise; learn how to use free weights; get access to a universal exercise machine.

Strategy 3:   Find substitutes for nighttime eating.

Tactics: Take a bath; drink water; leave the house; call a friend; start a diary; clean a closet; call my therapist; call my mother; scream; yell; sing; play my guitar; go for a walk; exercise; go to a movie; make a list of things to do; balance the checkbook; eat only celery and carrots; tell myself to wait 10 minutes before having something to eat; polish my nails; give myself a facial; brush my teeth; floss my teeth.

Strategy 4:   Accept my looks.

Tactics: Say to myself, "It doesn't matter how I look"; refuse to look in the mirror; refuse to get on a scale; refuse to buy new clothes; look in the mirror and say "You're all right just the way you are"; say to myself "It's not awful to be overweight."

Strategy 5:   Improve my wardrobe.

Tactics: Buy some new clothes; buy a jogging suit; get clothing that hides fat; consult Omar the tentmaker; buy only dark-colored clothes; ask friends what types of clothes look good on me; get a professional consultation on what clothes would help my appearance; wait until I lose some weight to buy new clothes; use buying clothes as a reward for losing weight.

Strategy 6:   Lose weight.

Tactics: Join Weight Watchers; go on a total fast for 2 to 3 days; try the Stillman diet; go to a diet doctor to get reducing pills; stop eating breakfast and lunch; become a vegetarian; try the Cambridge Diet; join a weight loss group at the local YWCA; eliminate all sweets from my diet.

Clinical Example of Generating Alternatives

The following is an example of how the generation of alternatives can be implemented in a clinical situation. Robert C. was a 35-year-old Vietnam veteran with a history of two psychiatric hospitalizations, each precipitated by suicidal ideation. Following a monthlong hospitalization, he was discharged and referred for outpatient psychotherapy. After completing an assessment, he and his therapist compiled a list of problems confronting him. One of the high-priority items on the list was the problem of employment. At the time he was hospitalized, Robert was driving a truck for a private sanitation firm. Just prior to admission, he had failed to show up at work for an entire week saying he was too depressed to even telephone his boss and explain he would not be in. In using the problem-solving approach, Robert was initially resistant to the suggestion that he try brainstorming to generate possible solutions to his employment problem. Reluctantly, he agreed to participate and did so half-heartedly at first. As the session progressed, he got into the spirit of creative thinking and even smiled as he generated ideas.

THERAPIST (TH): It sounds like you have been feeling more depressed than usual, and one of the things that has been particularly upsetting for you is this problem of not being able to find work.

PATIENT (P): Yeah. It's hard, especially when you don't have any education. Nobody will hire me. Nobody will give me a break. It's impossible for a guy like me.

TH: Impossible is probably too strong a word. Difficult may be a more reasonable way to look at it.

P: That's easy for you to say, Doc. You're the guy with the diplomas on the wall. I don't have a college education, and I never finished high school. Who's going to hire someone like me?

TH: Let's look at the situation a little more closely. Right now you're feeling upset. One of the main things that's bothering you is not being able to find work. One of your goals is to find work.

P: Right, but not just any job. I'm not going to work at McDonald's or work for peanuts you know.

TH: I think it might be helpful if at this point we don't worry too much about the pros and cons of particular jobs, but instead try to make a list of all the possibilities. Let's write down and keep track of each of the ideas we come up with, and let's try to come up with as many ideas as possible.

P: It's going to be a short list. I don't see too many possibilities when you don't have an education.

TH: Let's give it a try.

P: I've been a truck driver and that's all I really know.

TH: OK, that's one possibility. Let's write it down.

P: I don't know what you're getting at. That's the only thing I've done, and I'm not sure that I want to do it again. When I get behind the wheel of a truck, I spend a lot of time thinking about how bad my situation is and I feel really depressed. Sometimes I think I'm lucky I never got into an accident.

TH: So one of the things you are saying is that you would like to consider some possibilities other than driving a truck. What else would you like to consider?

P: You don't understand what I'm saying. I only know one thing, driving a truck, and doing that only makes me more depressed. You know talking about this makes me feel worse. It makes me realize that I'm trapped. I'm depressed. I don't have any skills. I don't have an education. I don't have a job, and the only thing I know how to do, I can't stand.

TH: It sounds like you feel stuck at this point without many options.

P: That's what I've been trying to tell you.

TH: I'd like to try an exercise with you that is sometimes quite helpful in situations like this. It's called "brainstorming." It's a technique for coming up with a lot of possible ways for handling a problem situation so that you can increase your chances of developing a good way of dealing with the problem. There are a couple of things to do that help make it work. First, let's try to come up with as many ideas as possible, and second, let's not worry about how silly an idea might sound. Let's just be creative and put off until later judging whether a particular job possibility might be a good one for you.

P: That doesn't make too much sense to me. I could say I want to be a lawyer. Put that down on the list. But putting it on the list doesn't mean that I could really do it.

TH: Putting it on the list may help us in several ways. It may get us to think about some things that we otherwise might not have considered.

P: Like what?

TH: Well, what would you have to do to become a lawyer?

P: I'd have to finish my education.

TH: Let's put that on the list.

P: You know when I got my G.E.D. (graduate equivalency diploma), the teacher told me that the G.I. bill might pay for me to take some college credits.

TH: Great! I like the way you're thinking now. You see thinking up even wild possibilities—like becoming a lawyer—has already got you thinking about other possibilities that you might not have considered.

P: OK so you're saying I've got two options, either drive a truck or go to college.

TH: No. We're not done yet. We've just begun. One of the rules of brainstorming is to try to come up with a lot of job possibilities. The more options we come up with the more likely we will be to come up with a good one.

P: Well, I guess I could drive a cab, but I don't think I'd like that. The hours are long and the pay is lousy.

TH: Whoa. Whoa. Wait a second. Let's not forget our other rule. Remember we are not going to be critical about the possibilities at this point. We are going to judge how good each option is later on. Let's just make a long list of possibilities at this point. So, let's add driving a taxicab as another option on our list.

P: I could also drive my motorcycle.

TH: Tell me a little more about that. I'm not sure how driving a motorcycle is relevant to your objective of finding work.

P: I really like my motorcycle. It's one of the few things that I really enjoy. I heard that there is this place in the city that hires messengers on motorcycles because a bike can get through traffic better than a car.

TH: Terrific. That definitely sounds like a very relevant option. Let's add it to the list.

P: I guess I could always go back to my old job. I don't know if they would take me back.

TH: OK. That's an option that can be explored. Other ideas?

P: Gee, I don't know. Maybe there's another private trash-collecting outfit that might hire me. I know some guys who work for other companies. I could ask around and find out if anyone else is hiring drivers.

TH: Let's list that as an option.

P: You know I've thought about driving an 18-wheeler. There's good money in that, but you have to be on the road a lot.

TH: We've got several truck-driving options listed.

P: Yeah. That's true. That's about all I can think of.

TH: Why don't we look at what we have here on the list and see what other ideas might come to mind. Sometimes changing an option or combining possibilities leads to new alternatives that you might not have thought of before. Here's what we have on the list:

Drive a truck

Become a lawyer

Go back to school and get a degree

Drive a taxi

Become a motorcycle messenger
Return to your old job as a driver for a private sanitation company
Find a truck-driving job for another private sanitation company
Drive a tractor-trailer

TH: Let's use another brainstorming procedure at this point. It's called the strategy-tactics principle. What it suggests is that a good list should have several different general strategies for attacking a problem and for each general strategy we should identify several specific tactics or ways of putting the strategy into action.

P: I'm not sure I know what you mean.

TH: OK. Let's look at your list and group together those alternatives that seem to go together.

P: They all seem to go together.

TH: In what way?

P: Well, they are all things I could do.

TH: Right, but a couple of the possibilities are very different from the others. Look over the list and see if you can tell me which ones seem to go together as a group.

P: Well, I guess a lot of them are jobs that involve driving.

TH: Right. One general strategy or approach to the problem of finding work involves getting a job that involves driving. So we might label it the "Driving" strategy. Each of the different types of driving jobs—driving a truck, driving a taxi, driving a motorcycle—is an example of a tactic or a specific way of putting the strategy into action.

P: OK. I follow you now, and becoming a lawyer or going to school are different strategies.

TH: Right. And I think we can improve your list if we think of more strategies at this point.

P: Do you mean different ways of going about getting a job or do you mean different jobs?

TH: Let's consider both.

P: I guess I could look at the classified section of the newspaper.

TH: That's a terrific idea. Let's add it to the list as another strategy.

P: (Long pause) I really don't know what I would like to do or what I would be good at.

TH: Let's turn that around and make it a strategy.

P: What do you mean?

TH: Let's add: "Find out what jobs I would like and what jobs I would be good at" to the list.

P: But how do I find that out?

TH: One tactic that you could use might be to see a vocational counselor, someone whose main job is helping people to discover their occupational interests—what they like—and their occupational aptitudes—what they would be good at.

P: That sounds like something I should definitely have on the list.

TH: Let's put it down.

P: Can we go back to something else on the list.

TH: Sure.

P: You know these other strategies we have down—becoming a lawyer or getting more education—well, I just thought of something that combines the two of them. Maybe I could take some courses to become a legal assistant.

TH: Good thinking! Combining ideas to make new ideas is a great way to come up with creative possibilities. Let's list "Taking courses to become a legal assistant" as a tactic under the strategy, "Getting more education."

P: I've got another combination strategy. Maybe I should think about working and taking courses, maybe night classes, at the same time.

TH: You are really getting the hang of it. Let's keep going. Remember, the more ideas we come up with . . .

Clinical Comment

As illustrated in the preceding example, combining the three principles of brainstorming can lead to both productive and flexible thinking. Robert's initial approach to job finding was not only dichotomous (i.e., no job vs. taking an unsatisfying job), but also quite hopeless. By generating a wide range of possible options not previously identified, he was able to pursue other problem-solving tasks with more optimism and enthusiasm. The belief that one has only restricted options tends to also increase the sense of having little control, which can lead to further despondency and hopelessness. This problem-solving process, in particular, should be geared toward relieving, in part, the patient's pessimism.

ADDITIONAL AIDS FOR GENERATING ALTERNATIVES

Several additional sets of heuristics can be used by the therapist to assist patients in generating a wide range of creative solution possibilities. These include the use of combinations, modifications, models, and visualization (cf. D'Zurilla, 1986). Sample instructions to the patient for each of these procedures follow.

> *Combinations.* Combining ideas is sometimes an excellent way to develop new alternatives. Let's review your list of potential solutions and see if we might be able to combine some of the alternatives to develop new solutions that have advantages over the options already listed. As we review each alternative on the list, let's ask ourselves whether the item might be combined with some other alternative to produce a new solution.
>
> *Modifications.* As we review the list, let's also see if any of the solutions can be changed or elaborated on to improve the range of solution possibilities. Let's see if we can modify some of the alternatives and give them a new twist. Often, we can improve an alternative by magnifying it, making it stronger, larger, longer, or more intense. Sometimes, we might improve a solution by simplifying it, by making it smaller, slower, lower, lighter, or more streamlined. In other cases we might modify and improve an alternative by substituting another ingredient, process, place, or person, or by rearranging components, patterns, or approaches. So let's be sure to think about the possibility of modifying and elaborating our options to produce improved solution possibilities.
>
> *Models.* In developing new solution possibilities, it is sometimes helpful to bring to mind a person whom you admire and respect. Then ask yourself how he or she would approach this problem. What actions would that person take if faced with the same problematic circumstances? If you cannot think of a person whom you know personally, consider someone from the world of movies, books, or current events. For example, you might ask yourself how would 'Rocky,' Ghandi, or Oliver North, handle this problematic situation. Considering how others might approach a problem can help you to think of new solution options.
>
> *Visualization.* Another technique that can be used for generating solutions is visualization. Take a moment to close your eyes and imagine yourself in the problematic situation. Imagine yourself successfully coping with the problem. Think of what you would say and do to deal effectively with the situation. While you are imagining yourself in this situation, try to think of a different strategy or tactic that you can visualize yourself using to cope successfully with the problematic situation.

DIFFICULTIES IN GENERATING ALTERNATIVES

Three common difficulties can represent obstacles to the depressed patient's ability to generate a wide variety of solution possibilities. These include (1) emotional distress, (2) habit and convention, and (3) a lack of information (cf. D'Zurilla, 1986). This section presents several procedures for dealing with such difficulties.

Emotional Distress

Feelings of distress, such as anxiety or depression, can interfere with a patient's attention, concentration, and general ability to explore and manipulate ideas. It can inhibit the capacity to conceptualize fluently and flexibly and to generate appropriate and creative solution possibilities. In addition to problem-orientation training (see Chapter 7), several therapeutic strategies can be utilized to help patients overcome emotional distress in generating alternatives. They are cognitive restructuring, self-instruction, and relaxation training.

   1. *Cognitive Restructuring.*   Patients' emotional reactions are often direct consequences of the ways in which they perceive and interpret information about their problems (see Chapter 1). Frequently, their beliefs and expectations are inconsistent with the realities of the situation. The therapist can reduce emotional distress during problem solving by helping the patient to identify and correct cognitive distortions.

   Consider the following examples of the use of cognitive restructuring. Depressed patients often view themselves as inadequate and incapable of successfully dealing with their problems. In that situation, the therapist should attempt to identify invalid assumptions in the patient's thinking by asking questions such as: "What facts support the assumption that you are inadequate and incapable of changing your situation?" "What facts contradict this assumption?" "What alternative assumptions are possible?" The therapist can remind the patient to continue to be an investigative reporter in order to accurately obtain this information (see Chapter 8).

   Another common emotional block for depressed patients is anxiety centered around fear of failure. Fears that inhibit the generation of alternatives are often based on unrealistic and catastrophic appraisals of the likely consequences of change. To develop a more realistic assessment of the situation, the therapist might ask questions such as: "What have you got to lose by trying to change?" "What is the worst thing that can happen if you try but are unsuccessful in solving this problem?" and "What would happen to you if everything went wrong?" By making such information explicit, the patient can often successfully use analytic ability to overcome the fear of failure.

   2. *Self-Instruction.*   In addition to helping the patient correct distortions in thinking, the therapist can also utilize self-instructional techniques

to reduce emotional distress during the generation of alternatives. Constructive self-statements can divert attention away from unproductive, distress-producing thoughts. Constructive self-statements include "Slow down," "Easy does it," "One step at a time," "I can handle this situation," "Let me look at this as a challenge rather than a problem," "This is an opportunity for personal growth," "I have the skills to handle this, all I have to do is try," "I'm going to feel good about myself when I solve this problem." The patient can use such self-instructions to help replace emotionally arousing, dysfunctional worries and ruminations with coping statements that are likely to result in positive emotions and creative thinking.

3. *Relaxation Training.* In some situations, the patient's level of emotional arousal may be so high as to prevent meaningful attention to the task of generating alternatives. In such circumstances, the therapist should consider the use of relaxation methods to reduce the intensity of emotional distress directly. A variety of procedures may be employed including progressive muscle relaxation, deep breathing exercises, meditation, and imagery. Two advantages are inherent in the use of such techniques. First, it often lowers the patient's emotional arousal to the point of allowing attention to and concentration on the tasks of problem solving; and second, the relaxation procedure represents an additional coping strategy the patient can use to cope with emotional distress in the future (see Chapter 11).

Habit and Convention

A second set of common obstacles in the development of creative coping options are *habit* and *convention*. Frequently, patients feel uncomfortable in trying to change the way they have always approached coping with a problem. Often they may be reluctant to approach a real-life problem, particularly a personally difficult one, in a new and different way. As a consequence, it is not unusual for a patient to react automatically or cautiously with previously learned habits. The therapist may need to question the appropriateness and applicability of the patient's old way of generating solutions. Moreover, the therapist must challenge the patient to break out of the mold of conventional thinking and to approach the problem from a fresh and creative perspective.

In order to improve the development of new and original ideas, the therapist should focus initially on impersonal exercises for practice in overcoming the blocks of habit and convention. Sample exercises can include the use of brainstorming to develop creative uses for (1) a broom, (2) a wire coat hanger, or (3) a bar of soap. Once the patient has demonstrated the ability to generate creative and original solutions for impersonal problems, the therapist can initiate practice targeted at generating creative solutions for the real-life difficulties facing the patient.

Insufficient Information

A third difficulty that occurs in generating alternatives is a lack of relevant information about solution possibilities. For some difficult and highly specialized problems, the patient may not be able to come up with many solution alternatives with the potential to be effective. In such circumstances, the therapist should assist the patient in seeking information or advice about possible solutions. In some cases, another professional may be the appropriate expert to consult, and the therapist can provide a referral. For example, in the case of Robert, the depressed veteran who was unemployed (described earlier in this chapter), the therapist referred the patient to a vocational counselor for an assessment of the patient's occupational interests and aptitudes. In other situations, an appropriate expert may be another person who has had experience with a similar type of problem. In addition, patients can often gather relevant information by using community resources, such as libraries and public agencies. The therapist should take care to encourage the patient to ask for information about both the pros *and* cons of the different solution possibilities. By gathering information about the advantages and disadvantages of different options, the patient can later make an independent decision about which alternative to pursue.

PRACTICE WITH REAL-LIFE PROBLEMS

The keys to success in generating alternatives to real-life problems are practice, practice, and more practice. Figure 9.1 is a worksheet that may be helpful to patients. Note that a reminder is included concerning the three guiding principles of the brainstorming process.

SUMMARY

Training in the generation-of-alternatives procedure is geared to increase the likelihood of identifying solutions that are effective. According to the model, individuals are taught to use three brainstorming principles: quantity; deferment-of-judgment; and the strategy-tactics procedure. Use of these techniques can often help depressed individuals to recognize that

Name: _____   Date: _____

State the problem-solving goal (or subgoals if applicable):

Generate alternatives in concrete, unambiguous terms. Remember to use the following principles of idea production:

QUANTITY
DEFERMENT OF JUDGMENT
STRATEGIES-TACTICS

Figure 9.1. Generation of Alternatives Worksheet.

a wide variety of coping options are, in fact, available. In this manner, this problem-solving operation can be especially helpful in overcoming feelings of hopelessness and poor self-control.

The flexibility of thinking engendered in this training can also minimize the influence of certain depression-associated cognitive distortions (e.g., dichotomous thinking, catastrophizing). Moreover, this generalized flexible approach can facilitate the success of later problem-solving tasks (e.g., generating all possible consequences that might occur as a function of implementing a given alternative).

CHAPTER 10

Training in Decision Making

To be, or not to be: that is the question.
Whether 'tis nobler in the mind to suffer
The slings and arrows of outrageous fortune,
Or to take arms against a sea of troubles,
And by opposing end them?

SHAKESPEARE

During a problem-solving therapy group with a population of recently hospitalized psychiatric patients, one of the participants had criticized another member's contribution while the group was engaged in generating alternative solutions to a problem. The therapist reminded the judgmental patient that when generating alternatives, evaluation should be deferred in order to promote creativity and brainstorming. The patient smiled and stated, "Oh, that's right, we're just listing alternatives now. I'll wait until the next step [decision making] . . . then I'll tell him how stupid his ideas are!"

Although this patient could have provided more encouragement to his fellow group participant and was evaluating solution alternatives both prematurely and harshly, he was accurate in his recognition of a specific methodological point in the problem-solving process devoted to evaluating the available solution alternatives. His actual response, however, demonstrates the consequence of pursuing this process without a systematic and educative approach. The purpose of focusing specifically on decision making is to train individuals to strategically evaluate alternative solutions for a problem in a way that increases the likelihood of choosing the most effective solution(s). The ultimate goal is to select the best alternative or combination of alternatives, so as to maximize positive outcome and benefits for the individual while minimizing negative consequences or costs. Prediction of consequences for each solution alternative, or combination of alternatives, remains the central activity in this course of treatment. Patients are presented with the concept that the utility of any particular alternative is a joint function of the value and likelihood of

197

predicted consequences. In other words, for individuals to make the best decision possible, they need to assess both the long and short-term consequences, as well as the likelihood of carrying through each of the various alternatives. The solution that is chosen is the one that has the greatest utility (value and likelihood) associated with it.

It is helpful to estimate value and likelihood of alternatives separately in order to make the task of assessing utility more manageable. The most important criterion is an evaluation of the likelihood that a given alternative will produce outcomes that attain one's goals and overcome the relevant obstacles. As such, it is the first assessment made.

PREDICTING GOAL ATTAINMENT

Therapeutic Principle

The purpose of this strategy is to collaborate with the patient in predictively evaluating each alternative concerning the likelihood that, when implemented, it would provide a solution that meets the major goals established during the problem-definition-and-formulation process. Evaluation of each alternative in overcoming the identified obstacles is also a necessary part of this process. This procedure frequently reinforces past therapeutic work aimed at decreasing the patient's overgeneralizations. For most defined problems, there may exist several goals (one or two primary goals and subgoals) and several existing obstacles. By predicting each alternative's probability of successfully accomplishing goals and overcoming obstacles, individuals are encouraged to identify each solution's strong and weak points, rather than viewing them in overgeneralized or dichotomous terms such as "That's no good" or "That sounds silly, I couldn't do that." The individual is continually reminded, while engaging in this process, that no solution is perfect. However, by increasing problem-solving skills, the patient can achieve greater confidence in developing effective solutions.

Procedure

Prior to beginning this strategy, the patient is provided with a decision making worksheet on which to rate the various alternatives (see Figure 10.1). Because the patient may initially react to this aid as involving more paperwork, it is useful to explain that this worksheet helps to demonstrate the process at a slow-motion pace in order to illustrate the subtle benefits of coping with stressful problems in a more systematic way. The patient

ALTERNATIVE # RATING SCALE: 0 = Not likely 1 = Moderately likely 2 = Very likely	PRIMARY GOALS	SUBGOALS	OBSTACLES	LIKELIHOOD of IMPLEMENTATION	TIME/EFFORT	EMOTIONAL GAIN	MORALS/ETHICS	PERSONAL GROWTH	PHYSICAL	OTHER	FAMILY/FRIENDS	COMMUNITY	SHORT-TERM	LONG-TERM	OTHER	TOTAL

Figure 10.1. Decision Making Worksheet.

should also be instructed that there will be a cumulative tally of the overall adequacy of each alternative at the end of the process. Meanwhile, however, each alternative (as represented by a number on the worksheet) will be rated during this exercise for only the likelihood of meeting stated goals and overcoming obstacles.

The process may begin by quickly scanning the list to determine whether any alternatives stand out as obviously unrelated, or contraindicative, toward the relevant problem-solving goals. Such alternatives are discarded. Following this step, the therapist and the patient review each alternative and predict the probability that a particular solution will result in goal attainment. They follow this step with a similar prediction regarding the alternative's potential for successfully overcoming the major obstacles. It is important to remember that any impact upon intrapersonal and environmental concerns will be evaluated later, thus continuing the separation of an individual alternative's strengths and weaknesses. This separation helps to minimize or avoid the patient's overgeneralization. For example, the individual who has a loneliness problem may rate the alternative of visiting a singles bar to be a strong possible solution for the goal of meeting new people, as well as for overcoming the obstacle of having insufficient time to devote to this goal. The same alternative, however, may be rated less effective in overcoming obstacles when considering fears related to sexually transmitted diseases or the personal criterion of wanting intellectual stimulation to be part of a new companionship.

Following a brief task-oriented discussion, each alternative is then rated on a scale of 0–2, indicating the likelihood of successful completion of goals and coping with obstacles. According to this simple scale, 0 = Not likely, 1 = Moderately likely, and 2 = Very likely. The chief strategy for the therapist during this process is to keep the patient task focused, forestalling the patient's tendency to rate each alternative prematurely for criteria that will be addressed later.

Clinical Example

Terry was an 18-year-old high school student living in an urban area. She first entered treatment while residing in a youth residence, which occurred upon being rejected by her family. Initially referred following a brief hospitalization for a second suicide attempt (she had consumed an overdose of tranquilizers on both occasions), Terry appeared to be quite depressed (initial BDI score was 49). Her clinical symptoms included sadness, anger and crying outbursts, and strong feelings of hopelessness concerning what she perceived to be overwhelming problems and stressful life circumstances. She originally defined her chief problem areas as the following: poor family relationships (arguments and physical aggression toward her siblings and mother), social isolation at the youth residence, difficulty controlling her anger, confusion over future plans upon graduating from high school in a few months, and financial destitution.

During the process of problem definition, the first area she decided to address involved her recent separation from her family. Terry had left her family following a heated argument during which she criticized her mother for allowing her sister's boyfriend to live in the family home. She had engaged in an intensely emotional and physical argument with her sister and was told to leave the house after becoming violent. Terry had experienced extreme guilt and sadness concerning this event, and believed, "I will never be able to be with Mom again without terrible tension and anger." Additionally, her sister's boyfriend had continued to live with the family.

Over several sessions, Terry defined her chief problem in terms of the following goal: "To spend increased amounts of time visiting with my mother without the presence of heated arguments." Obstacles that were currently impeding goal attainment consisted of the following: (1) the level of guilt and anxiety she experienced whenever she visited her home, causing her to feel extremely vulnerable to any statements of criticism from her family; (2) her habituated pattern of responding to anxiety with angry and violent behavior over which she perceived having little control; and (3) the continued presence of her sister's boyfriend in the family home, which seemed to serve as a discriminative stimulus for her hostile outbursts.

During several brainstorming sessions, the following alternative solutions were generated by the patient:

1. Talk to older sister and tell her to have boyfriend leave the house
2. Make a special time to talk with mother alone when other family members are not present
3. Visit home as if nothing happened and make a special effort to be cordial to sister's boyfriend
4. Begin family visits by taking out younger brother and sisters in order to break the ice with older sister and mother
5. Approach mother and sister in a totally different way, expressing feelings in an assertive, but nonthreatening manner
6. Bring a trusted counselor (Laurie) from the youth center along on home visit in order to have an ally to keep her under control
7. Write a letter to her mother and sister prior to a family visit stating her goals in a positive and constructive fashion

8. Talk to her sister's boyfriend secretly and ask him to leave their home
9. Talk to her mother and sister during a planned family therapy session
10. Apologize to her mother and sister for her past behavior and ask their forgiveness
11. Hire a street gang to threaten her sister's boyfriend so that he will leave the house
12. Accept the possibility that she may never be able to go home again
13. Accept the possibility that her mother will never understand her viewpoint
14. Bring her mother a gift to start out a visit on the right foot
15. Introduce her sister to some men at the youth residence to make her leave her boyfriend and kick him out of the house

The session represented by the therapy transcript that follows occurred during one of three sessions that focused on evaluating these alternatives. In this sequence, Terry has begun to rate each alternative for the likelihood of meeting her desired goals.

THERAPIST (TH): Bearing in mind that this is a time to focus on specific criteria for each alternative, let's review and rate the solutions you have come up with in terms of the likelihood of meeting your goals. In looking over the list, can you immediately disregard any of these as very unlikely, if not impossible, in meeting your stated goals?

PATIENT (P): Well, it could be that what I said about getting the gang after Adam (sister's boyfriend), was 'cause I was so mad. That wouldn't make my relationship with my mother or sister any better, no way. Besides I don't have no money!

TH: We probably can rule out this alternative as very unlikely in helping you reach your goals. But remember, consideration of whether or not you can afford an alternative financially will be rated later. It may sound kind of picky right now, because you're disregarding this alternative anyway, but it's important while learning to find effective solutions for these very difficult problems to practice thinking systematically.

P: You mean that for now, even if I think that, for instance, it would be real hard for me to do one of these, but it would probably be a good choice for just meeting the goals, then I rate it high for meeting goals? I'll rate it low for how hard it is to do later . . . (refers to worksheet) like where it says "Likelihood of Implementation" or "Time/Effort"?

TH: That's it exactly! Good! Let's start with the first alternative that you listed—to try to talk your older sister into having her boyfriend leave the house. How likely would this alternative be in helping you meet your primary goal of spending increased time with your family without the presence of heated arguments?

P: If I could talk her into it and she don't jump on me, then I would say moderate, because I still have a lot of mistakes to make up for (enters 1 in the appropriate column).

TH: OK. Now consider the obstacles that are present. Would this alternative help you to overcome your feelings of sadness and tension when you go home?

P: Not much. I'd still have to face my mother. I have to give that a 0.

TH: OK. How helpful would this alternative be in helping you get over your past ways of coping with your anger?

P: Maybe a little if I really talked to her and communicated instead of just yelling at her. But I probably couldn't help myself any better than before. Give that a 1.

TH: And the obstacle concerning your sister's boyfriend in the house?

P: Well, if he was gone, that wouldn't even be an obstacle anymore! So, if I could talk her into getting rid of him, I'd give that a 2!

TH: Good work, Terry. Do you notice how, just in examining goals and obstacles, you can see that the same alternative can have several different ratings?

P: Yeah. I never really thought of it that way.

TH: What about the next alternative, Number 2? How would you rate it for its likelihood of meeting your goals?

P: Can I ask you something? What if, after going through all this, I still don't have a better relationship with my mom and family . . . what then?

TH: Terry, let's focus on the goals at hand. You've worked hard to define one goal toward a better relationship as spending more time with your family without the presence of heated arguments. At this moment we're getting so close to a well-planned solution for you to implement toward that goal. It's only natural, since this goal is important to you, that you have some concerns that things may not turn out as you had hoped. The only way to actually find out about its effectiveness, however, is to make some educated choices and put a plan into action. It's your goal . . . we can spend some time worrying together or continue to come up with our best prediction for a plan. Straying from our work is OK, just as long as you're aware of what you're doing. Want to take a break?

P: (Laughs) Not when you put it that way—I like the way you get me back on track—feels like it's my own idea.

TH: Isn't it?

P: I guess so.

TH: Where were we?

P: Rating alternative Number 2. OK. If I set up time to talk to my mother alone, without everyone else around, I will be spending more time with her. I guess I would give that a 2 rating.

TH: What rating would you give this alternative with reference to its usefulness in overcoming the three main obstacles you listed?

P: Well, I'm still going to feel real guilty and afraid I'll have a fight with her—so I'd have to say 0 in overcoming that obstacle. And I'll still have the same problem with my own hostility and temper, so 0 for that obstacle, too. But being able to see her without Adam around, even if he's still living there, will be a little better. At least I won't see him grinning at me, like he won, so I'll rate that a 1. After we're done, I might want to combine some of the best things to do.

TH: Excellent idea!

Clinical Comment

During this session, Terry appears to have been able to engage in a systematic evaluation of each alternative, targeting one criterion at a time. To her, it represents a new skill. Although she is oriented to the process, and working through the problem quite effectively, it is evident also that there are emotional intrusions concerning past habits of overgeneralization and fears of losing her family's love that serve to throw her off track without therapeutic supervision. At this point, it is important to acknowledge the presence of habituated, emotionalizing past ways of coping as predictable and acceptable, providing they are acknowledged as thinking habits that will occur less frequently if reinforced less often.

The patient's final comments in the transcript illustrate an additional benefit of rating each alternative on several different types of criteria. After the ratings are complete and the best alternative has been chosen, any given solution, despite its high overall cumulative rating, may have important negative points. It may be possible to strengthen the ultimate solution by adding components of other alternatives that were rated highly on those points of weakness. For example, Terry may recognize that although her second alternative is likely to meet her stated goals, it was not rated highly regarding its likelihood of overcoming all three major obstacles. If this alternative were to be chosen as the most desirable, it would be helpful to add at least a part of another alternative that received a rating of 1 or 2 on overcoming the first two obstacles.

ASSESSING THE LIKELIHOOD OF IMPLEMENTATION

Therapeutic Principle

Although the concept of developing likelihood estimates was initially introduced to the patient as an assessment of the likelihood that various alternatives can achieve stated goals, the next step is to assess the probability that the particular patient is able to carry out the alternatives. This step in the process frequently provides useful information concerning adjunctive therapeutic work that may be helpful in better preparing the patient to implement a difficult alternative that otherwise has high utility.

Further, several additional subgoals may be developed to facilitate a desirable alternative, where the main weakness lies in the patient's current ability to carry it out in its optimal form. For example, if Terry's alternative of buying her mother a present were to be highly rated in terms of the likelihood of meeting stated goals and overcoming obstacles, as well as highly rated on all the intrapersonal and interpersonal criteria that follow, not having the money to purchase the present might represent a low rating regarding her ability to implement an otherwise desirable alternative. In that case, she might develop a subgoal of identifying a means of obtaining enough money to buy a present as part of her eventual plan for implementation. Following is the actual transcript in which assessment of the likelihood of being able to carry out alternatives was discussed with the patient.

THERAPIST (TH): In looking over your list of alternatives and your first ratings of how likely it is that each one of these would actually achieve your goals, let's quickly review the list again and see how likely it is that you would be able to carry out these alternatives. How about Number 2, making time to talk to your mother alone without other people present. How likely would it be that you could carry this out?

PATIENT (P): Well, it would be pretty easy to find a time when my mother is alone, like when my little brother and sister are at school and my sister and her boyfriend are out working. But where do you think I got this stubborn personality from? My mother may say one thing, or I'll feel the tension, and I'll lash out and I won't be talking very calmly to her. I don't think I could stay calm in that situation— which means not likely at all.

TH: That may be the case with some otherwise very useful alternatives. Can you find any others that you listed and gave a high likelihood rating to as far as goals, but would have difficulty implementing?

P: Yes. All those alternatives where my hostility problem makes it too hard for me, like this one (points to Number 5)—approaching my mother and sister in a whole different way. That would be real good if I could change. I want to, but it's like some kind of evil force— how angry I get—and I can feel it sometimes now at the residence. I'm getting real mad at this one girl who knows everybody's business and makes people feel bad. Sometimes I want to tell her that she better watch out for me! I started telling my counselor, Laurie, about it, and she said she'd look into it, but she's leaving 'cause she's going to have a baby!

TH: Laurie is leaving? When did you find this out?

P: Two days ago. And I think I'm going to be different with my new counselor. I might give her a hard time because I'm getting mad about things going on at this residence!

TH: Do you think some of these angry feelings might have to do with Laurie leaving?

P: But I really like Laurie. She can't help it, it's not bad that she wants to have a baby. I feel like I just got to know her though and started to really trust her. Then she's leaving. I guess . . . sure I'm mad. But I shouldn't be. She's so nice. Now I'm starting to feel so tense when I'm with her, too.

TH: You know, Terry, these angry feelings appear to be very similar to how you were feeling when you first came here, shortly after you left your mother's house. You love your mother but felt kind of betrayed when your sister's boyfriend moved in without your approval. You felt bad and guilty when you were angry. Soon you started feeling sad at your mother and angry toward everyone else. Finally, you became aggressive and threatened your sister. Now you are starting to sound somewhat threatening toward your housemate and it's right after you experience a disappointment about someone who you care about losing.

P: Yeah . . . yeah. I see what you mean. My way of getting mad and hurt turns out to end up with me hurting someone. But I don't think I'm really like that. I wish I could learn a better way to talk with Laurie and my mother without being so uptight.

TH: Maybe there's a way you could turn the alternative of approaching your mother into a whole different way more likely for you to implement.

P: Could you help me with that? To have my feelings, but handle them different?

TH: I think we could work together on that as kind of a subgoal if this is the alternative you ultimately choose. It seems as though it might be helpful as well with the way you handle this current problem at the residence.

Clinical Comment

The therapist has found it useful to sidetrack a bit from the task at hand during this strategy, since the coping deficits that have surfaced as roadblocks to successful implementation of an otherwise useful alternative are particularly relevant to another current problem that the patient is experiencing. This suggests that there are very predictable interpersonal situations in which the patient appears more vulnerable to the triggering of angry emotional experiences, as well as more likely to become overtly threatening and aggressive. This is valuable information for the patient to obtain, since developing a subgoal of increasing anger management skills might also provide her with increased abilities to implement meaningful plans for other interpersonal problems that she is either currently experiencing or will experience in the future.

CONDUCTING A COST/BENEFIT ANALYSIS OF ALTERNATIVES

Therapeutic Principle

The purpose of this strategy is to provide the patient with a systematic set of guidelines by which to evaluate the value for each alternative. This set of ratings concludes the assessment of the total utility of each generated potential solution. The therapist helps the patient to complete the decision-making process by weighing the positive and negative consequences (cost/benefit analysis) of the various alternative solutions. This task requires the patient to shift to a new means of analyzing each alternative. Rather than asking whether or not a given solution can attain the stated goals, the patient now analyzes the likely effects of each solution regarding both positive and negative consequences across many intrapersonal and interpersonal criteria. Certain of these criteria are extremely idiosyncratic, such as moral, ethical, and religious concerns. Addressing such individual differences serves to state to the patient that *his* or *her* criteria are the most important. Further, it communicates respect for those values and a sense that the consequences that the patient will be required to live with concern the therapist, rather than the enforcement of a therapeutically "wise" or "mature" decision.

Procedure

This procedure consists of establishing a rating for each alternative, based on the previous 3-point scale, corresponding to the following values: mostly negative consequences (0); a relatively equal number of positive and negative consequences (1); and mostly positive consequences (2). The following consequences are provided, in the order presented, on the decision-making worksheet (see Figure 10.1): personal consequences; social consequences; short-term consequences; and long-term consequences. Below is a list of the specific consequences that are evaluated within the personal and social categories.

Personal Consequences

1. *Time/Effort.* Estimation of how much personal time and effort is involved in implementing each alternative and how it might impinge upon time committed to other important personal concerns.

2. *Emotional Cost or Gain.* Prediction of emotional ramifications for the individual that might occur by implementing a particular alternative.

3. *Consistency with Moral/Ethical Values.* Assessment of each alternative in terms of its consistency with one's current moral and ethical values. If for example, implementation of a given alternative involves a change in basic moral values, it is predictable that the emotional cost involved in making this change may be quite dramatic.

4. *Effects on Personal Growth.* Assessment of each alternative in terms of the opportunity it provides for new learning experiences, sense of achievement, or an increase in self-esteem or self-competency.

5. *Physical Well-Being.* Assessment of drain upon physical resources of individual.

6. *Other Problem-Specific Personal Consequences.* Assessment of predicted outcome in areas specific to the problem of concern (e.g., financial consequences).

Social (Interpersonal) Consequences

1. *Effects on Family and Friends.* Analysis of the impact of each alternative on those people involved in significant relationships with the individual, especially if they are involved directly with the problem at hand.

2. *Effects on Community/Neighborhood.* Assessment of how each alternative may affect an individual's social or employment environment. For example, a woman with a history of involvement in voluntary community service, if returning to compensatory employment, may want to consider the impact of various alternatives upon her relationship with the pertinent community agencies.

3. *Problem-Specific Social Consequences.* Assessment of any additional effects of each alternative on the social environment specific to the problem at hand.

Clinical Example

In a subsequent therapy session, Terry, the patient described earlier, continued her decision-making process by conducting a cost/benefit analysis of the various consequences for each alternative. The transcript presented here focuses on her evaluation of just one of the alternatives from the previously presented list.

THERAPIST (TH): Let's review the positive and negative consequences regarding the fifth alternative that you listed. What would you predict that increasing your assertiveness skills in therapy, prior to making a visit home, would cost you regarding investment of time?

PATIENT (P): A lot of time! I really have a problem with my hostility. I keep it all inside me, then when my mother "pushes my buttons," crash! I really feel like I could hit her or something. It would take me a long time before I wouldn't be afraid of hurting her. Give that a 0.

TH: What would you predict regarding emotional benefits to you?

P: I'd rate that a 2. That could only change my personality for the better— like now, with talking to Laurie about her leaving the residence.

TH: What would be the cost or benefits to your moral beliefs and values?

P: Well, the Bible says I should feel love, not hate or anger. I still feel bad getting so mad, but I guess God would want me to show it without hurting my family if I'm going to feel it. So I'd say, some good and some bad. Can I give that a 1?

TH: It's your rating. You're the best judge of the consequences concerning your own moral and religious principles. How about the other personal consequences?

P: My personal growth would definitely be a 2. If I could learn not to be so hostile, that would help a whole lot of problems . . . like with that girl at the youth residence . . . and when boyfriends start to remind me of my father and the way he abused me.

TH: I think so, too. We have spent some time understanding how upsetting those memories can be. If you gave yourself the chance, as you are doing now, we may be able to help you make them hurt less.

P: They say time heals wounds, but I guess there's some things we can do to help time.

TH: I couldn't have phrased it better. How about this same alternative regarding your physical well-being?

P: (Smiles) Well, if I could learn to show my anger better, I'd probably get in a lot less fights.

TH: True, but that's not exactly what I meant. One physical concern you may want to consider is all the stress-related physical symptoms you have described to me, like your headaches, body weakness, feeling drained, and fatigue. Do you see any negative or positive consequences that might occur regarding this alternative's impact upon your personal health?

P: Yeah. I bet if I didn't spend so much energy worrying and crying all the time, and I could get my feelings out and over with, I'd feel a little better. Give that a 1 or 2.

TH: Which one?

P: Give it a 1.

TH: Can you think of any other personal consequences?

P: My school stuff. Right now one of the only things that's been going right for me is school. I don't want to mess that up, but I feel like I'm so busy thinking about my family and how mad I am, I can't concentrate sometimes. That would probably get better too. Give that a 1 for "other."

TH: Moving on to the social consequences category, what would you predict in terms of cost/benefit to your friends and/or family?

P: Well, if I took time to communicate my anger better, my mother would probably not have such an "attitude" with me, but she still does not want to hear me tell her she is doing something wrong, so that would be a 1 at the most, even if it was that much.

TH: How about the community you live in, for example, at the youth residence?

P: For my family problem, it wouldn't make too much difference to them. I guess they would feel a little better around me if I wasn't so bothered by bad feelings—sometimes I take it out on them. Actually I do that a lot—give that a 2.

TH: Let's now predict consequences for the short term.

P: I don't want to criticize you, but I think it would take a lot to help me with my hostility—so nothing would change for awhile—I have to say 0.

TH: What about the long-term consequences?

P: Well, that's a different story. That would probably be better, but I still would never feel OK about Adam living in my mother's house, even if I could communicate that better. I'd have to say—give it a 1.

Clinical Comment

As the dialogue demonstrates, Terry is beginning to understand that specific alternatives may contribute to certain positive personal and social consequences but can be less satisfactory in other aspects. At several points during this session, it became evident that for this alternative (i.e., to become more assertive) to be chosen, the long-term, intrapersonal, and interpersonal positive consequences would have to outweigh the time, effort, and delay of gratification involved in its implementation. This illustrates the purpose in eventually providing a summed score for each alternative at the end of the process.

Further, despite many ratings of the various alternative solutions in the three strategies presented here, almost no alternative directly addresses the obstacle created by Terry's sister's boyfriend continuing to live in the family home. Terry mentions again, at the end of this sequence, some sense of futility concerning this one fact. In such a case, where a very limited number of solutions appear available to address an obstacle directly, the problem solver may need to consider several questions. These include: "Do I have enough information concerning this obstacle?" "Did I define the problem correctly?" "Are my goals too high?" and/or "Did I generate enough options?" Further, this may require a quick visit back to prior problem-solving tasks before continuing.

In Terry's case, a review of the problem-definition phase indicated that it was not the presence of her sister's boyfriend in the home that incited her so, but the fact that he spent most nights in her sister's room, which was shared by two younger siblings. Her third obstacle was modified to state that it was the presence of Adam in her sister's room that contributed to the problem. Alternatives listed previously regarding how to get Adam out of the house were also modified to describe means of facilitating a change in sleeping arrangements.

SUMMING UP AND MAKING FINAL ADJUSTMENTS

Using the ratings provided by the previously demonstrated strategies, the patient is then instructed to sum the ratings for each alternative in order to provide an overall score. The alternative solutions with the higher ratings are considered to possess the greatest utility and serve as the basis of a potential solution plan to be implemented. Several alternatives may be of value and combined for the following reasons. First, there may be several tie scores; it is not necessary to disregard an effective solution if both alternatives may be incorporated. Second, it is extremely helpful to review the individual ratings for the highest rated alternative and search for areas of weakness. The patient can then review the other alternatives to locate the ones that particularly address these areas of weakness, and if possible, incorporate them into the most highly rated solution.

The final worksheet completed by Terry demonstrates the strategy to combine alternatives. Shown in Figure 10.2, the highest rated alternative was the fifth one originally generated (i.e., approaching her family in an honest and assertive manner with the subgoal of increasing her anger management and assertiveness skills in therapy prior to the next home visit). Additionally, she chose to include initial visits with her younger siblings as a means of breaking the ice and providing her with some short-term benefits of increased satisfaction with family members while working with the therapist on skill-building techniques.

PLANNING THE STRATEGY

As the final step in the decision-making process, the patient in collaboration with the therapist devises the actual plan for implementation. Particularly when working on initial and complex problems, therapist involvement may be more direct. The therapist, however, should remain flexible in this regard, individualizing the needs of each therapy situation.

The plan should be as specific as possible, in order to predict areas of uncertainty, develop any subgoals that may have been overlooked, and maximize the patient's probability of achieving at least partial success with the first problem-solving effort. A positive result increases the likelihood that the patient will use the process in the future. Further, several

Figure 10.2. Terry's Completed Decision Making Worksheet.

ALTERNATIVE # RATING SCALE: 0 = Not likely, 1 = Moderately likely, 2 = Very likely	PRIMARY GOALS	SUBGOALS	OBSTACLES	LIKELIHOOD of IMPLEMENTATION	TIME/EFFORT	EMOTIONAL GAIN	MORALS/ETHICS	PERSONAL GROWTH	PHYSICAL	OTHER	FAMILY/FRIENDS	COMMUNITY	SHORT-TERM	LONG-TERM	OTHER	TOTAL
1	1		0/1/2	1	2	0	2	0	1		0	1	1	0		12
2	2		0/0/1	2	2	1	1	1	1		1	1	1	1		15
3	2		2/0/1	0	0	0	0	0	0		2	0	2	0		9
4	1		0/0/0	2	2	1	1	1	1		1	1	1	1		13
5	2		2/2/0	0	0	2	1	2	1	1	1	2	0	2		18
6	1		1/1/0	2	1	1	1	1	1		1	1	2	0		14
7	1		1/1/0	2	2	0	1	0	1		1	1	1	0		12
8	0		0/1/1	0	1	0	0	0	1		1	0	1	0		6
9	2		2/1/0	1	1	1	0	0	1		2	1	1	0		15
10	2		2/0/0	1	1	0	0	0	0		1	0	1	0		8
11	discard															
12	0		0/1/0	0	2	0	0	0	0		0	1	0	0		4
13	0		0/1/0	0	2	1	1	1	0		0	1	0	1		8

alternatives should be implemented simultaneously as a means of attacking the problem from a number of perspectives.

Clinical Example

Terry's final plan was developed as follows:

1. She would schedule additional therapy sessions (3 times per week) for 4 weeks in order to engage in anger management and assertiveness training. This would not only accelerate her learning, but would serve as a focus in her life and as a distraction from "just waiting" until she could feel comfortable spending time with her mother.
2. She would call her mother in order to explain her plan and ask her to mutually agree to meet together in the future.
3. She would practice her new skills, first in therapy sessions, using a roleplay format, and later at the residence with her counselor and fellow residents. Finally, she would use these new skills to better communicate with her family.
4. She would spend several hours on the weekend taking her two younger siblings to the park and museums, as a short-term reinforcement for herself as well as them.
5. She agreed to avoid all physical violence while this plan was in effect. If she believed that at any time she might lose control, she further agreed that she would call the therapist prior to any incidence of aggression.

SUMMARY

This chapter has presented the clinical guidelines involved in the process of decision making (evaluation and selection of previously generated alternatives). This process requires establishing which alternative or combination of alternatives has the greatest utility (likelihood and value) associated with it. Further, throughout the decision-making process, it is not only possible, but also helpful, to occasionally circle back to previous problem-solving phases of treatment in order to redefine goals, reassess orientation, or generate additional alternatives.

Finally, emphasis was placed on the importance of constructing with the patient a multifaceted and specific implementation plan, maximizing the probability of an initial successful problem-solving experience.

CHAPTER 11

Training in Solution Implementation and Verification

> *Thank Heaven! The crisis—*
> *The danger is passed,*
> *And the lingering illness*
> *Is over at last—*
> *And the fever called "Living"*
> *Is conquered at last.*
>
> EDGAR ALLEN POE

Up to this point, the quality or effectiveness of any identified solution to a given problem remains hypothetical only. Although many of the previous problem-solving tasks required certain behavioral skills (i.e., gathering information, generating alternatives), the activities thus far in the process were primarily cognitive in nature. The last component in the overall problem-solving model consists of the actual *implementation* of the identified solution alternative(s) and an evaluation of its effectiveness after it has been carried out.

From the perspective of a feedback loop, implementing a solution provides valuable information about (1) the effectiveness of the solution, and (2) the accuracy and/or efficacy of an individual's performance regarding previous problem-solving tasks (i.e., problem definition, generating alternatives, decision making). Further, it can facilitate a positive problem orientation given that the problem is resolved. More specifically, problem resolution or effective coping reinforces a sense of self-efficacy and adaptive beliefs concerning problems in living. This feedback cannot occur in the absence of solution implementation. Additionally, if the individual does not attend to or focus on the actual effects of the implemented solution plan, it is also possible to minimize the feedback potential.

Training in this last problem-solving component, then, involves the following four specific tasks:

1. Implementation of the solution
2. Observation of the actual outcome
3. Evaluation of the effectiveness of the solution
4. Self-reinforcement if problem is solved; troubleshooting if problem is not resolved

SOLUTION IMPLEMENTATION

Therapeutic Principle

After the patient has engaged in the four previous problem-solving components, it is possible to perceive the problem as now solved symbolically. However, in order to oppose the "slings and arrows of outrageous fortune," the patient now needs to carry out the identified solutions in real life. Depressed patients require much encouragement in order to implement their solutions. Feelings of hopelessness will often interfere with the patient's ability to put a solution into effect. It is possible also that a fear of failing may inhibit the desire to engage in this last problem-solving phase. Lastly, the patient may be unconvinced that his or her problem-solving ability has improved to the degree of really identifying effective solutions. At this point, the therapist may need to review that aspect of the orientation training that pertains to an approach/avoidance style (i.e., "It is better to confront a problem rather than to avoid it"). Additionally, it may be necessary to engage the patient in an exercise that focuses on predicting the consequences of *not* implementing a solution. This set of consequences can then be compared with those previously identified during the decision-making phase regarding the cost/benefit analysis.

Procedure

If a particular patient appears to be hesitant to implement a solution, the problem-solving therapist should encourage generation of a list of possible consequences if the problem is not resolved. Although this list will strongly resemble aspects of the patient's initial complaints (e.g., "If I don't get a new job, my family will starve!" "If my wife and I don't start relating to each other better, then we might wind up getting a divorce"), it is imperative to underscore the *realistic* consequences of the unresolved problem. Moreover, these consequences are compared to those predicted positive outcomes resulting from the cost-benefit analysis conducted during decision making. Figure 11.1 contains a worksheet that can be useful for such a comparison.

Name: _____ Date: _____

Instructions. In Column A, list as many possible outcomes that you can identify that might occur if your problem is *not* resolved. In Column B, list those positive effects associated with a potentially effective solution that you previously identified during the decision-making phase. To help generate these lists, use the brainstorming techniques that you have already learned.

A. Consequences if problem is *not resolved*	B. Predicted consequences of chosen solution plan

Figure 11.1. Solution Implementation Worksheet.

Clinical Example

One recent patient, Judy, responded well to the earlier parts of problem-solving training. However, when it was time to actually implement her solution plan, she remained hesitant, suggesting, "Maybe I should continue to generate more alternatives—it's possible that I may have missed some." Upon further probing, however, it became apparent that she harbored fears concerning her ability to cope effectively and to successfully resolve her major problems. At this point, the therapist decided initially to review the previous reversed advocate role-play exercise (see Chapter 7) conducted during problem-orientation training. As a second therapeutic strategy, Judy was encouraged to use the comparison worksheet. The following is a portion from a session that focused on this exercise.

THERAPIST (TH): OK, Judy. Last session I had requested that you complete the worksheet that I gave you. Did you have a chance to do it this week?

PATIENT (P): I was supposed to list some of the consequences if my problem of getting a new job wasn't solved, right?

TH: Yes, as well as listing some of the positive consequences that you identified when we first began evaluating the alternative solutions.

P: I did that also.

TH: Good! What were some of the consequences if you didn't get a new job?

P: Well, I guess that I would still feel horrible about myself. I know that I should get out of my present job . . . if I don't, I'll think of myself as a big chicken!

TH: So, one of the possible consequences involves a negative evaluation. Is that right?

P: Yeah . . . I really wouldn't feel good about myself at all.

TH: Are there any other consequences that you identified?

P: Actually, I thought of a whole lot. Another is that I would continue to have a lousy salary! Without more money, I'll never be able to get a place of my own and will continue to have problems with my dizzy roommate, Jan. Like I told you before, even though she seems nice on the outside, she always stabs people in the back, saying nasty things about them to others.

TH: OK. Staying in your present job, then, prevents you from having more money that can be used to satisfy certain of your other goals.

P: Yeah.

TH: Any others?

P: I've listed several more, but they all have to do with having to deal with my bitchy roommate.

TH: OK. Now let's review the possible consequences if you actually implement the solution plan that we talked about.

P: It almost seems like the exact opposite of the other list. If I get a new, high-paying job, which I think exists out there, I'll start to feel better about myself. After what we discussed, I realize that not all of my problems will be solved. But I believe I would be happier.

TH: Can you be a little more specific?

P: OK, like I was saying, it seems the exact opposite of the other list. If I get the new job, I can make more money. I would be able to get a small apartment of my own. Most important, I would feel really good about myself for taking a risk for once in my life!

TH: I can certainly understand how you might feel in that regard. Judy, when you looked over both lists, what was your reaction?

P: I started to actually get mad at myself for being afraid of trying! I realized that if I don't do something to help me, nobody else will. If I don't solve this problem, then I stay depressed.

TH: OK, Judy. What do you think you are going to do?

P: I'm going to give myself a chance and carry out my solution plan.

TH: Good!

Clinical Comment

In the preceding illustration, Judy, in comparing the possible consequences of *not* solving her problem with those associated with solving the problem, had begun to feel more motivated to implement her solution plan. This exercise can facilitate movement toward overcoming motivational difficulties or fears of failure. It may be important for the therapist to initially address subgoals that have a higher probability of being reached in order to provide for a reinforcing experience early in treatment. As noted in Chapter 6, this shaping procedure is especially relevant for depressed individuals with strong beliefs of poor self-efficacy.

In addition to motivation problems that may inhibit the solution-implementation process, it is possible that certain behavioral skill deficits prevent the individual from implementing a solution in its optimal form. Remember that an important criterion in evaluating alternatives during the decision-making phase is an estimation of the likelihood that the problem solver is actually capable of carrying out a particular solution optimally (see Chapter 10). Even if a solution is rated as potentially effective concerning its ability to attain one's goals, it may be rated poorly with regard to its probability of ever being carried out. At this point, the therapist and patient need to collaboratively decide whether training in specific skills may be necessary. For instance, in the above clinical example, Judy may need training in job-finding skills. If the therapist has some expertise in this area, it may be appropriate to change directions in treatment temporarily to focus on skills training. However, it may also be appropriate to suggest to Judy the possibility of seeking such training elsewhere (e.g., career development service).

Such training should be viewed as one alternative to pursue among the various additional solutions that the patient generated previously. For example, in the previous chapter, Terry, who was experiencing difficulties with her family, decided to implement various solutions while simultaneously engaged in assertiveness and anger management training with her therapist. Depending on the nature of both the problem and the identified solution plan, skills training may be conducted in tandem with the implementation of other patient-generated alternatives. Table 11.1 contains a list of common skills in which a particular patient may require additional training to facilitate the solution-implementation process. This table dis-

---

TABLE 11.1.   Cognitive-Behavioral Performance Skills (Problem-Focused and Emotion-Focused)

Problem-Focused Coping Skills

Assertiveness
Job skills (job finding, interview skills)
Parenting or child rearing
Financial management
Academics
Conflict resolution
Communication
Self-help or management
Social skills (interpersonal skills)

Emotion-Focused Coping Skills

Cognitive restructuring
Relaxation methods (muscle relaxation exercises, breathing
   exercises, meditation, biofeedback)
Positive imagery
Self-control desensitization
Distraction and perspective taking
Physical exercise
Positive/rational self-statements

---

tinguishes between problem-focused and emotion-focused strategies that might be included depending on the nature of the overall problem-solving goals.

In essence, following the philosophy of the problem-solving model, the decision to make at this point entails choosing between two directions: (1) returning to certain previous problem-solving operations (i.e., generation of alternatives and decision making) in order to identify a different solution plan; or (2) reformulating the overall definition of the problem situation so that it includes a statement about overcoming the obstacles related to effective coping *performance* (i.e., optimal solution implementation). In further keeping with the model, however, long-range treatment plans should focus on the second option if the skill deficit lies within an area that can continue to influence the likelihood of similar problems occurring in the future. If Judy, for example, attempts to find a new job by implementing a solution plan that, although hypothetically effective, she cannot carry out because of poor job-finding or interviewing skills, she may in fact become more depressed when her problem is not resolved (see also clinical example of Terry in Chapter 10).

MONITORING AND EVALUATING THE SOLUTION OUTCOME

Therapeutic Principle

After the solution is implemented, the problem solver's work still remains incomplete. The next phase of this operation entails monitoring the effects of the solution after it is carried out and evaluating the actual outcome relative to the desired goals. The first step involves a combination of self-monitoring and observation, whereby the therapist teaches the patient to keep track of the actual effects of the solution. Depending upon the nature of the problem and the implemented solution plan, self-monitoring can take a wide variety of forms. For example, Judy, in the preceding illustration, may record the actual number of job interviews that she obtains as a consequence of her solution plan. Terry, in the clinical example described in Chapter 10, may use a rating system that focuses on her degree of satisfaction in a family visit with her mother and sister. Other self-monitoring formats may focus on response frequency, intensity, duration, or latency (cf. Mahoney, 1977; Nelson, 1977).

Although the ultimate measure of problem resolution revolves around the actual products of the solution (i.e., presence or absence of goal attainment), it is also important to include additional assessment measures that focus on associated consequences as highlighted during the decision-making process. More specifically, in addition to recording whether or not one's goal has been reached (e.g., whether Judy actually obtained a new job), the patient should also focus on additional personal consequences (e.g., how much time and effort was involved, emotional well-being, etc.); interpersonal consequences (e.g., effects on others); and short- and long-term effects. In certain cases, even though the patient actually attains the goal, the presence of various negative consequences engendered by the implemented solution may create additional problems and make the solution less effective overall. To make these evaluations requires concrete information.

Keeping this record also minimizes the tendency for depressed individuals to focus on negative consequences as compared to positive outcomes. Collection of data concerning the actual consequences of a solution can facilitate more accurate appraisal of the overall impact.

Lastly, it is important to develop with the patient a time frame in which to monitor such consequences. On one hand, it is important to allow sufficient time for the solution plan to take effect. For example, for Judy to expect a job offer within a few days of sending out résumés is unrealistic. On the other hand, an upper time limit also needs to be identified in order to be able to decide whether the solution can ever be effective. After several months without job interviews, it may be important for Judy and her therapist to devise a new solution plan.

Essentially, after implementing a solution, the patient uses some form of a measurement system to concretely assess its overall effects. This task is a prerequisite for the next task of *evaluating* or judging the actual quality of the solution plan. At the end of the decision-making process, various predictions were made concerning the potential of the solution plan to have certain specific outcomes. With the information obtained through the self-monitoring procedure, the problem solver is now able to compare these predictions with the actual consequences in the real-life situation. This matching procedure should again focus on the overall effects of the solution, and not only on goal attainment.

Procedure

Figure 11.2 contains a solution verification worksheet that can be helpful in this matching process. Essentially, the patient is encouraged to list both the actual *and* predicted consequences of the solution plan and to evaluate how close a match was obtained. Note that this worksheet provides for an evaluation of the overall impact of a solution.

During the evaluation procedure, the therapist needs to be careful to minimize the possibility that lack of a perfect match does not result in a

Name: _____ Date: _____

A. Describe the effects of the solution in relation to meeting your goals.

How well did your solution plan meet your goals?

1	2	3	4	5
Not at All		Somewhat		Very Well

B. What were the *actual* effects on *you*? (emotional well-being, time and effort, consistency with morals, physical well-being, etc.)

How well did they match your original predictions?

1	2	3	4	5
Not at All		Somewhat		Very Well

C. What were the *actual* effects on others?

How well did they match your original predictions?

1	2	3	4	5
Not at All		Somewhat		Very Well

Figure 11.2. Solution Verification Worksheet.

negative evaluation. As noted in Chapters 1 and 4, depressed individuals can often be characterized by their overly perfectionistic and unrealistically high standards. Although this issue was addressed to some degree during the problem-definition-and-formulation process, this is another opportunity to reinforce the patient for identifying more realistic and attainable goals.

Clinical Example

The following therapist-patient dialogue represents a session that occurred subsequent to Judy's implementation of a solution plan that addressed the subgoal of obtaining several job interviews. This subgoal was previously decided upon as one prerequisite step toward reaching her ultimate objective of attaining new employment.

THERAPIST (TH): Well, Judy, did you have a chance to complete the worksheet I gave you last session?

PATIENT (P): Yeah, I did. Even though it was more paperwork (laughs), I did find it helpful.

TH: OK, let's look at what you put down (takes worksheet from Judy). I notice that you indicated that your overall solution plan met your goals of obtaining job interviews as "very well."

P: Yeah, that's right! Using several different ideas to form an overall plan really seemed to help me. I guess if I only used one alternative, maybe I wouldn't have gotten so many interviews lined up.

TH: That's probably true. As we have previously discussed many times, it generally is a good overall strategy to attack the problem from several different angles at the same time.

P: That's really true. People have always told me that sending out résumés to different companies didn't really get much results. But since I did that plus the other ideas, I guess the overall plan was helpful.

TH: I'm glad to hear that, Judy. I remember that some of the other strategies included listing yourself with several agencies, telling your friends that you were looking for a new job, calling up old friends and telling them about your new goals, anything else?

P: Yeah. In addition to those, I responded to all ads in the newspapers, went to the local college's job fair, and began that computer course in the adult ed program at my old high school.

TH: Seems like a bunch of useful strategies.

P: It really turned out that some of those ideas that I first thought wouldn't be too helpful turned out to be the best!

TH: Tell me more about it.

P: Well, responding to the newspaper ads only got me one interview so far. That was out of about 20 ads! But calling up my friends, both old and new, really turned out to be great. Several of my friends knew of openings in their companies and recommended me to the personnel department. That idea got me five interviews so far! Even though not all these jobs seem to be exactly what I want, I figure it's good practice to go on them. Right?

TH: I do think that's a good idea. Practicing your interview skills can only help to make them better. I notice that you seem to have been very organized with monitoring the actual number of job interviews you received depending on the actual alternative.

P: Yeah, I also figured that would be good practice for my organizational skills that I would like to better develop to continue to get better jobs in the future. But I also wanted to tell you that I might be able to get a part-time job next semester in that adult ed program where I'm taking the computer course! I'm really happy about that!

TH: How did that come about?

P: Well, since I'm doing so well in that class, the instructor asked if I would be interested in serving as a part-time teaching assistant next year! If that happens, I could get even more money, sharpen my computer skills, and be able to get my own apartment even sooner!

TH: That would be great!

P: Yeah, it certainly would be!

TH: OK, Judy, let's get back to the worksheet. I see here that you feel that the personal side effects were also generally very positive.

P: That's right—even though it took alot of time and effort, I think it might really pay off. Even if nothing comes of these job interviews real soon, I know that I should keep on trying. Taking these risks really does make me feel better about myself. I used to think that I would never amount to anything. That's what my parents always told me. I guess I really believed them. But since I started to do more for myself, I can really see how it's all up to me! If I don't start solving my own problems, nobody else will!

TH: I'm not sure if nobody can be helpful, but you are correct in stating that you are the most important person to help solve your own problems.

P: I didn't mean it that way. You know, I told my good friend, Liz, about this therapy and how she should start taking more responsibility for solving her own problems. In a weird kind of way, she has been very helpful to me. We used to get together and always complain about life. Now I see her and think about the way I used to be! Because I still care very much about her, I'm not going to stop being friends, even though she kind of gets me down sometimes. I figured that I should try to help her. I showed her these worksheets figuring that it might help her too. Is that okay?

TH: If you continue to feel comfortable about it, sure. Speaking of the worksheets, let's see how you rated the match concerning the effects of your plan on others . . . I see that you again rated it as positive.

P: Generally, yeah. I was kind of scared and embarrassed to talk to my friends about my getting a new job. I thought that they would think I was a failure or something. But I remembered what you said about taking a risk and gathering information like an investigative reporter and decided to try. It wasn't easy at first, but when the first phone call turned out OK, I felt that I should keep on trying. Like I said before, it was this idea that got me the most interviews so far.

TH: And the short-term effects?

P: Real good! I think the most important one is that I feel so good about myself. I don't think I'm Supergirl or something like that, but I do feel now that I can solve some of my problems. I hope it continues this way.

TH: And the long-term effects?

P: I really hope that my solution plan will actually get me a new job that I like. I think it will. If not in the next few weeks, maybe later on.

TH: So, to sum it up, it seems as though your particular solution plan appears to be both effective and positive thus far. I think that's excellent. I just wanted to highlight how much work you yourself did to make things happen this way. You deserve a pat on the back. Further, I noticed that the rather high standards that you used to have also changed dramatically.

P: Thanks. I realized also that shooting for the moon and expecting to succeed at it made me more depressed. I guess I always thought that if I really became a huge success in life, my parents would change their minds about me. I now realize that I was only hurting myself. They probably will never change their minds. It would be nice, but I can't spend my whole life trying to solve that problem.

TH: No, I don't think you should.

Clinical Comment

In this very positive session, it can be observed how this matching procedure can take place. The therapist can use the worksheets to highlight specific comparisons between the expected outcome and the actual consequences. Continued self-monitoring and observation should also be encouraged.

SELF-REINFORCEMENT VERSUS TROUBLESHOOTING

For other patients not as successful as Judy, the therapist should be careful to assess the discrepancy between the actual solution outcome and the predicted outcome. If this discrepancy exists, the therapist and patient need to collaboratively review the specific nature of the breakdown by attempting to identify the source of the discrepancy. As noted in Chapter 4, the difficulties might lie in either the problem-solving process itself, the performance of the solution, or both. If the therapist and patient determine that the new problem exists with the problem-solving process, then they should return to each of the previous problem-solving components and attempt to devise a more effective solution plan. For example, the reasons why a solution may have been ineffective may be a function of a poorly defined or formulated problem, insufficient number of alternatives that were generated, or ineffective decision making.

If, however, the difficulty involves ineffective solution implementation, the therapist and patient need to decide either to go through the problem-solving process once again to determine an equally effective solution plan that can be implemented more easily by the particular patient, or they must attempt to improve the patient's performance skills. Again, this choice highlights the continuous and significant interplay among the various problem-solving operations. Although many of the latter training stages are predicated on previous problem-solving skill acquisition, the dynamic interplay among these problem-solving operations needs to be emphasized. For example, due to unanticipated obstacles, training in other cognitive-behavioral skills (e.g., assertiveness skills, relaxation skills) may occur after a previously identified effective solution proves to be unsuccessful. Moreover, decision-making skills can be utilized in facilitating more realistic goal setting.

The more positive outcome of the verification process entails recognition that the problem is actually resolved. Although this set of circumstances may be highly reinforcing for the problem solver in and of itself, the last systematic component should be self-reinforcement. As noted in Chapters 1 and 4, depressed individuals tend to engage in low levels of self-reinforcement and high levels of self-punishment. In this light, actual problem resolution needs to be followed by a variety of self-reinforcing activities. On a minimal level, this might entail several positive self-statements, such as "I did a good job at solving that problem"; or "Congrats to me! I worked at it hard, and my efforts paid off!" More systematic procedures may begin with the completion of a reinforcement survey or use of the PES (see Chapter 6) as a means of identifying potential reinforcers. Patients can then either reinforce themselves with a pleasurable leisure activity (e.g., expensive weekend dinner at a favorite restaurant) or by the purchase of a tangible gift (e.g., new shirt or record album).

Patients often initially feel foolish about self-reinforcement procedures and hesitate to engage in this last problem-solving task. The therapist, however, should continue to point out that they previously and frequently punished themselves through negative self-evaluations (e.g., "I screwed up again"; "I can't do anything about this problem"). Therefore, self-reinforcement of successful problem resolution can further prevent old habits associated with depressive thinking from emerging again. The therapist should couch self-reinforcement within the context of connecting attempts at problem-solving with the reward (i.e., reinforcement of the behavior itself).

SUMMARY

This chapter has described training in this last problem-solving component as comprised of four specific tasks: (1) implementing the solution; (2) monitoring and observing the effects of the solution; (3) comparing the actual effects with those predictions made during the decision-making phase; and (4) reinforcing oneself if the problem was resolved or troubleshooting if it was not.

Strategies focusing on facilitating these operations were also described and addressed difficulties in motivation and performance skill deficits. The included worksheets should be used during training as an adjunctive aid.

Although it may appear that successful problem resolution represents the end of the problem-solving process, according to the philosophy espoused throughout this volume the effective problem solver accepts the belief that problems are a normal part of living and is sensitive to the existence of new problems. Advocating that the individual become hypervigilant to the appearance of a new stressful situation is certainly not appropriate. However, an effective problem-perception orientation (see Chapters 4 and 7) would be in agreement with the sentiments expressed by Emily Dickinson—

> *Low at my problem bending,*
> *Another problem comes.*

PART THREE

Conclusion

CHAPTER 12

Concluding Remarks

> *Surgeons must be very careful*
> *When they take the knife!*
> *Underneath their fine incision*
> *Stirs the Culprit—Life!*
>
> EMILY DICKINSON

Previous critical reviews of several major contemporary theories of depression have pinpointed the simplistic nature inherent in models that espouse linear causality and unitary etiological formulations (Coyne, 1982; Hammen, 1985). For example, Hammen suggests that more complete models of depression are necessary and should encompass a multivariate approach, besides considering the dynamic interplay among these variables as they change over time. The theoretical, research, and clinical aspects of the problem-solving formulation of depression delineate such an approach.

The big-picture analysis of this model involved three major areas. First, there is the need to utilize a transactional perspective focusing on the reciprocal relations among major negative life events, daily current problems, problem-solving coping, and depression as a means of better understanding individual differences in the expression of depressive symptomatology. Long-term negative affective states (i.e., clinical depression) can result from the interactions among different sources of stress (major life events and current problems), immediate emotional reactions, and the nature of the problem-solving coping process. More specifically, if the outcome of the interactions within this model, primarily as a function of problem-solving coping, is negative (i.e., unsuccessful problem resolution), then depression is likely to occur. On the other hand, if attempts at problem solving lead to effective coping, then the probability of experiencing clinical depression becomes greatly reduced.

The second general level of analysis focused on the predisposing and moderating influence of genetic and biological vulnerabilities on the model, as well as the role of previous learning and developmental history. Based on attempts to integrate diverse bodies of literature, it was suggested that biological vulnerabilities to depression, which may be genetically transmitted, lie in the individual's neurochemical reactivity threshold to stressful events. As such, biological correlates of depression may be the neurochemical sequelae to stressful events. Thus, biological propensity to depression may involve a heightened sensitivity (or lowered threshold) to stressful situations. However, whether this threshold in fact becomes reached or triggered also partially depends on various psychosocial variables, in particular, perceptions of control. Based on these research findings, it is hypothesized that effective problem-solving coping with stressful situations may serve to inhibit activation of the depression-related neurochemical patterns. An additional postulate is that individual differences in the complex interplay among environmental stress, coping, and biological propensity may account for the variability in differential types of depressive disorders, as well as the severity of the depressive symptomatology itself.

Moreover, prior learning experiences and developmental history can strongly influence each of the major variables within the transactional model. Prior learning can affect the perceived importance, potency, and impact of a particular stressor through respondent, operant, and vicarious learning processes. Learning history can also strongly influence the overall quality of problem-solving coping ability. Previous depressive episodes also influence the nature, pattern, and severity of current depressive reactions, especially if the prior experiences were associated with similar circumstances.

The third level of analysis addressed the nature of the problem-solving process itself and its specific relation to depression. As a function of the nature and purposes of the five major problem-solving components (problem orientation, problem definition and formulation, generation of alternatives, decision making, solution implementation and verification), problem solving actually encompasses several of the composite processes and depression-related variables that a number of cognitive-behavioral theories of depression identify as their major etiologic factors. In this manner, a problem-solving framework can provide for a heuristic metaphor that integrates these existing theories in a meaningful way.

More specifically, the five problem-solving components collectively incorporate a large number of the variables that the major cognitive-behavioral models of depression and negative emotions center on. For example, the problem-orientation component focuses on the influence on successful problem resolution of variables such as attributional processes, cognitive distortions, self-efficacy beliefs, irrational beliefs, and appraisal processes. These variables form the core etiologic foundations of various major cognitive theories. Similarly, aspects of a self-control model of depression were cited as inherent tasks to complete during the problem-definition-and-formulation, decision-making, and solution-implementation-and-verification phases of problem solving. Additionally, the causal importance of decreased positive reinforcement (the core explanatory factor within a behavioral model of depression), as a consequence of experiencing stressful problems, was also highlighted within the transactional framework.

Integration of these various models under a general problem-solving rubric represents an endeavor to describe how the various causal variables posited by these theories can collectively account for individual differences in reaction to stressful situations both among different individuals and across the same individuals over time. As stated previously, not all depressed individuals have social skill deficits, negative attributional styles, distorted cognitions, and/or self-control deficiencies. Group comparisons between depressed and nondepressed subjects can often obscure individual differences among a depressed population concerning these variables (cf. Craighead et al., 1984). The problem-solving formulation of depression was presented as an attempt to explain how such individual differences exist in a dynamic fashion. The amount of variance accounted for by each of the five problem-solving components in serving as a risk factor for depression also vary as a function of individual differences. Moreover, deficiencies in one process can, in fact, be compensated for by other factors.

Inherent in the model, then, is the proposition that the onset and maintenance of clinical depression is influenced by a multitude of biological and psychosocial factors. In this manner, the model is consistent with recent calls for more pluralistic approaches. The model also attempts to delineate a set of heuristic principles that can guide both assessment and therapy for depression. More specifically, inherent in the clinical application of the model is the recommendation that assessment be broad-based in nature with the goal of identifying specific problem-solving deficits that idiosyncratically account for a given person becoming depressed. In this light, the model attempts to provide for a nomothetic framework that guides an idiographic therapeutic application of problem-solving principles. Therapy for depression should be geared toward remediation of specific problem-solving deficits associated with the onset and maintenance of a depressive episode for a particular person.

Part Two of this volume provides a detailed therapist manual highlighting problem-solving treatment for depression. Each specific problem-solving task that was described in essence has two major purposes: (1) to facilitate overall problem-solving effectiveness; and (2) to remediate various depression-related causal variables. In other words, each of the five major problem-solving components was described as having a specific function within the prescriptive model geared to increase one's overall coping abilities. Training in various problem-solving tasks was also characterized as addressing specific depression-related problems (i.e., those factors that have been linked causally to depression).

For example, training in the problem-orientation component is directed at facilitating a positive approach toward problems in living and problem solving as a means of coping. However, an additional purpose of this training is to ameliorate certain variables characteristic of depression (i.e., negative attributional style, negative cognitive distortions, negative appraisals, poor self-efficacy beliefs, and irrational thinking). Similarly, training in each of the remaining four problem-solving components is also geared toward changing specific depression-associated deficits (see Chapter 4).

FUTURE DIRECTIONS

Although this conceptual framework appears to be consistent with recent calls for multivariate approaches to depression, the utility and validity of any model must stand the test of continued empirical scrutiny. It is hoped that the present explication of both the theoretical model and its associated treatment approach will engender future research and clinical attention. In particular, there is a need for research to further evaluate the generalization and long-term effects of problem-solving therapy. Additional dismantling investigations should also be conducted to identify the crucial and most important ingredients of this therapy model. The relative efficacy of problem-solving therapy for depression among the elderly and among children and adolescents is another important research area. Since a problem-solving approach has been advocated as a general coping model, its utility as a preventive strategy for high risk groups may also be worthy of empirical scrutiny. Finally, the speculations in this volume concerning the relation between biological and psychosocial factors of depression especially need investigation. Huge separate bodies of literature related to these areas sorely need an integrative bridge.

As the poem by Emily Dickinson which opened this chapter suggests, life is full of problems. The ubiquity of both life's problems and the experience of depression are sufficient justification to investigate meaningful ways of coping more effectively in general, and of treating depression in particular. Is problem-solving therapy the ultimate solution? Probably not. It may, however, prove to be a particularly important and useful "alternative" toward that goal. More importantly, the hope is that this volume has sufficiently "defined the nature of the problem" and stimulated the reader to participate in generating and empirically evaluating more alternatives.

Format of Problem-Solving Group Treatment for a 10-Week Program

Components to Cover Each Session

Session 1

Introduction and Rationale

1. Introduce overall program, including description of structure (i.e., 10 sessions, group format, use of homework, etc.)
2. Facilitate sense of "groupness" (i.e., have all members introduce themselves and discuss reasons for joining program)
3. Provide detailed rationale underlying a problem-solving treatment approach to depression
4. Provide definitions of stress, problems, and problem solving
5. Provide overview of the five training components and their relation to depression
6. Explain homework assignment: completion of 2–3 Record of Coping Attempts Worksheets

Session 2

Problem-Orientation (PO) Training

1. Discuss previous week's homework
2. Provide therapeutic rationale for PO training
3. Facilitate adoption of positive orientation via Reverse Advocacy Role-Play exercise
4. Discuss common problems
5. Discuss personally relevant problems

6. Develop concept of using feelings as cues or signals that a problem exists
7. Discuss use of "STOP and THINK" technique
8. Practice with relevant examples
9. Summarize major points
10. Explain homework: completion of PO Worksheets; continued completion of Record of Coping Attempts Worksheets

Session 3

Problem-Definition-and-Formulation (PDF) Training

1. Discuss previous week's homework
2. Provide therapeutic rationale for PDF training
3. Discuss gathering information—becoming a personal investigative reporter
4. Discuss use of concrete and unambiguous terms
5. Explore ways to minimize cognitive distortions
6. Identify factors that make the situation a problem
7. Develop concept of setting realistic goals
8. Practice with relevant examples
9. Summarize major points
10. Explain homework: completion of PDF Worksheets

Session 4

Generation-of-Alternatives (GOA) Training

1. Discuss previous week's homework
2. Provide therapeutic rationale for GOA training
3. Develop concept of brainstorming techniques (quantity, deferment, and variety principles)
4. Discuss use of concrete and unambiguous terms
5. Practice with impersonal problems (i.e., creativity exercises)
6. Practice with relevant problems

7. Summarize major points
8. Explain homework: completion of GOA Worksheets

Session 5

Decision-Making (DM) Training

1. Discuss previous week's homework
2. Provide therapeutic rationale for DM training
3. Discuss: Anticipating solution consequences
   a. Expected effectiveness of solution in reaching problem-solving goals
   b. Expected personal ability to implement a particular solution in its optimal form
   c. Expected personal consequences
   d. Expected social consequences
   e. Expected short-term consequences
   f. Expected long-term consequences
4. Explain how to evaluate overall cost/benefit ratio
5. Consider ways to devise a solution plan
6. Practice with relevant problems
7. Summarize major points
8. Explain homework: completion of DM Worksheets

Session 6

Solution-Implementation-and-Verification (SIV) Training

1. Discuss previous week's homework
2. Provide therapeutic rationale for SIV training
3. Discuss implementing solution plan
4. Explain how to observe and monitor solution outcome
5. Discuss evaluating actual solution outcome
6. Explore rationale of self-reinforcement for problem resolution
7. Define and elaborate troubleshooting and recycling
8. Practice with relevant problems

9. Summarize major points
10. Explain homework: implementation of solutions and completion of SIV Worksheets

Sessions 7–9

Maintenance and Generalization Training

1. Discuss previous week's homework and attempts at problem resolution
2. Integrate skills—apply entire model for relevant current problems
3. Explain homework: completion of Record of Coping Attempts Worksheets

Session 10

Wrap-Up and Termination

1. Discuss previous week's homework
2. Review model
3. Review individual progress
4. Encourage use of model in future via handouts and homework worksheets
5. Discuss termination difficulties

APPENDIX B

Patient Handout

PHILOSOPHY OF PROGRAM

Our philosophy concerning depression is that it is a common problem in our society. We view depression as being due to the everyday problems in living and general stresses that we all experience, rather than being due to some disease or illness. Therefore, we believe that people such as yourself, who may be currently experiencing depression, can learn new ways of dealing with these problems that will help them to cope more effectively in general and thus reduce the depressive feelings.

Further, we believe that if you can continually resolve new problems and cope better with the everyday strains and stresses of living, then you will be able to prevent experiencing severe bouts of depression in the future.

Therefore, our goal in offering this program was to teach you a new approach to solving problems in living. The following is a brief overview of the concepts and suggestions that you have already learned in the program. Hopefully, some of what follows will sound familiar to you. This overview is intended to provide some reminders for your future application of the problem-solving process.

PROBLEM-SOLVING PROCESSES

According to the model described during the program, there are five major components involved in effective problem solving: problem orientation; problem definition and formulation; generation of alternatives; decision

Note: Patients receive this handout at the final session of problem-solving therapy as a reminder for future coping attempts. In this way, treatment maintenance can be enhanced. However, by changing the verb tense of some of the sections, the following can also be distributed *during* treatment at the appropriate training phase to further reinforce the lesson of the particular session.

making; and solution implementation and verification. Each of these five problem-solving operations has specific suggestions to remember.

Problem Orientation

Having a rational, realistic, and positive attitude towards problems in living goes a long way towards resolving them. The next time you encounter a problem, remember the following ideas.

Remember:

Problems are COMMON to everyone—if you have a problem, that means you are NORMAL!

Many people have similar kinds of problems—you are NOT alone!

It is NOT catastrophic or awful when things do not go right in your life!

Do NOT avoid facing a problem, no matter how large or small—it is better to attempt to deal with it and try to solve it!

There is NO such thing as THE perfect solution to any problem—look for the best solution(s) for YOU!

It is best to STOP and THINK before solving a problem—the first idea is not always the best!

You CAN change if you want to!

You CAN solve your problems and have CONTROL over your life!

Also Remember:

Use your feelings as cues or signals ("red light flashing") that something is going wrong—recognizing that a problem exists allows you to attempt to resolve it effectively.

Always STOP and THINK about how you are feeling about the problematic situation!

Having problems simply means you are a human being—solving them means you are a happy one!

Problem Definition and Formulation

After you recognize that a problem exists, you should attempt to define the situation in such a manner that makes it easier to understand. Determine the *who, what, where, when, why,* and *how* of the problem in order to better understand what is making it problematic (play scientist, detective, or investigative reporter).

Remember:

STOP *and* THINK *about defining the problem(s) and your goals.*

Describe all the available facts in clear, specific, and concrete terms.

Separate relevant from irrelevant information, and facts from assumptions (opinions, inferences).

Identify the factors and circumstances that are making the situation a problem (obstacles and conflicts).

Identify your goals—discriminate between rational and irrational goals.

Generation of Alternatives

After you clearly define your problem(s) and goals, generate as many alternative solutions as possible.

Remember:

Use the following brainstorming principles:

"Quantity breeds quality": the more the better.

"Deferment of judgment": withhold evaluation of alternatives.

Be concrete.

Be appropriate and relevant.

Combine and improve upon ideas in order to produce new ones.

STOP and THINK of alternative solutions to your problem(s).

Decision Making

After you produce an exhaustive list of possible solution alternatives, attempt to evaluate them according to the criteria listed here. Those solutions that appear to be the best (more positive than negative expectations) then become the ones to implement.

Remember:

Consider the following criteria in making a decision.

Value of Alternative

"What is the likelihood that this alternative will achieve my goal?"

"What is the likelihood that I can implement this solution in its optimal form?"

Personal Consequences

Time
Effort
Emotional cost or gain
Consistency with moral/ethical values
Physical well-being
Other problem-specific personal consequences

Social Consequences

Effects on family
Effects on friends
Effects on community/neighborhood
Other problem-specific social consequences

Short-Term Consequences

"How will this decision affect me now?"

Long-Term Consequences

"How will this decision affect me in the future?"

Solution Implementation and Verification

After you select those alternatives that are the best or most effective, attempt to carry out each one in its optimal form; that is, in the best way possible.

Remember:

Observe outcome of alternative.
Match actual outcome to expected outcome.
Troubleshoot through the stages again if necessary (see below).
End problem-solving process if match is satisfactory.
Reinforce your efforts in applying the problem-solving process to your problem—regardless of whether the problem was resolved, you deserve praise for trying!

Troubleshooting

If the match between the observed outcome and the problem-solving goal is not satisfactory, make an attempt to determine whether the source of the difficulty is in: (1) the problem-solving process, or (2) the performance of the solution.

If it is in the former, then you can go back to one or more of the previous stages and try to work out an alternative solution that might be more effective for you. If, however, it is in the performance, you might attempt to improve upon the implementation of the solution.

What Happens if Nothing Works?

If you cannot succeed after attempting these corrective strategies, then the "best solution" might be to seek help from someone who is either more familiar with the particular problem or more adequately trained to assess the situation and provide appropriate recommendations. For example, if the problem is financial difficulties, and repeated problem-solving attempts fail to correct the situation, it might be better to consult a financial advisor for expert help.

Remember that problem solving is a *process*, not simply a step-by-step procedure. The skills you use during one phase can also be applied at later stages (i.e., objectively recognizing your feelings is important when orienting yourself to the problem as well as when deciding between solution alternatives).

Also, remember that problems may be small, medium, or large. Work on smaller ones and build yourself up for the bigger ones. Through the continued use of the problem-solving approach, it will become more automatic for you and will enable you to stop that vicious cycle of problems leading to depression leading to more problems. Instead, by taking control over your problems, you can feel better about yourself and cope more effectively with life's problems.

Remember to use the problem-solving worksheets!
Good luck in your future problem solving!

References

Abramson, L. Y., Alloy, L. B., & Rosoff, R. (1981). Depression and the generation of complex hypotheses in the judgment of contingency. *Behaviour Research and Therapy, 19*, 35–45.

Abramson, L. Y., & Sackheim, H. A. (1977). A paradox in depression: Uncontrollability and self-blame. *Psychological Bulletin, 84*, 835–851.

Abramson, L. Y., Seligman, M. E. P., & Teasdale, J. (1978). Learned helplessness in humans: Critique and reformulation. *Journal of Abnormal Psychology, 87*, 49–74.

Adams, J. L. (1976). *Conceptual blockbusting: A pleasurable guide to better problem solving.* New York: Norton.

Akiskal, H. S., & McKinney, W. T. (1975). Overview of recent research in depression: Integration of ten conceptual models into a comprehensive clinical frame. *Archives of General Psychiatry, 32*, 285–305.

American Psychiatric Association (1952). *Diagnostic and statistical manual of mental disorders* (DSM-I; 1st ed.). Washington, DC: Author.

American Psychiatric Association (1968). *Diagnostic and statistical manual of mental disorders* (DSM-II; 2nd ed.). Washington, DC: Author.

American Psychiatric Association (1980). *Diagnostic and statistical manual of mental disorders* (DSM-III; 3rd ed.). Washington, DC: Author.

American Psychiatric Association (1987). *Diagnostic and statistical manual of mental disorders* (DSM-III-R; 3rd ed.–revised). Washington, DC: Author.

Anisman, H., & LaPierre, Y. (1982). Neurochemical aspects of stress and depression: Formulations and caveats. In R. W. J. Neufeld (Ed.), *Psychosocial stress and psychopathology* (pp. 179–217). New York: McGraw-Hill.

Anisman, H., Pizzino, A., & Sklar, L. S. (1980). Coping with stress, norepinephrine depletion, and escape performance. *Brain Research, 191*, 538–588.

Bandura, A. (1971). Vicarious and self-reinforcement processes. In R. Glaser (Ed.), *The nature of reinforcement* (pp. 228–278). New York: Academic Press.

Bandura, A. (1977). Self-efficacy: Toward a unifying theory of behavior change. *Psychological Review, 84*, 191–215.

Bandura, A. (1978). The self-system in reciprocal determinism. *American Psychologist, 33*, 344–358.

Barlow, D. H. (Ed.). (1981). *Behavioral assessment of adult disorders*. New York: Guilford.

Baugh, J. R. (1981). *Solution training: Overcoming blocks to problem solving.* Gretna, LA: Pelican.

Baumgardner, A. H., Heppner, P. P., & Arkin, R. M. (1986). The role of causal attribution in personal problem solving. *Journal of Personality and Social Psychology, 50,* 636–643.

Beck, A. T. (1963). Thinking and depression: 1. Idiosyncratic content and cognitive distortions. *Archives of General Psychiatry, 9,* 324–333.

Beck, A. T. (1967). *Depression: Clinical, experimental, and theoretical aspects.* New York: Harper & Row.

Beck, A. T. (1974). The development of depression: A cognitive model. In R. Friedman & M. Katz (Eds.), *Psychology of depression: Contemporary theory and research* (pp. 3–28). Washington, DC: Winston-Wiley.

Beck, A. T. (1976). *Cognitive theory and the emotional disorders.* New York: International Universities Press.

Beck, A. T., & Hurvich, M. S. (1959). Psychological correlates of depression: 1. Frequency of "masochistic" dream content in a private practice sample. *Psychosomatic Medicine, 21,* 50–55.

Beck, A. T., Rush, A. J., Shaw, B. F., & Emery, G. (1979). *Cognitive therapy of depression: A treatment manual.* New York: Guilford.

Beck, A. T., & Ward, C. H. (1961). Dreams of depressed patients: Characteristic themes in manifest content. *Archives of General Psychiatry, 5,* 562–571.

Beck, A. T., Ward, C. H., Mendelson, M., Mock, J., & Erbaugh, J. (1961). An inventory for measuring depression. *Archives of General Psychiatry, 5,* 462–467.

Becker, G. M., & McClintock, C. G. (1967). Value: Behavioral decision theory. *Annual Review of Psychology, 18,* 139–286.

Beckham, E. E., & Adams, R. L. (1984). Coping behavior in depression: Report on a new scale. *Behaviour Research and Therapy, 22,* 71–75.

Bedell, J. R., Archer, R. P., & Marlowe, H. A. (1980). A description and evaluation of a problem solving skills training program. In D. Upper & S. M. Ross (Eds.), *Behavioral group therapy: An annual review* (pp. 92–121). Champaign, IL: Research Press.

Billings, A. G., Cronkite, R. C., & Moos, R. H. (1983). Socio-environmental factors in unipolar depression: Comparisons of depressed patients and nondepressed controls. *Journal of Abnormal Psychology, 92,* 119–133.

Billings, A. G., & Moos, R. H. (1981). The role of coping responses and social resources in attenuating the impact of stressful life events. *Journal of Behavioral Medicine, 4,* 139–157.

Billings, A. G., & Moos, R. H. (1982). Psychosocial theory and research on depression: An integrative framework and review. *Clinical Psychology Review, 2,* 213–237.

Billings, A. G., & Moos, R. H. (1984). Coping, stress, and social resources among adults with unipolar depression. *Journal of Personality and Social Psychology, 46*, 877–891.

Billings, A. G., & Moos, R. H. (1985). Psychosocial processes of remission in unipolar depression: Comparing depressed patients with matched community controls. *Journal of Consulting and Clinical Psychology, 53*, 314–325.

Black, D. R., & Scherba, D. S. (1983). Contracting to problem solve versus contracting to practice behavioral weight loss skills. *Behavior Therapy, 14*, 100–109.

Black, D. R., & Threlfall, W. E. (1986). A stepped approach to weight control: A minimal intervention and a bibliotherapy problem-solving program. *Behavior Therapy, 17*, 144–157.

Blaney, P. H., Behar, V., & Head, R. (1980). Two measures of depressive cognitions: Their association with depression and with each other. *Journal of Abnormal Psychology, 89*, 678–682.

Bloom, B. S., & Broder, L. J. (1950). *Problem-solving processes of college students.* Chicago: University of Chicago Press.

Brady, J. V. (1980). Experimental studies of stress and anxiety. In I. L. Kutash, L. B. Schlesinger, and Associates (Eds.), *Handbook on stress and anxiety* (pp. 129–158). San Francisco: Jossey-Bass.

Breslow, R., Kocsis, J., & Belkin, B. (1981). Contribution of the depressive perspective to memory function in depression. *American Journal of Psychiatry, 138*, 227–229.

Butler, L., & Meichenbaum, D. (1981). The assessment of interpersonal problem-solving skills. In P. C. Kendall & S. D. Hollon (Eds.), *Assessment strategies for cognitive-behavioral interventions* (pp. 197–226). New York: Academic Press.

Caple, M. A., & Blechman, E. A. (1976, December). *Problem-solving and self-approval training with a depressed single mother: Case study.* Paper presented at the meeting of the Association for the Advancement of Behavior Therapy, New York.

Cartwright, R. D. (1983). Rapid eye movement sleep characteristics during and after mood-disturbing events. *Archives of General Psychiatry, 40*, 197–201.

Carver, C. S., & Scheier, M. F. (1982). Control theory: A useful conceptual framework for personality-social, clinical, and health psychology. *Psychological Bulletin, 92*, 111–135.

Chaney, E. F., O'Leary, M. R., & Marlatt, G. A. (1978). Skill training with alcoholics. *Journal of Consulting and Clinical Psychology, 46*, 1092–1104.

Churchman, C. W. (1961). *Prediction and optimal decisions.* Englewood Cliffs, NJ: Prentice-Hall.

Christensen, J. F. (1981). Assessment of stress: Environmental, intra-personal, and outcome issues. In P. McReynolds (Ed.), *Advances in psychological assessment* (Vol. 5, pp. 63–123). San Francisco: Jossey-Bass.

Ciaranello, R. D. (1983). Neurochemical aspects of stress. In N. Garmezy & M.

Rutter (Eds.), *Stress, coping, and development in children* (pp. 85–106). New York: McGraw-Hill.

Ciminero, A. R., & Steingarten, K. A. (1978). The effects of performance standards on self-evaluation in depressed and nondepressed individuals. *Cognitive Therapy and Research, 2,* 179–182.

Claerhout, S., Elder, J., & Janes, C. (1982). Problem-solving skills of rural battered women. *American Journal of Community Psychology, 10,* 605–612.

Clayton, P. (1979). Course of depressive symptoms following the stress of bereavement. In J. E. Barrett (Ed.), *Stress and mental disorder* (pp. 201–219). New York: Raven.

Coche, E., & Douglas, A. A. (1977). Therapeutic effects of problem-solving training and play-reading groups. *Journal of Clinical Psychology, 33,* 820–827.

Coche, E., & Flick, A. (1975). Problem-solving training groups for hospitalized psychiatric patients. *Journal of Psychology, 91,* 19–29.

Cofer, C. N., & Apply, M. H. (1964). *Motivation: Theory and research.* New York: Wiley.

Copas, J. B., & Robin, A. (1982). Suicide in psychiatric patients. *The British Journal of Psychiatry, 141,* 503–511.

Cormier, W. H., Otani, A., & Cormier, S. (1986). The effects of problem-solving training on two problem-solving tasks. *Cognitive Therapy and Research, 10,* 95–108.

Costello, C. G. (1980). Loss as a source of stress in psychopathology. In R. W. J. Neufeld (Ed.), *Psychological stress and psychopathology* (pp. 93–124). New York: McGraw-Hill.

Costello, E. J. (1983). Information processing for decision making in depressed women: A study of subjective expected utilities. *Journal of Affective Disorders, 5,* 239–251.

Coyne, J. D. (1976a). Depression and the response of others. *Journal of Abnormal Psychology, 85,* 186–193.

Coyne, J. D. (1976b). Toward an interactional description of depression. *Psychiatry, 39,* 28–40.

Coyne, J. D. (1982). A critique of cognitions as causal entities with particular reference to depression. *Cognitive Therapy and Research, 6,* 3–13.

Coyne, J. D., & Gotlib, I. H. (1983). The role of cognition in depression: A critical appraisal. *Psychological Bulletin, 94,* 472–505.

Craighead, W. E. (1980). Away from a unitary model of depression. *Behavior Therapy, 11,* 112–128.

Craighead, W. E., Kennedy, R. E., Raczynski, J. M., & Dow, M. G. (1984). Affective disorders—unipolar. In S. M. Turner & M. Hersen (Eds.), *Adult psychopathology and diagnosis* (pp. 184–244). New York: Wiley.

Dahlstrom, W. G., & Welsh, G. S. (1960). *An MMPI handbook.* Minneapolis: University of Minnesota Press.

DeLongis, A., Coyne, J. C., Dakof, G., Folkman, S., & Lazarus, R. S. (1982). Relationship of daily hassles, uplifts, and major life events to health status. *Health Psychology, 1,* 119–136.

Dempsey, P. (1964). A unidimensional depression scale for the MMPI. *Journal of Consulting Psychology, 28,* 364–370.

Derry, P. A., & Kuiper, N. A. (1981). Schematic processing and self-reference in clinical depression. *Journal of Abnormal Psychology, 90,* 286–297.

Dewey, J. (1910). *How we think.* Princeton, NJ: Princeton University Press.

Dixon, D. N., Heppner, P. P., Petersen, C. H., & Ronning, R. R. (1979). Problem-solving workshop training. *Journal of Counseling Psychology, 26,* 133–139.

Dobson, D. J., & Dobson, K. S. (1981). Problem-solving strategies in depressed and nondepressed college students. *Cognitive Therapy and Research, 5,* 237–249.

Doerfler, L. A., & Richards, C. S. (1981). Self-initiated attempts to cope with depression. *Cognitive Therapy and Research, 5,* 367–371.

Dohrenwend, B. S., & Dohrenwend, B. P. (Eds.). (1974). *Stressful life events: Their nature and effects.* New York: Wiley.

Durlak, J. A. (1983). Social problem solving as a primary prevention strategy. In R. D. Felner, L. A. Jason, J. N. Moritsugu, & S. S. Farber (Eds.), *Preventive psychology: Theory, research, and practice* (pp. 31–48). New York: Pergamon.

D'Zurilla, T. J. (1986). *Problem-solving therapy: A social competence approach to clinical intervention.* New York: Springer.

D'Zurilla, T. J., & Goldfried, M. R. (1971). Problem solving and behavior modification. *Journal of Abnormal Psychology, 78,* 107–126.

D'Zurilla, T. J., & Nezu, A. (1980). A study of the generation of alternatives process in social problem solving. *Cognitive Therapy and Research, 4,* 67–72.

D'Zurilla, T. J., & Nezu, A. (1982). Social problem solving in adults. In P. C. Kendall (Ed.), *Advances in cognitive-behavioral research and therapy* (Vol. 1, pp. 201–274). New York: Academic Press.

D'Zurilla, T. J., & Nezu, A. M. (1987). The Heppner and Krauskopf approach: A model of personal problem solving or social skills? *The Counseling Psychologist, 15,* 463–470.

D'Zurilla, T. J., & Nezu, A. M. (1988, November). *Development and preliminary evaluation of the Social Problem-Solving Inventory (SPSI).* Paper presented at the meeting of the Association for the Advancement of Behavior Therapy, New York.

Edwards, W. (1961). Behavioral decision theory. *Annual Review of Psychology, 12,* 473–498.

Edwards, W., Lindman, H., & Phillips, L. D. (1965). Emerging technologies for making decisions. In T. M. Newcomb (Ed.), *New directions in psychology* (pp. 291–324). New York: Holt, Rinehart, & Winston.

Elias, M. J., Larcen, S. W., Zlotnow, S. F., & Chinsky, J. J. (1978, August). *An innovative measure of children's cognitions in problematic interpersonal situ-*

ations. Paper presented at the meeting of the American Psychological Association, Toronto.

Ellis, A. (1962). *Reason and emotion in psychotherapy.* New York: Lyle Stuart.

Ellis, A. (1985). *Overcoming resistance: Rational-emotive therapy with difficult clients.* New York: Springer.

Endicott, J., Cohen, J., Nee, J., Fleiss, J., & Santakos, S. (1981). Hamilton Depression Rating Scale, extracted from regular and change versions of the Schedule for Affective Disorders and Schizophrenia. *Archives of General Psychiatry, 38,* 98–103.

Endicott, J., & Spitzer, R. L. (1978). A diagnostic interview: The Schedule for Affective Disorders and Schizophrenia. *Archives of General Psychiatry, 35,* 837–844.

Erickson, R. C., Post, R. D., & Paige, A. B. (1975). Hope as a psychiatric variable. *Journal of Clinical Psychology, 31,* 324–330.

Feighner, J. P., Robins, E., Guze, S. B., Woodruff, R. A., Winokur, G., & Munoz, R. (1972). Diagnostic criteria for use in psychiatric research. *Archives of General Psychiatry, 26,* 57–63.

Ferster, C. B. (1966). Animal behavior and mental illness. *Psychological Record, 16,* 345–356.

Fisher-Beckfield, D., & McFall, R. M. (1982). Development of a competence inventory for college men and evaluation of relationships between competence and depression. *Journal of Consulting and Clinical Psychology, 50,* 697–705.

Flowers, J. V. (1979). Behavioral analysis of group therapy and a model for behavioral group therapy. In D. Upper & S. M. Ross (Eds.), *Behavioral group therapy: An annual review* (pp. 5–38). Champaign, IL: Research Press.

Folkman, S., & Lazarus, R. S. (1980). An analysis of coping in a middle-aged community sample. *Journal of Health and Social Behavior, 21,* 219–239.

Freedman, B. I., Rosenthal, L., Donahoe, C. P., Schlundt, D. G., & McFall, R. M. (1978). A social-behavioral analysis of skill deficits in delinquent and non-delinquent adolescent boys. *Journal of Consulting and Clinical Psychology, 46,* 1448–1462.

Frost, R. O., Graff, M., & Becker, J. (1979). Self-evaluation and depressed moods. *Journal of Consulting and Clinical Psychology, 47,* 958–962.

Funabiki, D., & Calhoun, J. (1979). Use of a behavioral-analytic procedure in evaluating two models of depression. *Journal of Consulting and Clinical Psychology, 47,* 183–185.

Gagne, R. M. (1966). Human problem solving: Internal and external events. In B. Kleinmutz (Ed.), *Problem solving: Research, method and theory* (pp. 171–196). New York: Wiley.

Getter, H., & Nowinski, J. K. (1981). A free response test of interpersonal effectiveness. *Journal of Personality Assessment, 45,* 301–308.

Glazer, H. I., Clarkin, J. F., & Hunt, H. F. (1981). Assessment of depression.

In J. F. Clarkin & H. I. Glazer (Eds.), *Depression: Behavioral and directive intervention strategies* (pp. 3–30). New York: Garland.

Goldfried, M. R., & Davison, G. C. (1976). *Clinical behavior therapy.* New York: Holt, Rinehart & Winston.

Goldfried, M. R., & D'Zurilla, T. J. (1969). A behavior-analytic model for assessing competence. In C. D. Spielberger (Ed.), *Current topics in clinical and community psychology* (Vol. 1, pp. 151–196). New York: Academic Press.

Goldfried, M. R., & Merbaum, M. (Eds.). (1973). *Behavior change through self-control.* New York: Holt, Rinehart & Winston.

Goldstein, A. P. (1975). Relationship-enhancement methods. In F. H. Kanfer & A. P. Goldstein (Eds.), *Helping people change* (pp. 192–221). New York: Pergamon.

Golin, S., & Terrell, F. (1977). Motivational and associative aspects of mild depression in skill and chance tasks. *Journal of Abnormal Psychology, 86,* 389–401.

Gotlib, I. H. (1984). Depression and general psychopathology in university students. *Journal of Abnormal Psychology, 93,* 19–30.

Gotlib, I. H., & Asarnow, R. F. (1979). Interpersonal and impersonal problem-solving skills in mildly and moderately depressed university students. *Journal of Consulting and Clinical Psychology, 47,* 86–95.

Gottschalk, L. A. (1974). A hope scale applicable to verbal samples. *Archives of General Psychiatry, 30,* 779–785.

Halberstadt, L. J., Andrews, D., Metalsky, G. I., & Abramson, L. Y. (1984). Helplessness, hopelessness, and depression: A review of progress and future directions. In N. S. Endler & J. M. Hunt (Eds.), *Personality and the behavioral disorders* (Vol. 1, 2nd ed., pp. 373–412). New York: Wiley.

Hamberger, L. K., & Lohr, J. M. (1984). *Stress and stress management.* New York: Springer.

Hamilton, M. (1960). A rating scale for depression. *Journal of Neurology, Neurosurgery and Psychiatry, 23,* 56–62.

Hamilton, M. (1967). Development of a rating scale for primary depressive illness. *British Journal of Social and Clinical Psychology, 6,* 278–296.

Hammen, C. L. (1981). Assessment: A clinical and cognitive emphasis. In L. P. Rehm (Ed.), *Behavior therapy for depression: Present status and future directions* (pp. 255–278). New York: Academic Press.

Hammen, C. L. (1985). Predicting depression: A cognitive-behavioral perspective. In P. C. Kendall (Ed.), *Advances in cognitive-behavioral research and therapy* (Vol. 4, pp. 29–71). New York: Academic Press.

Hammen, C. L., Miklowitz, D., & Dyck, D. (1986). Stability and severity parameters of depressive self-schema responding. *Journal of Social and Clinical Psychology, 4,* 23–45.

Hansen, D. J., St. Lawrence, J. S., & Christoff, K. A. (1985). Effects of interpersonal problem-solving training with chronic aftercare patients on problem-solving component skills and effectiveness of solutions. *Journal of Consulting and Clinical Psychology, 53,* 167–174.

Harris, R., & Lingoes, J. (1955). *Subscales for the MMPI: An aid to profile interpretation.* Unpublished manuscript, University of California, San Francisco, Department of Psychiatry.

Hathaway, S. R., & McKinley, J. C. (1943). *Manual for the Minnesota Multiphasic Personality Inventory.* New York: Psychological Corporation.

Hauri, P. (1976). Dreams in patients remitted from reactive depression. *Journal of Abnormal Psychology, 85,* 1–10.

Hedlund, J., & Vieweg, B. (1979). The Hamilton Rating Scale for Depression: A comprehensive review. *Journal of Operational Psychiatry, 10,* 149–162.

Henry, J. P. (1980). Present concepts of stress theory. In E. Usdin, R. Kvetnansky, & I. J. Kopin (Eds.), *Catecholamines and stress: Recent advances* (pp. 7–29). New York: Elsevier Press.

Heppner, P. P., & Anderson W. P. (1985). The relationship between problem-solving self-appraisal and psychological adjustment. *Cognitive Therapy and Research, 9,* 415–427.

Heppner, P. P., Baumgardner, A. H., & Jackson, J. (1985). Problem-solving self-appraisal, depression, and attributional style: Are they related? *Cognitive Therapy and Research, 9,* 105–113.

Heppner, P. P., Baumgardner, A. H., Larson, L. M., & Petty, R. E. (1983, August). *Problem-solving training for college students with problem-solving deficits.* Paper presented at the meeting of the American Psychological Association, Anaheim, CA.

Heppner, P. P., Hibel, J. H., Neal, G. W., Weinstein, C. L., & Rabinowitz, F. E. (1982). Personal problem solving: A descriptive study of individual differences. *Journal of Counseling Psychology, 29,* 580–590.

Heppner, P. P. Kampa, M. & Brunning, L. (1987). The relationship between problem-solving self-appraisal and indices of physical and psychological health. *Cognitive Therapy and Research, 11,* 155–168.

Heppner, P. P., Neal, G. W., & Larson, L. M. (1984). Problem-solving training as prevention with college students. *Personnel and Guidance Journal, 62,* 514–519.

Heppner, P. P., & Petersen, C. H. (1982). The development and implications of a personal problem solving inventory. *Journal of Counseling Psychology, 29,* 66–75.

Heppner, P. P., Reeder, B. L., & Larson, L. M. (1983). Cognitive variables associated with personal problem-solving appraisal: Implications for counseling. *Journal of Counseling Psychology, 30,* 537–545.

Hersen, M., Bellack, A. S., & Himmelhoch, J. M. (1980). Treatment of unipolar depression with social skills training. *Behavior Modification, 4,* 547–556.

Hollon, S. D., & Beck, A. T. (1979). Cognitive therapy of depression. In P. C.

Kendall & S. D. Hollon (Eds.), *Cognitive-behavioral interventions: Theory, research and procedures* (pp. 153–204). New York: Academic Press.

Hollon, S. D., & Kendall, P. C. (1980). Cognitive self-statements in depression: Development of an automatic thoughts questionnaire. *Cognitive Therapy and Research, 4,* 383–395.

Horowitz, H. M., Weckler, D. A., & Doren, R. (1983). Interpersonal problems and symptoms of depression: A cognitive approach. In P. C. Kendall (Ed.), *Advances in cognitive-behavioral research and treatment* (Vol. 2, pp. 81–125). New York: Academic Press.

Hussian, R. A., & Lawrence, P. S. (1981). Social reinforcement of activity and problem-solving training in the treatment of depressed institutionalized elderly patients. *Cognitive Therapy and Research, 5,* 57–69.

Hyland, M. E. (1987). Control theory interpretation of psychological mechanisms of depression: Comparison and integration of several theories. *Psychological Bulletin, 102,* 109–121.

Intagliatia, J. C. (1978). Increasing the interpersonal problem solving skills of an alcoholic population. *Journal of Consulting and Clinical Psychology, 46,* 489–498.

Jacobson, N. S. (1981). The assessment of overt behavior. In L. Rehm (Ed.), *Behavior therapy for depression: Present status and future directions* (pp. 279–300). New York: Academic Press.

Jahoda, M. (1953). The meaning of psychological health. *Social Casework, 34,* 349–354.

Jahoda, M. (1958). *Current concepts of positive mental health.* New York: Basic Books.

Janis, I. L. (1982). Decisionmaking under stress. In L. Goldberger & S. Breznitz (Eds.), *Handbook of stress: Theoretical and clinical aspects* (pp. 69–87). New York: The Free Press.

Jannoun, L., Munby, M., Catalan, J., & Gelder, M. (1980). A home-based treatment program for agoraphobia: Replication and controlled evaluation. *Behavior Therapy, 11,* 294–305.

Kahneman, D., & Tversky, A. (1979). Prospect theory: An analysis of decisions under risk. *Econometrica, 47,* 263–291.

Kanfer, F. H. (1970). Self-regulation: Research, issues, and speculations. In C. Neuringer & J. L. Michael (Eds.), *Behavior modification in clinical psychology* (pp. 351–389). New York: Appleton-Century-Crofts.

Kanfer, F. H. (1971). The maintenance of behavior by self-generated stimuli and reinforcement. In A. Jacobs & L. B. Sachs (Eds.), *The psychology of private events: Perspectives on covert response systems* (pp. 219–243). New York: Academic Press.

Kanner, A. D., Coyne, J. C., Schaefer, C., & Lazarus, R. S. (1981). Comparison of two modes of stress measurement: Daily hassles and uplifts versus major life events. *Journal of Behavioral Medicine, 4,* 1–39.

Kendall, P. C., & Fischler, G. L. (1984). Behavioral and adjustment correlates of problem solving: Validational analyses of interpersonal cognitive problem solving measures. *Child Development, 55,* 879–892.

Kovacs, M. (1980). Rating scales to assess depression in school-aged children. *Acta Paedopsychiatrica, 46,* 305–315.

Krantz, S., & Hammen, C. (1979). The assessment of cognitive bias in depression. *Journal of Abnormal Psychology, 88,* 611–619.

Kuiper, N. A., Olinger, L. J., & MacDonald, M. R. (1988). Vulnerability and episodic cognitions in a self-worth contingency model of depression. In L. B. Alloy (Ed.), *Cognitive processes in depression* (pp. 289–309). New York: Guilford.

Kunreuther, H. C., & Schoemaker, P. J. H. (1981). Decision analysis for complex systems. *Knowledge: Creation, Diffusion, Utilization, 2,* 389–412.

Lazarus, A. A. (1968). Learning theory and the treatment of depression. *Behavior Research and Therapy, 6,* 83–89.

Lazarus, R. S. (1981). The stress and coping paradigm. In C. Eisendofer, D. Cohen, A. Kleinman, & P. Maxim (Eds.), *Theoretical bases for psychopathology* (pp. 47–82). New York: Spectrum.

Lazarus, R. S., & Folkman, S. (1984). *Stress, appraisal, and coping.* New York: Springer.

Lazarus, R. S., & Lanier, R. (1978). Stress-related transactions between person and environment. In L. Pervin & M. Lewis (Eds.), *Internal and external determinants of behavior* (pp. 53–79). New York: Plenum.

Lee, W. (1971). *Decision theory and human behavior.* New York: Wiley.

Lefcourt, H. M. (1966). Internal-external control of reinforcement: A review. *Psychological Bulletin, 65,* 206–220.

Levine, S. (1983). A psychobiological approach to the ontogeny of coping. In N. Garmezy & M. Rutter (Eds.), *Stress, coping, and development in children* (pp. 107–132). New York: McGraw-Hill.

Levine, S., Weinberg, J., & Ursin, H. (1978). Definition of the coping process and statement of the problem. In H. Ursin, E. Baade, & S. Levine (Eds.), *Psychobiology of stress: A study of coping men* (pp. 3–28). New York: Academic Press.

Levine, J., & Zigler, E. (1973). The essential-reactive distinction in alcoholism: A developmental approach. *Journal of Abnormal Psychology, 81,* 242–249.

Levitt, E. E., Lubin, B., & Brooks, J. M. (1983). *Depression: Concepts, controversies, and some new facts* (2nd ed.). Hillsdale, NJ: Lawrence Erlbaum.

Lewinsohn, P. M. (1974). A behavioral approach to depression. In R. J. Friedman & M. M. Katz (Eds.), *The psychology of depression: Contemporary theory and research* (pp. 157–178). New York: Winston-Wiley.

Lewinsohn, P. M., & Atwood, G. (1969). Depression: A clinical research approach; the case of Mrs. G. *Psychotherapy: Theory, Research and Practice, 6,* 166–171.

Lewinsohn, P. M., & Graf, M. (1973). Pleasant activities and depression. *Journal of Consulting and Clinical Psychology, 41*, 261–268.

Lewinsohn, P. M., & Libet, J. (1972). Pleasant events, activity schedules, and depression. *Journal of Abnormal Psychology, 79*, 291–295.

Lewinsohn, P. M., & MacPhillamy, D. J. (1974). The relationship between age and engagement in pleasant events. *Journal of Gerontology, 29*, 290–294.

Lewinsohn, P. M., Mischel, W., Chaplin, W., & Barton, R. (1980). Social competence and depression: The role of illusory self-perceptions. *Journal of Abnormal Psychology, 89*, 203–212.

Lewinsohn, P. M., & Shaw, D. A. (1969). Feedback about interpersonal behavior as an agent of behavior change: A case study in the treatment of depression. *Psychotherapy and Psychosomatics, 17*, 82–88.

Lewinsohn, P. M., & Talkington, J. (1979). Studies on the measurement of unpleasant events and relations with depression. *Applied Psychological Measurement, 3*, 83–101.

Lewinsohn, P. M., Weinstein, M., & Alper, T. (1970). A behavioral approach to the group treatment of depressed persons: A methodological contribution. *Journal of Clinical Psychology, 26*, 525–532.

Libet, J. M., & Lewinsohn, P. M. (1973). Concept of social skill with special relevance to the behavior of depressed persons. *Journal of Consulting and Clinical Psychology, 40*, 304–312.

Lloyd, C. (1980). Life events and depressive disorder reviewed: II. Events as precipitating factors. *Archives of General Psychiatry, 37*, 542–548.

Lobitz, W. C., & Post, R. D. (1979). Parameters of self-reinforcement and depression. *Journal of Abnormal Psychology, 88*, 33–41.

Loeb, A., Beck, A. T., Diggory, J. C., & Tuthill, R. (1967, August). *Expectancy, level of aspiration, performance, and self-evaluation in depression.* Paper presented at the meeting of the American Psychological Association, New York.

Lubin, B. (1965). Adjective checklists for measurement of depression. *Archives of General Psychiatry, 12*, 57–62.

Lubin, B. (1967). *Manual for the Depression Adjective Check Lists.* San Diego, CA: Educational and Industrial Testing Service.

Lubin, B. (1977). *Bibliography for the Depression Adjective Check Lists.* San Diego, CA: Educational and Industrial Testing Service.

Luce, R. D. (1959). *Individual choice behavior.* New York: Wiley.

MacPhillamy, D. J., & Lewinsohn, P. M. (1971). *Pleasant Events Schedule.* Mimeograph, Department of Psychology, University of Oregon.

MacPhillamy, D. J., & Lewinsohn, P. M. (1974). Depression as a function of desired and obtained pleasure. *Journal of Abnormal Psychology, 83*, 651–657.

MacPhillamy, D. J., & Lewinsohn, P. M. (1982). The pleasant events schedule: Studies on reliability, validity and scale intercorrelation. *Journal of Consulting and Clinical Psychology, 50*, 363–380.

Mahoney, M. J. (1974). *Cognition and behavior modification.* Cambridge, MA: Ballinger.

Mahoney, M. J. (1977). Personal science: A cognitive learning therapy. In A. Ellis & R. Grieger (Eds.), *Handbook of rational-emotive therapy* (pp. 219–247). New York: Springer.

Mahoney, M. J., & Thoresen, C. E. (1974). *Self-control: Power to the person.* Monterey, CA: Brooks/Cole.

Maier, N. R. F., & Hoffman, L. R. (1964). Financial incentives and group decisions in motivating change. *Journal of Social Psychology, 64,* 369–378.

Mandler, G. (1982). Stress and thought processes. In L. Goldberger & S. Breznitz (Eds.), *Handbook of stress: Theoretical and clinical aspects* (pp. 88–104). New York: The Free Press.

Mayer, J. M. (1977). Assessment of depression. In P. McReynolds (Ed.), *Advances in psychological assessment* (Vol. 4, pp. 358–425). San Francisco: Jossey-Bass.

McFall, R. M. (1982). A review and reformulation of the concept of social skills. *Behavioral Assessment, 4,* 1–33.

McLean, P. (1981). Remediation of skills and performance deficits in depression: Clinical steps and research findings. In J. F. Clarkin & H. I. Glazer (Eds.), *Depression: Behavioral and directive intervention strategies* (pp. 179–204). New York: Garland.

Meadow, A., & Parnes, S. J. (1959). Evaluation of training in creative problem solving. *Journal of Applied Psychology, 43,* 189–194.

Meadow, A., Parnes, S. J., & Reese, H. (1959). Influence of instructions and problem sequence on a creative problem solving task. *Journal of Applied Psychology, 43,* 413–416.

Mechanic, D. (1968). The study of social stress and its relationship to disease. In D. Mechanic (Ed.), *Medical sociology* (pp. 103–126). New York: The Free Press.

Mechanic, D. (1970). Some problems in developing a social psychology of adaption to stress. In J. E. McGrath (Ed.), *Social and psychological factors in stress* (pp. 65–89). New York: Holt, Rinehart & Winston.

Meijers, J. J. (1978). *Problem-solving therapy with socially anxious children.* Amsterdam: Alblasserdam.

Mendlewicz, J. (1985). Genetic research in depressive disorders. In E. E. Beckham & W. R. Leber (Eds.), *Handbook of depression: Treatment, assessment, and research* (pp. 795–815). Homewood, IL: Dorsey.

Miller, W. T. (1975). Psychological deficit in depression. *Psychological Bulletin, 82,* 238–260.

Miller, G. A., Galanter, E., & Pribram, K. H. (1960). *Plans and the structure of behavior.* New York: Holt, Rinehart & Winston.

Miller, W. R., & Seligman, M. E. P. (1973). Depression and the perception of reinforcement. *Journal of Abnormal Psychology, 82,* 62–73.

Mitchell, R. E., Cronkite, R. C., & Moos, R. H. (1983). Stress, coping, and depression among married couples. *Journal of Abnormal Psychology, 92,* 433–448.

Mitchell, J. E., & Madigan, R. J. (1984). The effects of induced elation and depression on interpersonal problem solving. *Cognitive Therapy and Research, 8,* 277–285.

Mooney, R. L., & Gordon, L. V. (1950). *Manual: The Mooney Problem Checklist.* New York: Psychological Corporation.

Neal, G. W., & Heppner, P. P. (1982, March). *Personality correlates of effective problem solving.* Paper presented at the meeting of the American Personnel and Guidance Association, Detroit.

Nelson, R. E., & Craighead, W. E. (1977). Selective recall of positive and negative feedback, self-control behaviors, and depression. *Journal of Abnormal Psychology, 86,* 379–388.

Nelson, R. O. (1977). Methodological issues in assessment via self-monitoring. In J. D. Cone & R. P. Hawkins (Eds.), *Behavioral assessment: New directions in clinical psychology* (pp. 217–240). New York: Brunner/Mazel.

Nelson, R. O., & Hayes, S. C. (1986). *Conceptual foundations of behavioral assessment.* New York: Guilford.

Nezu, A. M. (1985). Differences in psychological distress between effective and ineffective problem solvers. *Journal of Counseling Psychology, 32,* 135–138.

Nezu, A. M. (1986a). Cognitive appraisal of problem-solving effectiveness: Relation to depression and depressive symptoms. *Journal of Clinical Psychology, 42,* 42–49.

Nezu, A. M. (1986b). Effects of stress from current problems: Comparison to major life events. *Journal of Clinical Psychology, 42,* 847–852.

Nezu, A. M. (1986c). Efficacy of a social problem-solving therapy approach for unipolar depression. *Journal of Consulting and Clinical Psychology, 54,* 196–202.

Nezu, A. M. (1986d). Negative life stress and anxiety: Problem solving as a moderator variable. *Psychological Reports, 58,* 279–283.

Nezu, A. M. (1987). A problem-solving formulation of depression: A literature review and proposal of a pluralistic model. *Clinical Psychology Review, 7,* 121–144.

Nezu, A. M., & Carnevale, G. C. (1987). Interpersonal problem solving and coping reactions of Vietnam veterans with posttraumatic stress disorder. *Journal of Abnormal Psychology, 96,* 155–157.

Nezu, A., & D'Zurilla, T. J. (1979). An experimental evaluation of the decision-making process in social problem solving. *Cognitive Therapy and Research, 3,* 269–277.

Nezu, A., & D'Zurilla, T. J. (1981a). Effects of problem definition and formulation on decision making in the social problem-solving process. *Behavior Therapy, 12,* 100–106.

Nezu, A., & D'Zurilla, T. J. (1981b). Effects of problem definition and formulation on the generation of alternatives in the social problem-solving process. *Cognitive Therapy and Research, 5*, 265–271.

Nezu, A. M., & D'Zurilla, T. J. (in press). Social problem solving and negative affective states. In P. C. Kendall & D. Watson (Eds.), *Anxiety and depression: Distinctive and overlapping features* . New York: Academic Press.

Nezu, A. M., & Kalmar, K. (in press). Stressful life events, problem solving, and psychological distress among young adolescents: An exploratory investigation. *Journal of Child and Adolescent Psychotherapy.*

Nezu, A. M., Kalmar, K., Ronan, G. F., & Clavijo, A. (1986). Attributional correlates of depression: An interactional model including problem solving. *Behavior Therapy, 17*, 50–56.

Nezu, A. M., & Nezu, C. M. (1987a, November). *Interpersonal aspects of humor as a coping strategy.* Paper presented at the meeting of the Association for the Advancement of Behavior Therapy, Boston.

Nezu, A. M., & Nezu, C. M. (1987b). Psychological distress, problem solving, and coping reactions: Sex role differences. *Sex Roles, 16*, 205–214.

Nezu, A. M., & Nezu, C. M. (Ed.) (in press). *Clinical decision making and judgment in the practice of behavior therapy.* Champaign, IL: Research Press.

Nezu, A. M., Nezu, C. M., & Blissett, S. E. (1988). Sense of humor as a moderator of stress: A prospective analysis. *Journal of Personality and Social Psychology, 54*, 520–525.

Nezu, A. M., Nezu, C. M., & Nezu, V. A. (1986). Depression, general distress, and causal attributions among university students. *Journal of Abnormal Psychology, 95*, 184–186.

Nezu, A. M., Nezu, C. M., & Perri, M. G. (in press). Psychotherapy for adults within a problem-solving framework: Focus on depression. *Journal of Cognitive Psychotherapy.*

Nezu, A. M., Nezu, C. M., & Peterson, M. A. (1986). Negative life stress, social support, and depressive symptoms: Sex roles as a moderator variable. *Journal of Social Behavior and Personality, 1*, 599–609.

Nezu, A. M., Nezu, C. M., Saraydarian, L., Kalmar, K., & Ronan, G. F. (1986). Social problem solving as a moderating variable between negative life stress and depressive symptoms. *Cognitive Therapy and Research, 10*, 489–498.

Nezu, A. M., & Perri, M. G. (1987, November). *Problem-solving therapy for unipolar depression: An initial dismantling investigation.* Paper presented at the meeting of the Association for the Advancement of Behavior Therapy, Boston.

Nezu, A. M., Perri, M. G., & Nezu, C. M. (1987, August). *Validation of a problem-solving/stress model of depression.* Paper presented at the meeting of the American Psychological Association, New York.

Nezu, A. M., Perri, M. G., Nezu, C. M., & Mahoney, D. J. (1987, November). Social problem solving as a moderator of stressful events among clinically depressed individuals. Paper presented at the meeting of the Association for the Advancement of Behavior Therapy, Boston.

Nezu, A. M., Petronko, M. R., & Nezu, C. M. (1982, November). Cognitive, behavioral, or cognitive-behavioral strategies? Using a problem-solving paradigm for clinical decision making in behavior therapy. In A. M. Nezu (Chair), *Clinical issues in cognitive-behavior therapy: Critical examination and future directions*. Symposium conducted at the meeting of the Association for the Advancement of Behavior Therapy, Los Angeles.

Nezu, A. M., & Ronan, G. F. (1985). Life stress, current problems, problem solving, and depressive symptoms: An integrative model. *Journal of Consulting and Clinical Psychology, 53,* 693–697.

Nezu, G. F., & Ronan, G. F. (1987). Social problem solving and depression: Deficits in generating alternatives and decision making. *The Southern Psychologist, 3,* 29–34.

Nezu, A. M., & Ronan, G. F. (1988). Stressful life events, problem solving, and depressive symptoms among university students: A prospective analysis. *Journal of Counseling Psychology, 35,* 134–138.

O'Hara, M., & Rehm, L. (1983). Hamilton rating scale for depression: Reliability and validity of judgements of novice raters. *Journal of Consulting and Clinical Psychology, 51,* 318–319.

Osborn, A. (1963). *Applied imagination: Principles and procedures of creative problem solving* (3rd ed.). New York: Scribner's.

Overmier, J. B., & Seligman, M. E. P. (1967). Effects of inescapable shock upon subsequent escape and avoidance learning. *Journal of Comparative and Physiological Psychology, 63,* 23–33.

Parnes, S. J. (1962). The creative problem-solving course and institute at the University of Buffalo. In S. J. Parnes & H. F. Harding (Eds.), *A source book for creative thinking*. New York: Scribner's.

Parnes, S. J. (1967). *Creative behavior handbook*. New York: Scribner's.

Parnes, S. J., & Meadow, A. (1959). Effects of "brainstorming" instructions on creative problem solving by trained and untrained subjects. *Journal of Educational Psychology, 50,* 171–176.

Payne, J. W. (1982). Contingent decision behavior. *Psychological Bulletin, 92,* 382–402.

Pearlin, L. I., & Schooler, C. (1978). The structure of coping. *Journal of Health and Social Behavior, 19,* 2–21.

Perri, M. G., McAdoo, W. G., McAllister, D. A., Jordan, R. C., Lauer, J. B., Yancy, D. Z., & Nezu, A. M. (1987). Effects of peer support and therapist contact on long-term weight loss. *Journal of Consulting and Clinical Psychology, 55,* 615–617.

Perri, M. G., McAllister, D. A., Gange, J. J., Jordan, R. C., McAdoo, W. G., & Nezu, A. M. (in press). Effects of four maintenance programs on the long-term management of obesity. *Journal of Consulting and Clinical Psychology*.

Peterson, C., Semmel, A., von Baeyer, C., Abramson, L. Y., Metalsky, G. I., & Seligman, M. E. P. (1982). The Attributional Style Questionnaire. *Cognitive Therapy and Research, 6,* 287–299.

Phillips, E. L. (1978). *The social skills basis of psychopathology: Alternatives to abnormal psychology and psychiatry.* New York: Grune & Stratton.

Phillips, S. D., Pazienza, N. J., & Ferrin, H. H. (1984). Decision making styles and problem solving appraisal. *Journal of Counseling Psychology, 31,* 497–502.

Phillips, L., & Zigler, E. (1961). Social competence: The action-thought parameter and vicariousness in normal and pathological behaviors. *Journal of Abnormal and Social Psychology, 63,* 137–146.

Phillips, L., & Zigler, E. (1964). Role orientation, the action-thought dimension, and outcome in psychiatric disorder. *Journal of Abnormal and Social Psychology, 68,* 381–389.

Pitz, G. F., & Sachs, N. J. (1984). Judgement and decision: Theory and application. *Annual Review of Psychology, 35,* 139–163.

Platt, J. J., Scura, W. C., & Hannon, J. R. (1973). Problem-solving thinking of youthful incarcerated heroin addicts. *Journal of Community Psychology, 1,* 278–281.

Platt, J. J., & Siegel, J. M. (1976). MMPI characteristics of good and poor social problem solvers among psychiatric patients. *Journal of Community Psychology, 4,* 245–251.

Platt, J. J., & Spivack, G. (1972a). Problem-solving thinking of psychiatric patients. *Journal of Consulting and Clinical Psychology, 39,* 148–151.

Platt, J. J., & Spivack, G. (1972b). Social competence and effective problem solving in psychiatric patients. *Journal of Clinical Psychology, 28,* 3–5.

Platt, J. J., & Spivack, G. (1973, August). Studies in problem-solving thinking of psychiatric patients: Patient-control differences and factorial structure of problem-solving thinking. *Proceedings, 81st Annual Convention of the American Psychological Association, 8,* 461–462.

Platt, J. J., & Spivack, G. (1974). Means of solving real-life problems: I. Psychiatric patients versus controls, and cross-cultural comparisons of normal females. *Journal of Community Psychology, 2,* 45–48.

Platt, J. J., & Spivack, G. (1975). *Manual for the means-end problem-solving procedure (MEPS): A measure of interpersonal cognitive problem-solving skills.* Hahnemann Community Mental Health/Mental Retardation Center, Philadelphia.

Platt, J. J., Spivack, G., Altman, N., Altman, D., & Peizer, S. B. (1974). Adolescent problem solving thinking. *Journal of Consulting and Clinical Psychology, 42,* 787–793.

Polivy, J., & Herman, C. P. (1985). Dieting and binging: A causal analysis. *American Psychologist, 40,* 193–201.

Rabkin, J. G. (1982). Stress and psychiatric disorders. In L. Goldberger & S.

Breznitz (Eds.), *Handbook of stress: Theoretical and clinical aspects* (pp. 566–584). New York: The Free Press.

Rehm, L. P. (1976). Assessment of depression. In M. Hersen & A. S. Bellack (Eds.), *Behavioral assessment: A practical handbook* (pp. 313–364). New York: Pergamon.

Rehm, L. P. (1977). A self-control model of depression. *Behavior Therapy, 8,* 787–804.

Rehm, L. P. (1981). A self-control therapy program for treatment of depression. In J. F. Clarkin & H. I. Glazer (Eds.), *Depression: Behavioral and directive intervention strategies* (pp. 68–110). New York: Garland.

Rehm, L. P., & O'Hara, M. W. (1980). The role of attribution theory in understanding depression. In I. H. Frieze, D. Bar-Tal, & J. S. Carroll (Eds.), *Attribution theory: Applications to social problems* (pp. 74–102). San Francisco: Jossey-Bass.

Richards, C. S., & Perri, M. G. (1978). Do self-control treatments last? An evaluation of behavioral problem solving and faded counselor contact as treatment maintenance strategies. *Journal of Counseling Psychology, 25,* 376–383.

Robins, E., & Guze, S. B. (1972). Classification of affective disorders: The primary-secondary, the endogenous-reactive and the neurotic-psychotic concepts. In T. A. Williams, M. M. Katz, & J. A. Shields (Eds.), *Recent advances in the psychobiology of the depressive illnesses* (pp. 23–51). Washington, DC: Government Printing Office.

Rogers, C. R. (1957). The necessary and sufficient conditions of therapeutic personality change. *Journal of Consulting Psychology, 21,* 95–103.

Rosenbaum, M. (1980). A schedule for assessing self-control behaviors: Preliminary findings. *Behavior Therapy, 11,* 109–121.

Roth, D., & Rehm, L. P. (1980). Relationships between self-monitoring processes, memory and depression. *Cognitive Therapy and Research, 4,* 149–158.

Roth, D., Rehm, L. P., & Rozensky, R. A. (1980). Self-reward, self-punishment and depression. *Psychological Reports, 47,* 3–7.

Rotter, J. B. (1966). Generalized expectancies for internal versus external control of reinforcement. *Psychological Monographs, 80,* 1–28.

Rotter, J. B. (1978). Generalized expectancies for problem solving and psychotherapy. *Cognitive Therapy and Research, 2,* 1–10.

Rozensky, R. H., Rehm, L. P., Pry, G., & Roth, G. (1977). Depression and self-reinforcement behavior in hospitalized patients. *Journal of Behavior Therapy and Experimental Psychiatry, 8,* 31–34.

Sacco, W. P., & Graves, D. J. (1984). Childhood depression, interpersonal problem solving, and self-ratings of performance. *Journal of Clinical Child Psychology, 13,* 10–15.

Sackheim, H. A., & Weber, S. L. (1982). Functional brain asymmetry in the regulation of emotion: Implications for bodily manifestations of stress. In L. Goldberger & S. Breznitz (Eds.), *Handbook of stress: Theoretical and clinical aspects* (pp. 183–199). New York: The Free Press.

Sansbury, D. L. (1979). The role of the group in behavioral group therapy. In D. Upper & S. M. Ross (Eds.), *Behavioral group therapy: An annual review* (pp. 39–54). Champaign, IL: Research Press.

Sarason, B. R. (1981). The dimensions of social competence: Contributions from a variety of research areas. In J. D. Wine & M. D. Smye (Eds.), *Social competence* (pp. 2–31). New York: Guilford.

Sarason, I. G., Johnson, J. H., & Siegel, J. M. (1978). Assessing the impact of life changes: Development of the Life Experiences Survey. *Journal of Consulting and Clinical Psychology, 46,* 932–946.

Sarason, I. G., Levine, A. M., & Sarason, B. R. (1982). Assessing the impact of life changes. In T. Millon, C. Green, & R. Meagher (Eds.), *Handbook of clinical health psychology* (pp. 377–399). New York: Plenum Press.

Schildkraut, J. J. (1974). Biogenic amines and affective disorders. *Annual Review of Medicine, 25,* 338–348.

Schinka, J. A. (1986). *Personal problems checklist.* Odessa, FL: Psychological Assessment Resources.

Schoemaker, P. J. H. (1982). The expected utility model: Its variants, purposes, evidence and limitations. *Journal of Economic Literature, 20,* 529–563.

Schotte, D. E., & Clum, G. A. (1982). Suicide ideation in a college population. *Journal of Consulting and Clinical Psychology, 50,* 690–696.

Schotte, D. E., & Clum, G. A. (1987). Problem-solving skills in suicidal psychiatric patients. *Journal of Consulting and Clinical Psychology, 55,* 49–54.

Schwartz, J. L. (1974). Relationship between goal discrepancy and depression. *Journal of Consulting and Clinical Psychology, 42,* 309.

Secunda, R., Friedman, R. J., & Schuyler, D. (1973). *The depressive disorders.* Washington, DC: Government Printing Office.

Seligman, M. E. P. (1975). *Helplessness: On depression, development, and death.* San Francisco: Freeman.

Seligman, M. E. P., & Maier, S. F. (1967). Failure to escape traumatic shock. *Journal of Experimental Psychology, 74,* 1–9.

Selye, H. (1983). The stress concept: Past, present, and future. In C. L. Cooper (Ed.), *Stress research: Issues for the eighties* (pp. 3–36). New York: Wiley.

Shaw, B. F. (1979). The theoretical and experimental foundations of a cognitive model for depression. In P. Pliner, K. R. Blankenstein, & I. M. Sigel (Eds.), *Advances in the study of communication and affect* (Vol. 5, pp. 81–119). New York: Plenum.

Sherry, P., Keitel, M., & Tracey, T. J. (1984, August). The relationship between person-environment fit, coping, and strain. Paper presented at the meeting of the American Psychological Association, Toronto.

Shipley, C. R., & Fazio, A. F. (1973). Pilot study of a treatment for psychological depression. *Journal of Abnormal Psychology, 82,* 372–376.

Shure, M. B. (1981). Social competence as a problem-solving skill. In J. D. Wine & M. D. Smye (Eds.), *Social competence* (pp. 98–120). New York: Guilford.

Siegel, J. M., Platt, J. J., & Peizer, S. B. (1976). Emotional and social real-life problem-solving thinking in adolescent and adult psychiatric patients. *Journal of Clinical Psychology, 32,* 230–232.

Siegel, J. M., & Spivack, G. (1976). Problem-solving therapy: The description of a new program for chronic psychiatric patients. *Psychotherapy: Theory, Research, and Practice, 13,* 368–373.

Skinner, B. F. (1953). *Science and human behavior.* New York: Macmillan.

Smolen, R. C. (1978). Expectancies, mood, and performance of depressed and nondepressed psychiatric patients on chance and skill tasks. *Journal of Abnormal Psychology, 87,* 91–101.

Spielberger, C. D. (1972). Anxiety as an emotional state. In C. D. Spielberger (Ed.), *Anxiety: Current trends in theory and research* (Vol. 1, pp. 2–30). New York: Academic Press.

Spitzer, R. L., Endicott, J., & Robins, E. (1978). Research diagnostic criteria: Rationale and reliability. *Archives of General Psychiatry, 36,* 773–782.

Spivack, G., Platt, J. J., & Shure, M. B. (1976). *The problem-solving approach to adjustment.* San Francisco: Jossey-Bass.

Spivack, G., & Shure, M. B. (1974). *Social adjustment of young children: A cognitive approach to solving real-life problems.* San Francisco: Jossey-Bass.

Teasdale, J. D., & Fogarty, S. J. (1979). Differential effects of induced mood on retrieval of pleasant and unpleasant events from episodic memory. *Journal of Abnormal Psychology, 88,* 248–257.

Thase, M. E., Frank, E., & Kupfer, D. J. (1985). Biological processes in major depression. In E. E. Beckham & W. R. Leber (Eds.), *Handbook of depression: Treatment, assessment, and research* (pp. 816–913). Homewood, IL: Dorsey.

Thierry, A. M., Blanc, G., & Glowinski, J. (1971). Effect of stress on the disposition of catecholamines localized in various intraneuronal storage forms in the brain stem of the rat. *Journal of Neurochemistry, 18,* 449–461.

Tisdelle, D. A., & St. Lawrence, J. S. (1986). Interpersonal problem-solving competence: Review and critique of the literature. *Clinical Psychology Review, 6,* 337–350.

Truax, C. B., & Carkhuff, R. R. (1967). *Toward effective counseling and psychotherapy.* Chicago: Aldine.

Turner, R. W., Ward, M. R., & Turner, D. J. (1979). Behavioral treatment for depression: An evaluation of therapeutic components. *Journal of Clinical Psychology, 35,* 166–175.

Tversky, A., & Kahneman, D. (1981). The framing of decisions and the psychology of choice. *Science, 211,* 453–458.

van Pragg, H. M. (1979). Psychopsychiatry: Can psychosocial factors cause psychiatric disorders? *Comprehensive Psychiatry, 20,* 215–225.

Velten, E. (1968). A laboratory task for induction of mood states. *Behavior Research and Therapy, 6,* 473–482.

von Neumann, J., & Morgenstern, O. (1944). *Theory of games and economic behavior*. Princeton, NJ: Princeton University Press.

Wallerstein, J. S. (1983). Children of divorce: Stress and developmental tasks. In N. Garmezy & M. Rutter (Eds.), *Stress, coping, and development in children* (pp. 265–302). New York: McGraw-Hill.

Weiss, J. M., Glazer, H. I., & Pohorecky, L. A. (1976). Coping behavior and neurochemical changes: An alternative explanation for the original "learned helplessness" experiments. In G. Serban & A. Kling (Eds.), *Animal models in human psychobiology* (pp. 215–240). New York: Plenum.

Wener, A. E., & Rehm, L. P. (1975). Depressive affect: A test of behavioral hypotheses. *Journal of Abnormal Psychology, 84,* 221–227.

Wheeler, D. D., & Janis, I. L. (1980). *A practical guide for making decisions*. New York: The Free Press.

White, R. W. (1959). Motivation reconsidered: The concept of competence. *Psychological Review, 66,* 297–333.

Wortman, C. B., & Brehm, J. W. (1975). Responses to uncontrollable outcomes: An integration of reactance theory and the learned helplessness model. In L. Berkowitz (Ed.), *Advances in experimental social psychology* (Vol. 8, pp. 279–315). New York: Academic Press.

Wrubel, J., Benner, P., & Lazarus, R. S. (1981). Social competence from the perspective of stress and coping. In J. D. Wine & M. D. Smye (Eds.), *Social competence* (pp. 121–153). New York: Guilford.

Youngren, M. A., & Lewinsohn, P. M. (1980). The functional relation between depression and problematic interpersonal behavior. *Journal of Abnormal Psychology, 89,* 333–341.

Zemore, R., & Dell, L. W. (1983). Interpersonal problem-solving skills and depression proneness. *Personality and Social Psychology Bulletin, 9,* 231–235.

Zigler, E., & Phillips, L. (1961). Social competence and outcome in psychiatric disorders. *Journal of Abnormal and Social Psychology, 63,* 264–271.

Zigler, E., & Phillips, L. (1962). Social competence and the process-reactive distinction in psychopathology. *Journal of Abnormal and Social Psychology, 65,* 215–222.

Zung, W. W. (1965). A self-rating depression scale. *Archives of General Psychiatry, 12,* 63–70.

Zung, W. W. (1973). From art to science: The diagnosis and treatment of depression. *Archives of General Psychiatry, 29,* 328–337.

Author Index

Note: Page numbers in italics indicate references.

266

Subject Index